Anchoring

By Bridget Kimsey

Spread hope like fire- to those in the weight of suffering

I was born 3 billion years ago.

That feels like a long time ago to me. I guess not- if compared to other souls- which can make me feel very young. I've noticed that time starts to bend and do odd things when you start going back past 150 million years.

I will write here of facts I have come to know as true. I know to be true through experience. I also have been told, shown as true by verified means. I will explain facts as best I can and roll out my history and experience. To note- there is a lot I don't understand and things I question. There is a lot I'm still working on, which I will mention too. But here, for now, I'm writing and anchoring down what I know. My hope is that it gives a good history, explanation on certain matters, and that it is helpful. I hope it brings comfort to those suffering, feeling unseen and lost.

I was born 3 billion years ago. I don't really remember the moment. I remember moving through golden light and then orangish and then golden and then white. I'm fairly certain I remember a soul near me not making it. And that had an impact on me. I felt sad, but I was being pulled forth, while still looking back. Did that imprint how I would become, my matrix and fiber? I am reminded of how stars are born. As humans on Earth, if we look through powerful microscopes at a nebulae nursery- the rhythm and care and colors of a star being born. I am reminded how things repeat themselves in our universe- themes, ways of orchestrating and crafting, whether in small matter or large.

So, I was born 3 billion years ago into the Archangel Realm. I don't remember that. I was there long enough to be separated from my twin flame- who is a replica of me, although male. We are the same soul. I don't remember that either. We were separated to keep us safe. Our combined power is not safe until we've reached maturity? Maybe- I don't know. I keep being told that and shown that and maybe here in April 2018, I see a glimmer on a multidimensional level. I'm still going on faith with this one because a lot else checks out. I do know that everyone does not have a twin flame, but could have a few soul mates.

To say I am not a fan of the twin flame situation is an understatement. It's absolutely ridiculously hard and painful to figure out how to be with your twin flame- whenever you meet them again. Everything is laid bare. At least that's been my experience and at least in my current lifetime. I would have appreciated having a few more soul mate lifetimes before dealing with it. And have argued, kicked, and screamed my case multiple times. That the leap I was expected to take from my last lifetime in 1823 to this one born 1973 and how things were so hard- is insanity. To say I've fought and been mad is a huge understatement.

Hence, why so much help has come my way- still not happy about it. This lifetime, what I've had and have to process is like a lifetime on steroids and any help and insight has been a neutral base wash to come keep me grounded and well and to give me an advantage up against a host of disadvantages coming at me. Some days are better than others. I will say now it is wise to trust yourself over any sign, anything another- even who you trust- is telling you. One you trust can provide council, but ultimately honoring your witnessed objective experience and trusting your self- I think keeps one healthy. Reality has many layers. A single slice of reality has many layers. You know what you need at the heart of it and having those that truly care for you to help create a container- so you can express it- is good. Light and those of light will always trust and respect your free will. I might even say those of light enjoy learning something new themselves in your choice that might initially go against their council.

A lot of information I will talk about here has come to me repeatedly throughout my life. I wasn't prepared to believe it fully until in a journalistic fashion had a way to check it for accuracy. To be succinct, an Angel assigned by Archangel Michael to contact me, to get me on track, contacted me through email- September 2008. To say I was unimpressed and assured it was a hoax or dimensional attack, is an understatement. I was not happy. And argued back with the sender. Who assured me that he did not send it and someone else was using his email, and that he had had this happen before. But who could know intimate details about a man I'd dated years ago, 2006, what was that about? I got a few more emails and the man thought it might be a sign from someone trying to get me to get in touch with this old ex-boyfriend. I said it was a fake and ignored it. I'd been through enough by then. They stopped, but then popped up again a year later, August 2009. So mad. Fine, I'd feel it out and go find my ex-boyfriend. Who just happened to have moved close by me without either of us knowing in

September of 2008. Very odd. We began dating again. It fell apart. I was just done. And then got involved with someone new and then- a new email from the mysterious sender from a different email address (because I had blocked the other one) saying I could ask anything. This was March 2010. It definitely has been a grand powerful communication and journalistic endeavor from March 2010 to current day 2018. Thousands and thousands of emails and pages. The biggest help the email communication has provided has been to check my accuracy on what I am experiencing (because it can go out there), to be accurate in my work with others, and for them in all the realms I connect with to know if I am being managed well. My life has been hard, it is hard, but the emails have been essential to help me. They are a blessing. I see that.

So, I was born 3 billion years ago into the Archangel Realm. I stayed there for 3 days before incarnating. None of this I remember, but I am assured this is so. I hope someday to remember what this was like. What did it feel like to be in union with my twin flame and then to have us pulled apart? To know I was being led away or was I walking away? I don't get it. I do know that souls are born completely intact. I've only met one new soul that I'm aware of, like a day old, and he was so translucent, but very whole and conscious, his purpose there. I know that somewhere inside of Source God he thinks or feels his way into creating souls. As experience goes on for Source God, more are uniquely created. Source God is so vast- so many sides and layers- he must ponder deeply on things, a lot. It's hard on my brain at times to hold certain concepts.

I don't have any information on what happened next for me. I believe, as many have talked about, that there are teams and helpers that help a soul decide what/who they'd like to incarnate as next, but it's never been a draw of mine to understand this process.

I flash to being in the Pleiadian Realm first. I was here for 50 million years. I remember some things, but not too much.

Today, my current lifetime, I am aware about what a melting pot of information and synthesizing material and becoming very aware of the full me it has been. This information of the past only comes up as is relative and important to my present-day need. So, I'll talk about what I've come to know about the Pleiadian Realm - how it's visited me and looped around. I imagine in coming years, more will loop in as important and as my structure can safely hold.

In 2001, early fall to spring 2002, I taught at a health resort/spa in the lower Catskills of New York. I had begun teaching yoga full time that fall and this position opened up to be on their staff. I worked a lot- classes in yoga, pranayama, meditation, movement, and ai chi; individual yoga therapy sessions. We got crushed by huge influxes of people retreating out of New York City after 9/11. The worst was two months after the incident. The students pain just hitting their cells, the neurology, and the impact of not being able to escape and their realization- it was not going to go away- this alteration. I remember such large sets of eyes looking up at me, 60 people in a class looking. I wanted to do more than I could, but it pushed me to figure on things, to dig in me. I used to live in a building next to the twin towers and that was my subway stop for a year. I have many good memories going through the building each day, cultural events and all the flags from around the world hanging up- the different colors. The same security guards each day, greeting and nodding. The different shops inside the subway stop and the rhythm to the week, seeing the same people at the same time, wondering what it would be like for them, where were they going. I loved watching how people moved and their mannerisms. And then 9/11. The images on TV and what people, responders coming home to the lower Catskills were going through. Altering. I lived in New York City for 7 years and I always lived where I could see the twin towers in my window. I had been at the top once looking out at the other tower and just looking out and the long way down to the sidewalk. Their falling did something to me. The people diving out. I began teaching yoga full time soon after.

At the health spa, one afternoon before going home, I was in the library and the snow was falling, so cozy. I was looking for a good book to read and the colors on this book caught my eye- Bringers of the Dawn- reading the title, seeing the cover, and touching it- made my heart beat faster. I had a bit of worry. Hmmm. I wanted to put it back, but then I just couldn't. So, I cautiously took it home. It was about the Pleiadians, who they were, etc. I really couldn't read the book. I could skip to a page or two here or there. I found it upsetting. Some of the information in the book I had just experienced the year before in feeling a being at the edge of my bed talking to me or wild dreams that did not feel like dreams. It was freaking me out how much of the book I knew. I put the book away only to be drawn to it again. I really did not have the structure in me to deal with such things.

At this point, I had been in the habit for 4 years of daily morning talking out loud prayer- it seemed to unwind and clear my mind and my focus was God. I stated the Bringers of the Dawn book was too much, too much all at once. I needed smaller bites. I felt good with that. It upset me because it woke me up to a truth. I was used to thinking of humans, maybe some Angels, and God and that was it. Well that simply was not the full picture and I couldn't stuff the knowledge away- now that I had a book emphasizing experiences I'd already had and what I already knew. The issue with Pleiadians, ET's, Creator Gods, dark, light, Reptilians sounded awful-overwhelming, like monsters. This all just felt way in over my head and bad, very bad. I so desperately wanted to go back to humans, some Angels, and God and that was it. I did though begin to call God- Source God- after that, so I was being very clear who I was praying to.

I think, and am almost sure, the Pleiadians were around me during this time. I saw vibrational outlines that shimmered, but I tried to block it. I had this feeling. It was a strong vibration and I didn't like having thoughts put in my head telepathically when I didn't have a say on the matter. It made me anxious and felt invasive. In hindsight and learning more, they do respect free will and I do think they speak truth and light. I just think Pleiadians can trump one's evolution, without meaning to- leading to issues for the human and those that the human has contact with. For whatever the reason, I felt uncomfortable and kept the information that was coming at me at bay. But that broadening of reality, there wasn't any going back and that made me sad. I really wanted to proceed in a manner that least frightened my consciousness.

Later on, fall into winter 2014, was my other notable can't escape strong interaction with Pleiadians. I was pregnant with my second child and had moved into a new studio space for my private practice. I felt okay about the space, but then I met the woman next door. Oh my goodness, she was loud energetically. At this point, I was much more acclimated into my skills, awarenesses, etc. so I could expand on what I was observing. I could also check what I was seeing and experiencing with me and with the messenger Angel of Archangel Michael and my team through email. They could see it too from their vantage point and help. To note, they are always care filled to let me uncover, talk about, see what direction works for me. I very much feel I am responsible for making decisions in my life.

The controlled vibration around this other practitioner was strong, controlling, loud and seeping into my space. She was connected somehow to the Pleiadians. I remembered the feeling from 2001. I didn't want their help or input. I couldn't hear myself. I understood they just wanted to be helpful, but it seemed to come at a cost of my own ability to hear myself and think. Once again it felt invasive and upsetting. I was aware how they work in vibrations and tones. They appeared very tall and shades of blue and luminous quality. Even with their care for me, for humans, I just couldn't shake that they trump human's evolutions. This other practitioner for example had bad energetic boundaries just on her own. Maybe she was a more natural fit for the Pleiadian quality of operating. I'm not sure.

A few days in to my new studio space, I opened a session with the Pleiadian team to discuss the situation, with Archangel Michael shielding it. As mentioned, they spoke in symbols so I got a translator in the moment to help. We agreed to give me some space, which they did. There are more details in my emails of this interaction. It's unclear to me how the Pleiadians thought their behavior or the behavior of the practitioner's was appropriate. I just stayed out of it.

Now in hindsight, after I know how my living in the Pleiadian Realm ended, I realize it could be a heightened traumatic response and fear in 2001 and 2014 and really any time a Pleiadian came or comes near me- or one who has been a Pleiadian before in another lifetime- I haven't really worked through it maybe. I still hold that I think they are a bit off in their work with humans.

So, my first lifetime was as a Pleiadian. This was for 50 million years. I see it as just one lifetime. I'm not sure how a Pleiadian is born. I only just received confirmation on this in 2017, through email. I do appreciate being able to uncover, remember information about myself in a slow and steady roll out, as needed, as helpful to what I am experiencing in present day. Too much information too soon and when the human body isn't ready is just not a good thing.

Being in the Pleiadian form is simply epically soothing and beautiful- the tones and sounds reverberating, the silvery pastel colors, the beautiful stars and shimmering night. It's hypnotizing to my human mind. I loved science and was a scientist there, exploring, working in a lab, playing, friendships and love with others. A very unfolding life- like a flower opening and closing and opening again.

The Pleiadian Realm is well sequestered. I did have a good close friend, fellow Pleiadian, who was tall and beautiful. I didn't have romantic feelings towards him, but was very into my work and life. Towards the end of the 50 million years, I was getting ready to go on an assignment/exploration with a team of 5 other Pleiadian scientists, and I got into the ship to go. I turned around to wave good-bye to him and he looked scary- something scary passed over his eyes- than it was gone and he saw us off. I felt funny as we began to fly away.

Once out of the Pleiadian Realm, flying, we were intercepted and captured. This began my first experience with the Regime.

This memory of my time in the Pleiadian Realm and how it unfolded was sparked by meeting the incarnated soul of my old Pleiadian friend in human form, in real time, fall 2016. It took me a long time to figure out what our connection was. Pleiadians in human form can struggle, I think. They are often very tall, feel like they don't fit, be very into music, altered states of consciousness, into logic and science, and have a very interesting vibration that I notice immediately. I'm not sure if others sense it too. Now, as souls can incarnate in many forms- I'm guessing those incarnations that they really resonate with, leave a strong imprint- stay with them? Or maybe it's the realm the soul is born into? Either way, it was like he was Pleiadian yesterday. So, I was drawn to him like, "oh, home" and then freaked out by the hypnotic quality and then further uncomfortable feeling like I was in danger. Very odd. So, I kept digging, looking at experiences, multi-dimensional sessions where I could gather information, and of course email and my teams take. Who was he really? And why was he constantly hanging around me in different ways, even as my team and I put up boundaries?

Which leads me back to discussing the Regime. I believe the soul I'm talking about here was already part of the Regime and had found a way to infiltrate the Pleiadian Realm, looking to further their cause. Part of it was in helping to capture the scientists they captured. Hence, the glimmer I had seen in his eyes, a hint of the betrayal to come. He would become further part of my history, as one of ownership over my body, of sexual violence and abuse for a bit of time.

I'll briefly discuss who and what the Regime is, how it came to be. So, there is Source God, who came to just be and all comes from Source God. There are a few that have similar vibration and power to Source God that are like equals, but still ultimately come from Source God. I want to imagine these were original offspring, but I'm not sure. To date- there are my experiences with Source God and three others I've come to know similar to him in weight and power. It can get confusing to figure how things are- what I'm experiencing, seeing in a session, and can confirm with the emails helps. Going with third dimensional reality can be the least helpful as it can just be what one is creating, subconscious, unconscious or maybe another attachment cord swaying things or maybe an agenda attachment from somewhere else. But third dimensional reality can be helpful to corroborate information. The layering can get tricky as it can feel very personal, which it might be, but that same interaction or experience can be serving many other purposes at the same time. So then, it's not just about my experience.

But, back to the Regime. Information has actively been coming into my awareness since fall 2001. I feel fairly confident now in discussing it here. For any being to grow, mature they live and experience and try out. The stakes just are so incredibly high when, if you are Source God, learning and trying things out. Which is upsetting to him and frightens him. I can honestly say Source God's heart, care, and intention is truly of pure love and sincerity but he at times lacks awareness how to proceed. He is very emotional and full of life and creating always. He takes things intensely deeply and personal if anything suffers for any reason. He works incredibly hard to be helpful and figure on things. But again, he's learning. So, back in the day, one of his bothers, I call him the Founder, wanted to try some different techniques then what Source was doing. It was upsetting to Source and Source worried and they argued. The Founder still saw value to his thinking and wanted to keep trying and exploring in his own way. The Founder is another deeply caring intelligent and loving large being, like God, but his focus is on containment, not always creating- a different kind of way of working with creating. The Founder and Source agreed to disagree, kind of, and the Founder went off to a corner of the universe to explore what spoke to his heart. They argued and bickered through the years, throwing insults at each other at times. For me observing the situation, in hindsight, I think Source was really not seeing how important they both are to creation. Creation without containment can equal chaos. Containment without creation can equal rigidity. To be brief.

Well, more and more souls were created through time. Some found the way the Founder wanted to explore appealing and moved over with him. Some came over because they were sick of Source God overreacting or them not being able to have a voice in his part of the universe. There were also those that joined and wanted to be dark and pursue pure darkness. The Regime started from this. It was not the Founder's intention to start a dark army or a Regime operating in such darkness and such technical savvy in dark, but it is what occurred. He was the Founder, but there became a whole operational network that had little to do with him and that he had little control over.

I'd like to say this is the only pocket of such powerful darkness, of billions and billions of souls involved, but I don't think it is. I just don't have that information at this time and only have what I have experienced and been involved with. I do know that it hooks into other universes that are dark and have an agenda that wish to tip all 100 universes over into dark.

So, back to being captured. This 50 million mark of my existence so far. And again, so far, it's been blissful beauty, sound, kindness, and exploring science from a Pleiadian perspective. I don't remember the actual ship being overrun. I could guess a hostile takeover and being overrun. I do remember the prison area. This memory and awareness came back about a week after the Las Vegas shooting on October 1, 2017.

To note, I do keep briefly aware of events happening in the United States and around the world. I see what pulls me to focus on and quickly let go that which does not. I have felt guilty about this at times- why do I take an interest, even alert my team or intervene on one thing, but not multiple others? I was told it's probably because of what I specifically might be good at aiding. And it's not that Angels, and multiple teams aren't aware of what's already happening on Earth- it's my perspective and take on it, especially as I have aged, might actually be valuable. It's hard to sit with this at times. Because people are dying and enslaved, caught in odd crosshairs. I might glance at a conspiracy theory, but usually there is not much there, but sometimes there is and often it is of a multidimensional awareness- so then both parties are right, those seeing it purely from third dimensional, not much there and those seeing it from multidimensional. They don't know what they are picking up on, but they are actually correct in viewing the information through a different lens.

The Las Vegas massacre definitely had my attention. Not only for those suffering, but my focus narrowed in on the gunman, why? I kept thinking.

I know it sounds strange, and I'll open this up later, but it took a tremendous amount to wrestle off the Regime from our planet with it finally leaving midnight Sept. 21, 2017. It's not going to become truly apparent for probably a long time, but until the Regime moved- things were bad and going in a monstrous enslaving kind of direction. Timing was beyond tight. I hate that, but that's how it was. The Regime's methods of torture are like nothing I have seen or experienced. They are masters at getting so in there, so personal, so private places, and creating such pain. I mean it is genius and brilliant.

With the Las Vegas massacre on Oct. 1, 2017, I was confused. I was confused by rashes of violence happening after the Regime leaving shift in September 2017. I was told it had to do with those that the Regime didn't wish to take with them when they left, that those leaving were too damaged and the Regime didn't want them. That made me mad, what?! So just leave them crazed out of their minds on Earth with no hope and nowhere to go? I made a request when I saw the pattern for scouts to go out and find these lost beings and people and get them at least situated so they wouldn't harm others. I'm not sure if that did anything and maybe that plan was already in place. They still keep popping up here and there. I alert my team.

But something about this Las Vegas gunman, something. With the gunman dead, I knew he'd be in the spirit realm and I wanted to visit with him. I imagined he was connected to the Regime and he seemed technically gifted. I do have this session written out, confirmed in email as well, and of course anything I say or write here can always be found in the Akashic Records. The Akashic Records being the library of all recorded information in the great library in the Archangel Realm (except for my interactions with Source God- they are also in the

Akashic Records- but only Source and whoever he spoke with can access them).

I found the Las Vegas gunman in a well and heavily guarded prison contraption. His eyes were big and he seemed overwhelmed by everything. I saw him and felt instantly sad. I felt deep compassion and spoke with him. I could see the depth of pain he was in before he hurt so many and now as well. I talked with him and he removed a recorded tape from his heart/chest area and meant to hand it to me, but a guard took it. It was inspected for any traps and seen as clean. We put the tape in a machine and all looked at the screen as it came on. And it was me. Me talking into the recording. I was saying how we were going to get out of here and "Shhhh, be quiet, here they come." It became quite clear very quickly, he was one of the Pleiadian scientists with me on that ship so long ago that had been captured by the Regime. He was a brilliant scientist with an incredible mind.

I felt so sad, so deeply sad. I knew that all the scientists on the ship that day, except for me, eventually were so brutalized and broke and turned into the Regime's hands of darkness. The only reason I did not break was because of the tireless support, effort, love, and care of my twin flame working on me, our connection- from a distance- without me even knowing it.

I am thankful my old Pleiadian scientist friend could see I knew the real him and I loved him. I pray that that helped him in beginning to work through all that he would need to to recover.

I know there has been a lot of controversy- was there more than one gunman, were there other odd occurrences that happened? I can't say for sure. It is such a loaded time moment- did dark and light try to insert in differing ways to help or hinder the outcome? I don't know.

Through seeing myself talking to him on the video- way back in time- I remembered that time of being captured and in the holding area prison cell. I believe the Regime wanted information and the scientist's capabilities. The Regime intruders were loud and gruff, twinkly and violent eyes. I just kept breathing. I don't have much memory except for a few in the initial stages. I remember being interrogated and he just kept going on and on. I don't remember pain. I do remember starting to feel bad for the interrogator- like the experience and the harsh light against the pale gray stone walls- and the droning on, the repetitiveness- it lulled me into a state of seeing how much pain he was in and how he was trapped too. This didn't seem enjoyable for him or make his life force happy. As clearly something other than me being distressed was happening, this angered my captors. I wasn't sure what I was supposed to be doing. I imagine, that as I was under and in more pain, my twin was sending me more love- just a guess. I do see that this was the beginning of, out of survival, my soul DNA slowly and organically shaping and shifting to see and feel the light in dark areas. I was with the Regime for about 50 million years. My memories are confusing.

As mentioned in the fall of 2016, I met the human form of the soul that I thought had been my Pleiadian friend for so long, saw us off, and handed us over to be captured. He had really just infiltrated the Pleiadian Realm. Having him ongoing around in my life in present day- sparked memories. I'll continue on in the chronological history.

As I wasn't breaking, the Regime interrogators must have called in their supervisor to figure what to do with me. As we were waiting, my old who I thought was my Pleiadian friend appeared, now showing his true colors and form. Like a bratty spoiled Roman son of a Roman general- that's what he reminded me of. His father was a ranking higher up in the Regime and his son was....well he just was fraternity bro crass. How exactly did he pull off being so different in the Pleiadian Realm? How did I miss this? I still don't know. Maybe he was just relaxed and letting his guard down now. It was such a harsh contrast. He absorbed me into part of his household and I believe he wanted me to....have a relationship? Having no mother around and just a general for a father, I'm not sure he knew what care or kindness or affection was and definitely not love. I could see him wrestle, but there just wasn't much in there-robotic. Was the Regime breeding out these qualities in their off spring? But still- it was harsh, the verbal abuse, the sexual abuse, the fear, the tormenting and like before- I eventually felt sad for him as I could see a soul lost in there and sad for how he was being treated. I could see his attempts with me. I never developed feelings for him, but I could see the pain and it made me sad. It also was a strengthening of my soul DNA to survive by finding light, really digging through and honestly seeing the root.

In 2017, was a year I worked through a lot of transformation and a lot of multidimensional sessions. In one, it became clear- after I had read a news article about how a doctor was caught branding his initials in organs he transplanted. It became clear with physical symptoms I was having that something was wrong with me. In the session, we were able to see the branding on my field at the heart and through great technology able to pull it off. The greater detail on this is in an email. As always, after every session, I write my notes of what I experienced to my team, to check for accuracy and I imagine for them to check what translated and what did not. I am fierce about scientific accuracy and checking my findings over and over again in differing ways. It just is so important. Once the branding came off, my physical symptoms cleared up and the soul/human- past Pleiadian in present time stopped physically and energetically pursuing a continued connection with me.

As a side note- my skills and talent in the healing arts and sciences definitely comes from the amazing abilities, technology of other realms and my ability to merge realities and download it from these realms. The technology and capabilities are like nothing I've seen before. It's quite fascinating to me at least. I was aware of it starting in 1994, but I'd say this really began in earnest for me spring 2001.

Getting this Regime general's son off of me in present day was good, but what happened those billions/millions of years ago? I don't remember much. Still in the time frame of this 50 million years in the Regime Realm- my next memory is being in the hallway getting something and looking up and seeing the great Founder looking at me. I knew who he was and I was startled and I apologized and scurried off on my assignment. In this time frame, I was still dealing with the general's son and it was tiring. I started to notice though the Founder more and I felt him watching me. I could feel it in my body. It felt warm, but startled me and I'd look around and then see nothing. I'd try to think on something positive or see something positive and go about my day. And then something happened. I was told I would be working for the Founder now. And I never saw the general's son again. Oh, I was thankful.

The Founder had that twinkle in his eyes, which now scared me, but he wasn't violent- there was something there, but I wasn't sure. I was now part of his household and it was so much nicer. Again, my memory is fuzzy. I do know it was out of the deep Regime territory and the cult vibration it carried. The Founder's home was a large gray stone simple castle, drab, but quiet and simple. The landscape was green and rolling hills and sky and birds. Beings of all species tended their fields and families. Oh, it was heavenly compared to where I had just been. I was so relieved. I began to feel true happiness start to really come over me and I did my chores with grace and ease. I loved seeing the villagers and especially the children with their mothers. That made me the happiest. I had never really seen that before. Most of the beings I met were Reptilians and they were kind and loving and very family centered. Oh, I had fun. And then I'd come back to the castle and work where I was needed. The Founder would sometimes come in to give an instruction and I would just lower my gaze. I would notice though sometimes when I was gazing out the window in the kitchen, I felt something wash over me like someone watching me, but I turned and there was nothing there. Oh, I loved that castle so much. This time was just so special and unique. I'm not sure how long things went on like this. One day, I was asked to help the Founder directly, maybe it was dropping off tea or clothing needed. I just remember looking for something in a basket and him motioning me in to his room and being frightened. I felt overwhelmed by his presence and then he kissed me. Him kissing me and this intimacy, I just fell right into it. It caught me completely by surprise, but I fell in love with that first kiss.

Early on, now this is a strong memory and confirmed through a session and through email, early on I was laying asleep on his chest very happy and he took a sample of my DNA to have it tested by his personal science team. He was thinking of having my DNA altered so I would fall in love with him. On testing, they let him know I already was in love with him. I'm not a DNA specialist by any means, but there are different ways to work with DNA- there is hard DNA and then there is the soul of the DNA- they both have an impact. In learning how I was, he was stunned and relieved but stunned. He wove a spell over me as I slept and in my sleep my energy bodies agreed that we would always be together and contributed to the spell and the weaving. A vow. I could feel myself snuggle closer into him. Oh, I so loved him-intelligent, beautiful, kind, solid and mine. I was so in love.

I enjoyed caring for our home and making it special for both of us, especially for him and doting on him. I loved spending time in the villages and caring for the women and children especially. I loved working and being in the gardens a bit. I was deeply happy.

Now, the Founder might be gone for stretches of time and I could see him wrestling and sometimes he'd be angry. I could feel him troubled. In hindsight, I think this was trouble with the Regime and how darkness was proceeding, wishing to proceed, and the Founder was in the midst of it. With the Regime going against what he had intended for this place in the universe, it was hard for him. It would get better at times and us making love a lot always brought us close. I can say that he truly did not want to create off spring. The drive was not in him. I never felt this pull in him and I never knew why. I later came to find out his fear of the pain parenting can cause and fear of how Source or really anyone might take advantage of him if he had a child- worried him. Because he felt no pull and I as a Pleiadian don't remember ever seeing off spring and families in the traditional sense- it was just us enjoying us and was very freeing.

Around this time Source God sent scouts to check on how I was doing, which I don't really remember, but the Founder caught them and accused Source of spying and much worse. Leading to their deeper argument.

The episodes of the Founder's internal conflict became worse. I could hear how I was in danger because those in the deep Regime knew what I could do to the Founder- possibly helping him back to Light and the worry of what

I might do to the whole Regime operation if I was allowed to remain alive. I grew scared.

In our home and land, in the sky- dark clouds would roll in and then flow away. The Founder became more violent and was like mumbling to himself. I didn't understand what was happening. I don't remember. I'm thinking now, why didn't they just kill me then, what stopped them? It seems to me it would have been simple. If they saw I didn't break like the scientists I came with, why wait for 50 million years, what was the point? Maybe they had to wait for their own strength to develop or it was a timing issue? I was told later on that a plan was finally brought forth of what to do with me and it was brutal and bad. I don't like to think what that could have been.

It confuses me now that I could have felt such love and closeness with the Founder and as things started to shake, I just thought about myself? Or maybe I did plead with him and I could feel how I was losing him? I could feel the Regime coming. I knew the brutality of the Regime and it frightened me. I felt so young in trying to navigate a lot I didn't really understand.

At the time, I did not know that Light was trying to figure how to rescue me. I've just been told later that I was rescued. So, I will go with my imagination and see what images come up to describe. I may be right or off a bit. How the rescue looked factually is not something I can say. As an aside, what I have observed and experienced with any healer, shaman, doctor, or counselor- that is actually truly right on and helpful for their patient- are those that do not rely on their feeling, gut instinct. It can be part of the picture, but it isn't the picture to stake a diagnosis on or a practice going forward. I read a good Cree shamanic elder quote from the 1800's that stated- "you must not go with what you see or feel, but go with what you see repeating itself in nature". As a Lenape woman now, in this lifetime, through my father's family, and raised in the native tradition for the later part of my teenage years and young adulthood- and all that I've learned from my elders both here and in spirit and multidimensionally- I agree so strongly with this. To do otherwise is risky and can be downright dangerous.

But, back to my imagining what the rescue might have been like. I imagine a quiet moment. The Founder away, air is still, not much going on, simple village life and the dark clouds taking a break. And having my basket of vegetables with some flowers and meandering on the cobblestone back to the castle/house and just hearing like a whisper of my name and looking around me and then looking up. And then just seeing like a little opening and a beam of soft light that landed as a pool of light in front of me, small and stepping into it. Like if you've ever been in the forest and a beam of light comes through and you step into that little pool of light and it feels like nothing else exists. Well, it felt like that, but then stairs along that beam of light. And when I stepped up it cloaked me and what I was carrying just felt to the ground, what I had on fell to the ground, the clothes everything and it was just me effortlessly racing up those stairs. And then standing at the top and falling forward into arms and blacking out.

I could imagine how then that slice in the sky zippered shut and all that was left of me from that time was just a pile of clothes and objects on the path. I think now, what would the Founder have thought when he saw my objects piled so? I was told that he knew why I had to be rescued and he knew what the Regime and darkness were planning and he knew he was unable to stop the Regime from harming me. I just don't understand. It feels like if he loved me so much, he could have stopped it, and it feels like he gave up pretty quickly. I know in my heart that that isn't the case, but it stings. I struggle with not comprehending how a Source God figure of equal power in certain regards couldn't stop it. On the other hand, the reality- there are rules in creation and structure and it has to be weighed what can be broken, what simply can't without other consequences. It really isn't simple. I know Source and those like him are put in horrible positions at times.

I have come to be able to see in a session and been verified in email that the Founder had a piece of my soul he kept in a small dangling container and wore around his neck, tucked close to his heart. That is comforting. For me, it hurts more now to think about this than it seemed to hurt me then. Maybe because now the threat to me is limited, not gone, but limited. The Founder makes other appearances in my soul history and, excluding my present lifetime, he is always in the background. In them, my poor Founder has become so monstrous and brutal and mentally sick. It was many things that led him to this, but I wonder how losing me contributed.

Reflecting briefly on the rescue- it reminds me of times I've helped people in their dying process. Before I explain, I should note my current professional work is in integrative healthcare, my practice started moving in a more medical direction in 2008. My training and interest, but also all that I've been through, how much trauma in my present lifetime, the other lifetimes whether known or not, working on myself, getting help, learning- has put me in a unique situation to not be rattled by really hard stuff. I can meet people in such fear and suffering and be there with them in a real way. I have and do see it repeated so many times and so many ways that cells, energy fields, souls, tissue have it all in them-what they need to move forward in their highest and best good and comfort zone, they know in there. The body/being just needs a container, a listener, space for it to come forward and ground in the body/being in a bioavailable and organic way- to hold, take roots, and not create a kickback. This usually requires a multidimensional effort and follow up homework. It sounds simple maybe, but it isn't. It takes skill, practice and it's tricky- how to bridge a way for trust and the practitioner to truly have no agenda. The only thing I won't do is help people harm themselves. Holding right where they are or healing, I'm good with. I think it is a more pre-colonial native approach in my skill work. I rarely see it elsewhere as I describe.

I remember this one patient I had been working with for years. It was hard. She so wanted such help to heal certain ailments, but other parts of her did not want to heal. Would fight herself every step of the way. I've only seen this a few times in my practice. I saw how I could stay out of the drama and just meet her with some basic structural physical help and be a comfort. That seemed to work. The time came for the dying process and she moved into a respite house and I worked with her there. And we worked. Her fear of dying and what was coming was palpable. I could tell her from my other experiences what I saw and what I knew. Upon leaving the body a portal opens up of a different vibration than the third dimension and you see these colors that don't match what we have on Earth. At the doorway of the portal in this vibration, there is always a loved one waiting for you, always someone you know and are happy to see. It is so wonderful, indescribably beautiful, and you feel this freedom in your movement and joy. You feel right at home. (As an aside, I have seen where this is not the case, twice, but help can be gathered and brought in). But I think, what I described to her happens quite a bit and with me there and her asking for my help and trusting me to orchestrate it- I would do what I could. But still she just was so, so scared. I could be there with her terror and made a vow to her that we got this. I could see the portal and her husband waiting, the good light, but she couldn't. So, I thought and prayed for help and it dawned on me- we could in a very slow titrated manner raise the vibration of the whole room multiverse, multitime, multidimensions, multirealms, multirealities, physically, emotionally, mentally, and energetically- seal the room and a foot around the whole parameter. Meanwhile, I'm checking to make sure I'm not going to blow a fuse or harm the building or anyone else's process. The good thing about working in a medical facility- they usually are wired for a lot of power to move through- third dimensionally and thus otherwise. We proceeded in this manner. And sure enough, she settled for the remainder of that session and the next day coming. The room was noticeably just a hair different and it continued like that each day increasing, until just before she died- the vibration of the room had lifted up to just barely meet the portal, enough where she could with steadiness and peace walk in. When I am able to help with this, orchestrate and structure it well, I feel good. I feel like I've done my job well and figured out the bridge, puzzle that was needed. Even if no one understands me, I know her soul does. I firmly believe that while there are lots of lessons and things to be explored in our life, even really painful horrific things, it can still be done in a way that is honoring, a crafting, just something other than traumatic. Again, going back to my native upbringing, the rituals were/are scientific in what they were achieving with the human's neurology and tissues health and nervous system processing as well as so much else. At the time, the words were not there, but it was deeply rooted in science. My job is mentally tiring more than anything else, like a multidimensional chess game of all these moving parts on so many levels and ways. I don't get attached to the person or the outcome- just if I have done the best I can offer and understood the dynamics. I do care deeply, but it is the patient's journey and story and honoring what comes next for them- a deep honoring of their time.

So, I was reminded of this- thinking of my rescue at 100 million years old. It was more of an ascension process I guess, as my body did not remain in the Regime Realm. At the top of the stairs, blacking out and falling forward into the light, I just remember the hands catching me. The sheer exhaustion of what I'd been through for the last 50 million years and constant fear had taken a toll I imagine. I don't remember what happened after I woke up.

I could go back to my imagination and best sense. Where was I? Maybe in a simple place. I wasn't dead, but what realm, planet was I on or in? It just felt simple and therapy and basics and breathing and rhythm to my daily life. How long was I there? I really have no idea. I do wonder if in my healing certain memories were buried or held until an appropriate time. Still, the first 100 million years and my time with the Regime had an impact. I was told later that after this was a time of healing for me and a settling. That I needed quite a bit of time to heal before incarnating again.

The next lifetime I remember and where I have spent most of my time I think is in Reptilian form. The Reptilian race is vilified on Earth from books I've seen printed, posters and images, movies, TV shows, etc. To me and my experience, this is not how most Reptilians are. For sure there are those that have gone on over to be with the Regime and/or dark. The Regime is the largest dark organization I know, but I imagine there are others.

Who are Reptilians? Again, I can only speak from my experience. I can't say if there is like a particular planet, or is it a part of our universe, or is it a whole realm? I'm not sure. I imagine it's some kind of combination. I know they look reptilian human like and are tall, strong, and fast. It is an interesting combination to be both incredibly strong and fast at the same time. At some point in time, I think Dragons and Reptilians had a common descendancy structure. They have similar qualities.

Reptilians are extremely intelligent, scientifically brilliant, and master geneticists. They are extremely loyal, very family oriented, and dote on and love their young. As noted, my first experience with Reptilians was seeing some in the Regime, but more the Reptilian families in the villages outside the heart of the Realm. I felt their love for each other and generosity to me when I lived with the Founder. Reptilians are kind and brave and can be fierce if need be. They are very regal. Maybe there are pockets and sects of Reptilian nations spread out through the universe. They have been involved with much in our universe. For example, with the human project and helping in creating humans, genetically they helped a lot.

My incarnating into the Reptilian lifetimes- I know I was just happy, a lot of happiness, playing, and exploring. In one lifetime, I was born with my twin brother and we were very close. My first memory, which later was confirmed, it was like we were high school age and it was a summer night. We were seated outside on a bench, enjoying the night air. We were just joking and talking. We made a vow there that if anything ever happened to either of us, we would never give up on trying to help the other until they were free, safe, cared for. Always. I felt such love for my brother. We were different in some key ways though. I've always been more cautious than him, looking at something from a few angles, more hesitant, thinking on things. My brother was impulsive, quick to be enticed into a cause.

A few years from this point, which could in reality have been a few million years, it's hard to say, but relatively speaking those first Regime recruiters came into our world. Up until this point, we hadn't heard of the Regime. I didn't remember it. It gave me a chill while my brother thought it was great and amazing. The energy and drive they possessed. What they planned for the universe, for all species- more equality, less chaos, security. I saw the twinkling in their energy fields and eyes at times and I didn't like it. I could not put my finger on why. What they said made sense, but something felt off. My brother was excited and dove in. I held back, but over time the Regime took over our world. I was working as an assistant for a ranking officer, but I kept to myself. It was so rigid and made me sad. I tried not to think about it too much. I was in the minority- everyone else seemed excited and into it. I stayed to myself. The officer began to display romantic notions to me and I just skirted around it. I'm not sure what happened here. I know in myself now 2017, we had to do a roll back to this time frame. With Source God's help and Archangel Michael and others to do a rollback- where I firmly told him to stop and no and left him. As allowing it to stay as it was in time, was impacting me in an unhealthy way in present day lifetime 2018. This rollback correction- I would not say this was a time traveling experience. To note- time traveling is not a common phenomenon as it is highly dangerous for everyone and there are many rules and regulations. This was just a shift. I'm not super sure of the difference.

In the session, when I did the rollback to this Reptilian time, I felt and experienced it like it was yesterday. Source God was with me asking me questions- such as, it really is your choice to keep things exactly as they are. My concern was that if I broke the officer's heart, he would dive deeper into the Regime and the Regime would use this as fuel- how horrible love is and how horrible Source God is, etc. Source said to me, yes that could happen, but it's your choice. That was hard, worrying if by following what I wanted to do, not have sexual relations with this officer would it- would it have bad consequences for innocent beings? So sad and hard, I listened to myself deeply. I broke it off as gentle as I could. I instantly felt a freedom ripple through me all the way into present day body and being. I was glad I was able to make the choice that spoke closest to my heart. But as I did this, a shift occurred in that time frame. In the way background was the Founder, who was so dark, who just looked like pure manipulative evil. It frightened me. I said to Source God- he knows, he sees the whole thing what we are doing here, he sees you. In fact, is the Founder orchestrating this, orchestrating the officer to have romantic feelings towards me? To have an officer then become more cleaved to darkness? The Founder will hurt me- this is just bad. I had no other recollection of the Founder and thought him the whole mastermind behind the Regime and just evil. As predicted, I broke it off and the officer was so angry and exploded into rage and this was used by the Regime and he went deeper in. I felt more freed up from this roll back and the change needed in present day 2017 softened and shifted, but the price I worried about. Who was I to cause others suffering, but yet who was I to have to be a sex slave in fear to spare others?

To note- in any of my work- with myself, with patients, clients, students, homes, land, multidimensional work that could impact any part of our Earth or beyond- I made a choice a while back that I don't wish to be involved where innocent people or beings die. Even if there is a greater gain, I just can't live with it at this time. This happened for example in May 2010, and is documented in an email exchange- where I had a visitation about helping to move something. When I hooked in and helped it moved there was a huge earthquake in Chile and many people died. When I told the Angel communicator, he said- "so yes, see your power of how you can impact great change". But I was just very upset, and told him this, people had died. This was not okay with me. I was thankful the Angel communicator said I did not need to be involved in anything that made me uncomfortable. As an old human mentor who understood the multidimensional world and visitations once said to me in 2007- you have choice, you can state your boundaries and limits. And as another great teacher said to me in early 2008- light, those of light, always respect and encourage your free will, they don't have an agenda for you. These tenets have served me well and is truth I've seen.

There is much more with my Reptilian twin brother, but it seems better to weave in at another time point. To say he got lost and sucked into the Regime is an understatement. It caused me great grief to not understand what he was doing and to feel and see him alive, but that I'd lost him. The Regime was an awful cult.

I imagine before the rollback, back there, billions and millions of years ago in the now Regime occupied territory, I must have just muddled through. It was very sad. But still, this was other, my general experience and remembering of the Reptilian world is that of home, feeling home, settled and happy. This Regime experience became part of it, but not enough to flavor all the time I spent as a Reptilian.

My next Reptilian lifetime has rolled out in my understanding during my present lifetime- a slow roll out starting in the year 2000. It was extremely upsetting and confusing. There have been many helpers with this and experiences, of course the emails much later on confirming everything, which was settling. The following information was gathered during the last 18 years.

The next Reptilian lifetime I speak about is about 1 million years ago. I would be roughly close to about my current age of 3 billion years. All I write here- I remember clearly.

I grew up in the Reptilian Realm and I remember my Reptilian dad clearly, as later on he incarnated as my human father in my present-day lifetime. To note- my father in my present-day lifetime I can see now definitely had not recovered from what he'd been through in this past lifetime. It explains why I most likely was so tight and close and protective of him present time- although not knowing this as a human child. His soul was the same, personality traits, interests and of course our deep connection. I note how after my father died present lifetime, as he got more acclimated and happier in the spirit realm- he went back to carrying himself and presenting as Reptilian.

So, back to this Reptilian lifetime, the last lifetime I remember as Reptilian. I'm about 3 billion years old and

1 million years out from present day 2018. I remember having a beautiful home and interested in my studies at school. My memories start when I was going through puberty around 15 years old in whatever relevant Reptilian time frame that would be. My dad was a well-accomplished and successful scientist, specializing in genetics. A main project he had begun working on was the human project. He was aiding in the endeavor.

What was the human project? 12 Creator Gods had come forth to discuss something new, to work together on and later on gathering others to assist them. I should start though then with who are Creator Gods? To the best of my knowledge and what I have gathered through experience, sessions, and email confirmation- way back in time as Source God started to create- there were some like him. As I have mentioned, the Founder being one I know of. I'm thinking the number like the Founder is small, relatively speaking to other of our Source God's creations. In addition, originally were created the Ancient Ones- very deep and steeped in knowledge of our universe, all aspects of our universe. Ancient Ones help run and control the engine of our universe and are generally wise, powerful, and holders of deep knowledge. At around this time were also created the Creator Gods, some we see depicted in the Greek and Roman myths. I was surprised to learn that they are quite real. Creator Gods learn and grow just like any being, unfortunately collateral damage gets accumulated. They are powerful like Ancient Ones, but Creator Gods are more in to creating and I don't find them always as reflective. In fact, they are often very emotional, passionate, and highly reactive. I instinctively feel the

Ancient Ones are older, but that could be because they just have different aims and structure. I know that our Source God has often been overwhelmed and frustrated with his powerful yet unwieldy Creator Gods, not all, but a decent amount. Like, for example, they literally do not see that cornering, seducing, raping or pillaging young human women as an issue. Source God has put a hard stop to that finally, but this is an example of how things can get out of control. All beings have personalities, but Creator Gods are especially vibrant and displaying of their individuality, needs, and wants.

But what was the human project? 12 Creator Gods, I'm not sure of the complete full thinking behind this, were interested in creating beings that could house a library of a lot of information and ways in our universe. I'm not sure fully. What I do know is that 2 of the Creator Gods were connected to darkness and that Source God had not been able to contact this path into darkness for quite a while. The other 10 Creator Gods did not know of this connection. They all went to talk with Source God about their project as he would need to provide the life force and the souls- was he interested? Source God thought on this. He was most interested in having an avenue to reach the beings and the path in darkness he had not been able to reach for a very long time. He knew basically how things might ensue. He signed off on it and the project began in development.

My father at this time was aiding in looking at a genetic piece to the human project.

He had a good friend and colleague, another male Reptilian. Both my father and his friend were around 50 years old to my 15-year-old self, relatively speaking. I had known my father's friend for my whole life, as a child and up till now. In reflecting about this and all my lifetimes, I do detect a very common theme of feeling extremely simple, behind the scenes, plodding along in my curiosity of science, reality, and nature. I see the theme of my being observing, alone, and then being pursued for reasons I've never really understood. Sigh.

One day, I remember being in my room studying for school seated on my bed when my father's friend came in and began talking to me. Seated on a chair. I was so confused. I was flattered by his expressed feelings for me and it made me feel warm, but I did not think my dad would like it. One thing though did lead to another- it warmed me and made me feel good. I don't remember all the details, but we had a strong love affair and relationship. We kept it hidden from my father for about 4 years. In hindsight, I have to wonder now with him being so much older. At the time I was happy, but very young.

We did eventually tell my father and that we planned to marry. My father was extremely upset, forbade it, and forbade my ever having contact with his colleague again. To say this put a rift in their relationship is an understatement. In hindsight, I can see my love and I had a strong relationship and if my love had talked with my father- I think it would have worked out. I personally was so young, like a little deer in headlights- I was just scared. My dad did make good sense in that look at the age difference and this is just bizarre, etc., but I still hold it could have worked out.

For my father's friend, the turn this took hit him hard. It was devastating. I've come to know now that way back in the day, he had lost his wife and had never healed from it. I have to wonder now if I reminded him of a young version of her. The whole series of events was very triggering for him. For him to think of losing another that he already thought of as his wife was unbearable. He couldn't think straight, he couldn't reason, and he couldn't plead his case. He was just all emotional and the emotions and rage and pain spilled over.

My father's friend and my father had been working on the human project. It was coming to some fruition. As mentioned, 2 of the Creator Gods were not exactly as they appeared. They were in part with the Regime, yet only Source God knew this, and as the project began to complete- the 2 wrestled the project into more of their own hands. With, "but yes, we are doing this, we helped create them and we can mine them for needs we have, we built them". To note- much like how animals are in our current time raised on Earth or fields cultivated. The other 10 Creator Gods were angry- this was not the plan.

I'm not sure of all the ins and outs on this. I do know that my father's friend, my love, had rapidly descended into working with the Regime, darkness, and the 2 darkly aligned Creator Gods. My dad argued to protect the genetics he helped create for the human project- my father's friend, my love, threw my dad in jail. I was devastated. Seeing the pain in my father's eyes as he was shoved into prison by the Regime is something I will never forget. It was a deep loss and pain. Myself alone, my father thrown in jail, having lost the soul of my beloved, and the Regime gaining strength here- I was so upset. I don't remember what happened next, my memories go blank.

I do start to see a pattern. Some soul suffering in lifetimes I remember, some comes in flashes or is necessary to remember for my current lifetime healing, growth, and evolution to go through. But a lot- I just have blacked out. This seems healthy and wise. I do feel it's very important to one's health not to push memories.

In my current lifetime, 2017, due to events unfolding- it became important for me to visit my Reptilian love during this past time. It was important to have a session and check in with him after he had made the decision to be with the Regime and after my father was in jail. It wasn't time travel nor was it a rollback. It might have felt like I was in a dream to him or a hologram. I'm not sure. I opened the session and was at a window outside amongst the stars, looking in on him and in his high-rise, beautiful sequestered large suite. It was very luxurious. The colors were orange, red, and yellow. He looked to be alone, studying some writing or data. I tapped on the window. He looked around startled. He saw me and briefly smiled. His eyes though were so large and filled with such pain and deep sadness. I wanted to scoop him up and carry him so far away from there. He let me in and we hugged each other. He looked behind him at the door where a very large Regime sentry I could imagine stood. "You shouldn't be here," he said. We talked. He was so upset about the choices he had made. Then there was a knock on his door and the guard began to come in. He asked the guard to pause for a moment. I hurried behind a curtain. The guard came in and began sniffing. He looked around and saw nothing, but he kept sniffing like he could smell me. I was reminded how scent travels through time and dimensions. The guard left and I went back to the window to leave. We were both sad I could not take him with me. The full description of this session is documented in an email. It's painful to remember. How I couldn't save him or do anything- it made me very sad. But I do remember thinking, as I left, how much was this about me? And how much was he living in the past with me and just remembering his wife that had died? That he just was never truly seeing me or being present with me.

Part II. Earth

Again, my information and experiences are limited. As extremely odd as it may sound, the planet Earth was created by Source God as a beautiful loving present for his future wife to come. I have viewed the planet Earth though mostly as an amazing living library with all these incredible keys into all the abundance of life, beings, dimensions, and history in our universe. It's just stunning. And one doesn't need to go much of anywhere multidimensionally except look into the scale of a fish or the bark on a tree to see and experience so much. Most Indigenous cultures know this and their scientific exploration and profound rituals tapped into and learned all of what I share here plus so much more. This wealth of knowledge and wisdom was then given into the tribe in a manner that was teaching, healing, supportive, and available to where the tribe was. So many layers and richness.

I believe it was just Source God that created the planet Earth. I could be wrong on this though. I know the amount of intertwinedness that created the human project. I have wondered did the Reptilians help with populating the dinosaurs for a while while Earth matured to keep away any other beings that wanted to take over Earth? I can just imagine a population of beings looking down at Earth with all the dinosaurs and just thinking, "hmmm, no, we'll pass". It is sad that the dinosaurs were wiped out, but I imagine it was time for humans to start to come in. Again, I'm a bit fuzzy on this.

So, how did the human project get up and running? Again, I can only speak from my experiences, sessions, and confirmations in emails or deeper clarification when I struggle with a concept.

It is true that there was originally Eden on Earth. I'm not sure where exactly. And Eve and Adam came down. Inside of Eve were 6 souls and inside of Adam were 6 as well. This has confused me, but I was told it was necessary to package it this way for a larger pool of DNA to pull from. All of humans that exist came from these 12. One of the souls inside of Eve was Source God's wife and he knew this- although no one else did. He had kept this a secret from her and from everyone- for protection. The souls were going to separate out. But then, he realized his mistake pretty early on in Eve landing on Earth. He could not be with his wife unless she was connected back with her twin flame. Without this occurrence, Source God trying to be with his wife would be too much for her soul. As he was trying to figure what to do, 2 of the 12 souls wanted to do something different. They wanted to go explore. The others did not. But as they were all tied up into only two bodies, a decision had to be reached. Adam and Eve decided to leave the Garden of Eden. The tree was more of an offering of how dark and light could work together, but Adam and Eve (or really the two who wanted to leave) did not wish to see that. Source God let them leave. He was distraught at being so close to being able to claim his wife and having to watch her walk away.

Source God with a wife? It sounds odd, but I imagine billions of years of seeing other couples- like with the Creator Gods- it was something Source God longed for and felt it could help him grow as well. He did not tell anyone of his intentions. He thought and felt and programmed deeply and she was created, the soul that it is. She did not know it, but he saw her birth and I imagine just smiled to himself and began preparing. He let her evolve and try out things while keeping a watchful eye, just waiting. Around 10 million years ago, he recognized the right time frame in the future when he would propose and make it official to the universe.

Adam and Eve were placed on planet Earth about 300,000 years ago. Was this one possibility he saw an opening for, to court and propose to his future wife? It seems like it to me. As mentioned, he realized and quickly saw the necessity of bringing in her twin flame, too late. He was looking at correcting his error when the 2 souls in the package of souls in Adam and Eve pulled the rest out of the Garden of Eden. I can only imagine how crushed Source God must have been.

I've got to wonder what Source God was thinking. Even when he got the formula set up correctly, did he just assume his wife to be with her twin flame would be open to another relationship inside of it? He saw all the jealousy and backstabbing that went on with his kin close to him and between the Creator Gods. I sometimes wonder why didn't he just create an individual soul, why create a soul with a twin flame- wouldn't that complicate everything? Maybe the hardness of having to share your great love was part of the process? I don't know.

So, Earth- this beautiful, rich, and enchantingly gorgeous planet. My first lifetime memory on Earth is as one of the 6 as Eve in Eden. I do wonder how that came about. How was it chosen which souls would come forth and why, what was specific about our soul DNA? I remember having long brown hair and being very tall with pale white skin. I remember sitting down at a river and the colors. In hindsight, they looked like the colors I've seen in heaven when I've glimpsed inside- in helping others during their death process. The colors in Eden were denser than the Archangel Realm, but had that luminous flowing alive feel. In this first memory, I was talking to a plant by the river. It was easy to fall into extreme presentness in Eden and the beauty was astounding- so alive and talkative. It truly made my heart soar to be in such a beautiful place. I grew tired and laid down on a mossy mound underneath the Sun. Everything felt so sensuous and good. I was happy, but then I felt like I wasn't alone. I startled awake. There was a rustling behind thrushes. But more than that, it felt like someone was watching me. There was no one there. I tried to rest again, but was a bit on edge.

In hindsight, this was Source God checking in, but I don't remember having any connection or communication or knowledge of him. In fact, in none of my past lifetimes or memories- do I ever remember anyone mentioning Source God, much less my thinking about him. This strikes me as odd. I see a theme in my lifetimes and how I feel- scientific, very curious, observant, caring, concerned, emotional- but not spiritual. Is "spiritual" a thing off Earth though?

Regarding my Earthly lifetimes, I have a few lifetimes that I'm aware of prior to my present day one. I'm not completely sure of the order. I imagine a historian of human events would be better at this. I just have never pressed for the order and allowed my knowledge of the lifetimes to naturally unfold. As mentioned, these memories have come up as needed, organically, then been verified in differing ways. They usually come up to help me make sense of symptoms I have now or struggles I'm working in. At times, it's been about keeping me out of danger. It's never been linear, lots of repetition throughout the years, the emails have confirmed what I was experiencing, sessions were bringing up, etc.

After as Eve in Eden, my second lifetime memory is in Atlantis. My initial memory is very specific. I was working in a lab and under a microscope and saw something. I became very upset. I raced up to the lead scientist and showed him my findings, what I had documented. He was shocked and raced to find the king. But when he got there, it was too late. The Regime had crashed through into Atlantis and it was just chaos. I was outside the lab when I heard what was happening. I ran back in, knowing I couldn't get back out. The lab locked and began filling with water quickly. I dove under water, the water so crystal clear with a bluish tint, and found my notes there. I somehow had a trap door to stuff them in and hid them. I swam back up and was gasping for air until it completely flooded and then I don't remember. I assume I drowned. I gave up my life to hide the notes. Notes that I would ultimately go back in in 2018 in a session and find them again, handing them over to my multidimensional team.

So, it would come full circle in 2018, for me to uncover with help what I had hid, but even just thinking about it now fills me with deep soul anxiety like it was yesterday-my heart pounding and hands shaking. Did my uncovering this information cause Atlantis to fall? I've been assured not, that it was part of the equation, but not the whole picture. Which really doesn't settle well with me. What I'm still trying to wrap my head around is- with my uncovering certain information, was the Regime alerted and on our doorsteps within seconds? It makes no sense. Maybe they were already on their way? Or maybe they had been aware of markers that would lead to my discovery and really their uncovering? I've been told what we were doing in the lab made them worried so they stepped up their invasion. But still, there are things about time that I just don't understand. I'm reminded again for all that I understand- it is all so vast and complex.

Atlantis- myself was just a behind the scenes kind of person. I guess besides this memory, my soul has really not felt the need to reveal much more than this. Atlantis reminded me of what modern day Venice must be like- the light, the beauty, the closeness with water- although the connection with water in Atlantis goes deeper. Atlantis reminded me exactly of a bit denser Pleiadian Realm but on Earth- just in resonance with colors, twinklingness, science, awareness, multidimensions. The Atlantis people were humans and very kind, very involved, and evolved in their energy medicine modalities and science.

In present day, 2018, in a session, I did have a visit of what is left of Atlantis moved to another realm. It was good to see the king and his family and to be greeted so warmly. I opened the session to not quite knowing where I was. I was standing in all white and slightly pregnant with my third human child. I was accompanied by my closest three male beings- one on either side of me and behind me. I looked up a row of beautiful white stairs to see the royal family at the top. Much open air feel. As I ascended to greet them, I could see the light they exuded and they were warm offering me tea. We went to visit one of their labs in studying and caring for plants- as I was wondering about my own journey with plants, emphasized greatly of the importance for me to do so by my native elders. I felt happy exploring this in Atlantis and was most drawn to a little aloe plant. We were discussing what part of plants most appealed to me. The full description of this session is recorded in email.

To note- I could see myself in Atlantis doing this or even other realms, but I don't see it yet on Earth. Sigh. Which, as of 2018, is where I would like it to be happening, where I think it would be best if it were happening- this desire to be more unified within third dimensional reality.

What I did notice in the session with the Atlantis lab of plants, and have come across in my present life experiences, is that plants are the best third dimensional connection to many cultures, species, living libraries of vast quantities of information throughout our entire universe- incorporating the layers and dimensions. How brilliant and powerful. And for the most part, many have not been altered. Their intelligence and awareness are astounding and such a rich beautiful link into the cosmos.

The next lifetime, my third, I think of is in Avalon. Avalon happened somewhere in the current United Kingdom area. I believe I was more of a, blend into the background, priestess. I don't have much memory of this lifetime, except for a continued and full relationship with Merlin and his owl and dragon in my present lifetime.

Merlin, I became aware of in 2008 and he has been quite helpful. He fully understands the confusion of having awarenesses and talents and not sure how to manage them or what is going on. He has been a strong helper, guide, and mentor for me. He can easily cross most of the realms. I remember in 2008 when he would say how I reminded him of the Lady of the Lake, which I found endearing, but hoped to handle my powers better than she. He has pushed on me about my calling to be the "Goddess of Time" which felt like a riddle to understand. Literally sending me an owl in the physical realm to be by my side, a foot in front of me staring at me- till I figured it out later, what the message was. Merlin has helped me numerous times in healing sessions with others. For example, like learning from him in the moment how to protect my patient's neurology- who had stopped breathing, and was in a coma when I visited her in the hospital. I actually worked on her with Merlin right next to me, showing me what to do. The doctors were quite surprised when she awoke with no brain damage. I could have explained what I saw and what was done, but didn't see the point as no one would have believed me. I've worked on all kinds of people in all kinds of situations. People are kind and thankful, but refer to it as magic or ask me to do "that thing I do." It's not. It's science and physics and takes a lot of brain power and skill to work correctly. My fascination and interest are enough, but it's lonely and frustrating to be so misunderstood. Merlin's Dragon has been very kind and helped me with existential issues and his owl has kept watch over me, literally at times in the forest.

As an aside, as I think on this, I do have to measure my experiences and constantly keep weighing them on how to proceed. Things and awarenesses I can handle now, I simply could not years ago. I did not have the structure back then and it would just upset me tremendously to the point that I would be shaking and having a rapid heartbeat. Keeping some distinctions of the realms is important to me. For example, even if I know Merlin is around- I need to open a session or through email or during a healing session with a client. He can't just appear. And yes, I do see the difference between the third dimension and otherwise. For now, when Merlin's Owl has broken the barrier- just swooped down right next to me and is staring at me and talking to me telepathically, that is too much for me and I find scary. I may say differently someday, but I like boundaries and need them. I don't like to be surprised like that. I have had that no boundaries experience hard core from 2001-2003 and it caused great trauma for me to be that aware like that all the time and such a constant blending. To each his or her own, but for me- it's just scary.

As I think about humans and evolution, I just want to pause and comment. Evolution does exist, but so does the fact that humans as we see them did drop into sight fully intact by their makers and help of Source God. These same makers as described also created many other creatures- so there is a learning process. Evolution exists on Earth and evolution exists in the labs that created many of the said creatures that were brought to Earth.

Both forms exist. I could be wrong, but I don't think there is going to be found a human that came from an ape. Sure, we share a lot of the same DNA and properties- I imagine we share similar makers. Where does this leave Neanderthals? Maybe a prototype?

Well, back to my own human incarnations. I don't have many memories. My recollection continues to roll out as needed. Before my current lifetime, there is also one in Turkey, one in Greece, one in Egypt, one in Damascus, and two in North America. I'm not super sure of the order.

In Turkey, this lifetime memory came up because of being sparked by events in 2017. In September 2017, my team and I couldn't help but uncover what was pursuing me hard. In encountering the Disgraced Creator God for a few weeks and trying to figure it out, get it settled- our previous times together spilled out. I will say that my current lifetime seems such a crashing together of important times for me of the last 3 billion years. In 2017, while I was going through a lot of transformations and sessions in figuring on it all- certain attachments, I've had from so long ago did not like this change. The following Disgraced Creator God has caused some real damage and suffering for me and for many.

I'll start with the memory in what is now known as Turkey. Such beauty and color of gold, red, orange. I was a servant woman to a higher end woman with some royal birth. I was aloof. I liked spending my time by the river, in nature, with wild life. I tried to serve my lady well and knew I had it good. I had been with her ever since I could remember. As I began to enter puberty, I changed in height and increasing beauty, but I stuck close with my lady and felt safe with her. She was distant, but kind and I just kept to myself except maybe for a blind old elder that would be in the gardens by the river and we would chat. I loved the sunlight. One day, a new courtier arrived. He was charismatic, and dashing, and dressed in beautiful regal armor and such. All the maids and ladies were fawning all over him and he talked well. They all were under his spell. My lady was married and found him a bit dull. I just hid behind her. I didn't see what the other girls saw in him. I found him odd. This seemed to spark his curiosity about me. I just stayed out of his way.

One day though I was in my lady's chambers on the ground sweeping and picking something up and then he was there. I was startled. He found different ways to meet me. And then he really started to pursue me. I was frightened and confused. I know that I was raped and was confused by it and somehow ended up falling under his spell. But never fully. I was still myself and my interest in nature and little ways. He could never fully figure me out or be there with me in my heart. I could see he wanted something from me, but I wasn't sure what. I was very young in the ways of women and men and had no education really to speak of. I didn't associate with the other girls and was painfully shy. It didn't prepare me for anything. The attention was kind of nice and he was always nice to me, well not the first time, but in other times. I was just so confused. And then I became pregnant which made me very happy. He seemed happy too. I was humming away in my tasks happily and he said he would figure it all out. But then I began bleeding and lost the baby. I was so deeply sad. And completely shut down from him. I don't remember anything after that.

What I have come to learn since then, is that this was no ordinary man. This was the Disgraced Creator God, coming to try and collect me. I have learned that after myself being separated from my twin flame back 3 billion years ago and before I incarnated, I was marked. The Disgraced Creator God was hiding out- collecting, marking souls he thought might be able to join him at some future time. But what does that really mean? Wasn't I properly looked after, especially after being separated from my twin? How did the Disgraced Creator God find any way to have access to me?

So, who was the Disgraced Creator God? Way back in time, this Creator God had done something bad and repeatedly not listened to Source God. So, at that time, as Source was still learning, he stripped him of his status and banished him as punishment. As we can all see, including Source himself- this did not help anyone. Source God no longer does this, but back in the day, he did. Which really did not help the brain of the Creator God, which was already struggling. This Creator God had been born with a host of genetic markers towards mental health issues- like a collection of bipolar, schizophrenia, ADD- to name a few. Source God's treatment of him sent these markers into flipping on and into overdrive.

This poor Disgraced Creator God with all these powers and abilities, in a brain struggling, isolated and alone and confused. Not only did he become a tool for darkness at times, he tried desperately to create those he could be close to and could be close to him- family, friends. I'm not sure what he did to me after I was born in the marking process, but he was hanging out on the fringes of the place where new souls came out- looking for souls that had certain properties.

Even in the lifetime in Turkey, I didn't recognize him as anything other than just a man. Only much later on, did I understand and see where his first insertion in my soul history came in. Which is an awful long time to have waited to make a move? Maybe there are other lifetimes? I'm not sure.

As mentioned, I do recognize there are a lot of themes in my soul's history that keep repeating themselves. Repetition is so common in so many ways in our universe, in the dimensions, on Earth, in all the species.

The next lifetime I'll mention is Greece. I don't like to think about my lifetime in Greece. This memory got sparked a few different ways and again confirmation in email eventually. In my current lifetime, I've always wanted to visit Greece, as long as I can remember. In 1995, an opportunity arose for me to tutor and take care of two boys for the summer in a small town outside of Kalamata. I loved the countryside and it was one of the most beautiful places I have ever been. I loved the Mediterranean. And considering no one spoke English, except for the one boy I was tutoring- I sort of blended into the flora and fauna. Every night I slept outside. It was a powerful time and I knew it, but I wasn't sure what was happening. I would swim in the sea for hours every morning. The light was incredible. I loved all the little trips I took. One trip was to Delphi and as the bus climbed into the mountains, my heart started racing. It was odd.

And then standing outside the steps to the Oracle, I couldn't stop crying. I thought how horrible it was that young girls were chosen and forced to perform as priestesses. It upset me so much. I was also drawn to the sacred majesty of the place at the same time. I felt like I had been here. I couldn't put my finger on it. But all these feelings were rushing back- like why did no one help these girls?

Much later on, I would come to understand that I had been one of the virginal girls chosen and the fumes I was forced to inhale were like a drug making one delirious. It terrified me. It was very scary and traumatic. To this day, I don't like drugs or alcohol- altered states that can't be controlled terrify me. Being around others under the influence of drugs, upsets me tremendously. The one who put a stop to this abuse of me in my lifetime in Greece was whom I later came to know as Creator God Greg.

Creator God Greg, now that is a long, long, long story. I'll weave it in. He is one of the numerous Creator Gods who would argue with Source God about things, rightfully so. For Source God to look at his horrible behavior we see outlined at times in the Old Testament. Greg would hold him to task with basic questions like "what are you doing?"

Creator God Greg is interested in the light and dark play, trying to see how dark techniques could be used for good and opening up all the techniques more. A similar being, trying to understand slices of reality in a new way, like the Founder. This did not settle well with Source God. They still got along though and Source valued his input.

The Ancient Ones could see the intelligence, power, and compassion in this Creator God, uniquely unto him, and felt he had great promise.

Creator God Greg eventually grew frustrated with the rigid old school council of the other Creator Gods that wanted him to stop with his looking and figuring on the dark and light interplay. Creator God Greg finally got fed up and left and isolated himself from Source and the others. He didn't turn dark and he wasn't banished. In fact, he was greatly missed. He felt though misunderstood, not seen, and not valued. Somewhere in here, he had a female Creator Goddess counterpart like a twin flame, who he alienated and hurt. She eventually left him. It was a tremendous source of pain for him all around. Alone, he would explore his techniques, but he was deeply sad.

I'm told he found me about 500 million years ago. I don't have any strong memory of this, except being in a field-the Sun above me and feeling something around me. This would have been in the Reptilian times I'm assuming. I have to wonder with all that I've been through how do others figure when to step in or not? I know that Greg, once putting claim to me, kept off other Creator Gods, but that didn't seem to stop the Disgraced Creator God in Turkey. Was the Disgraced Creator God cloaking himself? I could have done a lot worse than Creator God Greg and in fact, our souls have a lot of similarities and interests. We are a good well-suited match. Compared to for example, Creator God Zeus who back in the day was a disaster inside of his numerous romantic craziness.

As mentioned, Creator Gods like everyone in this universe- Source God included- is learning and growing and evolving. I am thankful that Zeus has gotten better about his romantic/rape issues. I have come to know Zeus and am very thankful for his aid on the few projects I'm aware that he's helped me on. He really is an amazing warrior- extremely funny and playful and powerful; his lightheartedness and joy and sense of humor with his raw power is something awesome to watch in action.

Source God did put a mandate to stop Creator Gods from having sexual relations with humans eventually. Creator God Greg did not hear this mandate, as he was isolated, so- as Greg puts it, he didn't technically violate God's will later on. Sigh. Again, I feel and see how so much has come to a head in this current lifetime. Everything rushing in and crashing down all at once and me just trying to catch up, stay present, and ground.

Onward to my next lifetime I think, or at least the one I remember, in Egypt. This memory came about in 2008 when I began taking classes from a yoga teacher and I recognized him, but couldn't figure out from where. He had a strong energetic presence and bright, but strength and awareness about him that was a bit odd. He would be talking to me during or after class and it was the human him and then this other soul him that felt familiar. It was very distinct and different. I started digging into it and of course, later on confirmation. It really opened up what this was. I was a young boy, street orphan, in a city in Egypt, and for whatever reason an older male sorcerer/scientist/ healer took pity on me and brought me under his wing. Of course, maybe he just needed help, but oh my goodness how thankful I was. Food and a place to stay and above all protection- so thankful, so happy, just in complete thankfulness and service to my kind master. I would take care of the home and help in any way I could. I was not magically inclined, but I was curious when I would see him working out different things in his lab area. I was quick to follow what he needed help with- just the kindest man. And at this time in Egypt, things were creepy and weird, energy flowing all over the place, power struggles- it was so intense and scary. To have the protection of a strong sorcerer, seemingly out of nowhere was the best. But those in his field with more power and darker and ego, did not like him. I believe he was eventually thrown in jail or worse. I just remember them coming after him because he was different and I was frightened. My memory goes blank after that.

My lifetime in Damascus maybe comes next. Damascus is a city I've always wanted and hoped to visit someday in my current lifetime. I had a passing Italian friend in New Mexico who was on her way to visit and stay in Damascus and later on, she would write to me about the great beauty of this city and the kindness and grace of the people. It has quite upset me to see what has happened to present day Damascus, such an amazing ancient city. I can't comprehend that it is all but destroyed from fighting in Syria.

The following memory of my time in Damascus was initially sparked by my toddler daughter sleeping with her hand on my shoulder. It has rolled out more since then in differing ways.

It starts with me in the kitchen working on a meal for who I help care for, himself and the home of Saint Paul. He was often writing and I saw how hard he worked, how carefully he chose his words, his deep compassion for others and concern. He was always working very hard and deeply aware of other people. He would neglect himself so I always tried to take extra good care of him. I was older than him, I think. He always seemed pondering and thinking.

I've had other memories of this time. Viscerally racing through the streets to find him as Roman guards were coming and being panicked. Not understanding why he wouldn't at times reach up to God to save himself. Not understanding what was going on in his mind. I could not read, but his presence had such light when he smiled. It pains me when I think of racing to find him and not being able to help him more. I grew attached to him- the person, the behind the scenes daily struggle at times I saw him go through. He had such an internal process.

When I read his writing now in present day, I'm often reminded of the behind the scenes- of him soothing his own fears, of him bolstering himself. It's painful for me.

My next lifetime began my journey in North America. It takes place in the Massachusetts area. I have a very brief snap shot of myself at the stake in the woods to be burned for witchery. I only very recently fell on this image because of work I was doing in sessions in clearing some of my past up and making shifts in my cells. I think I remembered it because I was able to create a change and save myself much pain. I've suspected something like this lifetime for a long while. I just couldn't see it. In my present life, I've never been able to light a match well. I can be around fire, but my holding a flame, it takes a lot of discipline and control to reason with myself what is happening. I don't know if others feel this way about fire. I have always felt the flame is going to instinctively jump and leap onto my hand. That it will attack me and I won't be able to stop it or get it off. It has struck me as odd to have this fear. In my present life, I have tried a few times to live in the Boston area and I just can't do it which could be either from this past life in Massachusetts or the next one. The area is thick with levels of atrocities to healers of old, native peoples, and then a celebration of things and ways of being that make me uncomfortable.

My next lifetime, and the final one before my current lifetime, has been with me in my awareness for most of my present life. It started rolling out more fully winter 2001. My former high school classmate's mother and father were stabbed to death in their home in a quiet town in New Hampshire. It was a random act of violence after the parents spoke with a stranger who asked for help and they warmly invited him in. It was a shock. My high school best friend contacted me to tell me. She coincidentally used to be roommates with the daughter impacted, and who I had just visited the both of them only a few years prior. The pain in my right hip became extremely bad. To note, this right hip pain has always come and gone- later to learn that even in utero things were not firing on correctly with deeper muscles in this region. No understanding of why. The pain kept getting worse and worse. Something about the parents, taking in a stranger, being kind and helpful, and being stabbed to death. My hip pain got so bad that finally the following memory exploded into myself. After I revealed the memory to myself, the pain did stop. This memory has weaved its way through a tremendous amount of my current lifetime history.

The year is around 1823. I am a member of the Teton Sioux Nation in the Wyoming area. I'm about 15 years old. I have a new husband and an infant son. This started out as a very low key, happy lifetime, connected with family, tribe, and nature- so much, I loved to walk in the beauty. We heard of the trouble. It was a troubling time. I felt that my whole life to be sure. I was always a little on edge when the trouble brewing in the east would be talked on. Something was odd, not right what was happening in the east. Lots of talking and deliberating. And then after a party had gone- a few made it back and my husband fell off his horse with a knife wound in his belly and died in my arms. It was horrific. I was terrified. Two weeks later, an army came into our camp and slaughtered everyone. A man of the cavalry ripped my son from arms and dashed his head in against the rock. I was screaming and trying to protect him. I remember this like it was yesterday. It is so vivid and clear. I was stabbed in my right hip. I remember laying on the rock dying and hearing the screams and cries and I became very silent as I watched the clouds drift past and a few birds flying above and the trees sway in the wind. All witnessing, the Creator witnessing. And in that moment, I lost all faith in the Creator, I lost all faith in Source God.

It has been a beast to come back from that memory. I have come to understand and know there are three things that break a human being and that can break a soul- losing a child, being abused and harmed as a child, being unable to connect to the parent as a child. These three things I have seen repeated over and over in the wandering of souls looking for help and an easement in a suffering that is like a black hole. Until those areas are healed, the human is just spinning- harming themselves, harming others- the pain is deep. The death of a child or having a child forcibly removed from the parent condemns that soul for lifetimes to be in one of the most dangerous spots in their heart. A soul can come back from this, but it takes a lot of help and care.

Losing my son in this manner, it took me about 200 years of a lot of hard work to even open to the possibility of loving again and to trust Source God. Even if my mind was there before then, my soul was not and nor was my heart. To risk it all again. I did decide though it was better to risk again, then to live isolated.

All the native people I have met on the other side, have all healed amazingly. I feel very fortunate in this lifetime and in my current lifetime to be born in such rich and healthy lineage of how to be a human being- with all that is encountered, including great suffering, loss and grief. This pretty much goes for any Indigenous tribe that has been on Earth for 30,000 years or more. To be fair, a lot of these are basic principles one can observe with any animal or even plant species if you listen and watch.

Part III. Current Lifetime

This past 3 billion years lays the foundation of coming in for this lifetime. Now, I really wish, I so wish I could have had a few more lifetimes- crafting possibly an easing into this current present life. Like a lifetime where I had a great love, a soul mate even (but not my twin flame) to work through some of my trauma about love and attachment; maybe a lifetime where it was good with my family and community and I felt like I fit; maybe a lifetime where I was helped out of my shell and a bit more leadership skill development as all of my lifetimes have been about serving others and being behind the scenes more hidden; maybe a lifetime that was just basic, very basic and healing. I think that would have been good and best. But that is not what happened and I really can't understand why. Unless we look at time and there just wasn't time? Maybe my last lifetime was meant to be that and it got screwed up? It seems like something is always coming in, busting up my quest for calm.

I hope to not be shocking. I will give a brief bare bones outline of my current lifetime and then flesh it out, emphasizing what seems relevant to my writings here. All of this information has been verified in various multiple ways.

Myself, Bridget Randall Kimsey, born August 13, 1973, Baltimore Maryland- my baby picture looks nothing like me now and looks like a Native American infant, my right hip- deep lower transverse abdominal muscle never kicked in and have always had pain and weakness there; born of Irish and Lenni Lenape/Delaware descent;

United States citizen and member of the Delaware Tribe of Indians

Father, from Oklahoma, the Randalls are the Native side last name; my father was my father from Reptilian time 1 million years ago; my father pursued a career in science and worked for Johns Hopkins University and Medical Center with electron microscopes; he dealt with heavy depression and anxiety his whole life; our bond was powerful, pure unconditional love for each other- a powerful connection; he could throw some energy, not always the easiest to be around, very Reptilian; died 2011

Father's family- nothing large stands out

Mother, from Maryland- a ball of energy, very extroverted, ADD or ADHD, always talking, caring but seems to have something like split personality disorder, fractured self, becomes dangerous if feels threatened, a bully, manipulative to the highest degree; anxiety, strong denial of seeing herself; I remember as a child at the age of two and a half years old- there was nothing to hook into there, it was very odd; there was no ability to connect to anything in there; I know my mother loves me and I do love her- but because of her fierce energy and pit bull need to dominate- it's a no win situation, just vicious and toxic. I have pushed against it and tried to find a way in there, but it is and always will be very unsafe around her- unless she honestly wants and gets the help she needs. A lot of who my mother is, extends from her mother and how she was manipulated and never got the help or maybe didn't want the help to get out from underneath of it. I chose a different path than to stay and be brutalized, scapegoated, made crazy and to feel horrible about myself.

Mother's mother, from Maryland, born in 1904, her family from County Cork, Ireland; her mother died when she was a child; my grandmother was seriously deeply cruel, harsh, manipulative and a gaslighter; at a soul level and in other dimensions I got to really understand the real evil nature of her, where she came from, how she developed this way. Her soul ended up being destroyed- as she went after the Archangel Realm in 2017. I have not seen a soul destroyed prior to this. Source God and others go above and beyond to really see what options there are. But on this- as I stood inside the Archangel Realm- and she still came after to attack and kill me, she crossed a line and destroyed herself; she was given the option to stand down, but she chose her path.

My stepfather, from Connecticut- I think started off pretty well, but my maternal grandmother's lineage- what she set in place, no one has been able to escape it. He did get sucked in and started turning pretty dark over time- just dark. To the point that in his hatred of me, in summer 2017, he was approached by darkness, unconsciously to him that is, and made a deal with darkness. He would help darkness separate me from my twin flame to make me suffer. I don't believe he knew this would kill me, but it would- as it would leave me open to darkness's plan for me and essentially hand me over to them. I was devastated to learn this. From 2001 to 2017, I have not had any contact with him nor my mother and stayed out of their way, yet he would wish me this level of pain and to hurt me? I struggled greatly with this. Am

I that horrible of a person? Maybe I am. I struggled greatly being raised in part in a household where I could feel the level of sickness and abuse happening to me, but didn't know what it was or what to do. This is a deep pain in me, as I strive for understanding and objectivity and truth. I can only go with what my experiences, sessions, the emails, and teams working with me have shown. Even then, it's not something I've come to terms with. Thankfully, I have at this point some solid protection against darkness and the Regime, definitely not perfect though. There has been a target on my back for as long as I can remember. The attack on me by my stepfather and darkness was stopped by Creator God Greg, Archangel Michael, and others. My stepfather just forfeited where he will spend a good amount of time after he dies. Honestly, to me, it's just shocking and ugly and sad.

Rest of mother's family- not much to mention.

The following is a chronological history of influential events, people, and beings as pertains to this writing.

I have mentioned the biological family I grew up in.

As a 2- and 3-year-old I was aware of energy colors in a room and could hear people's thoughts without them speaking. I was confused how I would know something was about to happen before it happened, like a song on the radio or a cup falling.

At 3 years old, I fell in love with yoga. I have an active memory of doing shoulder stand and plow in the garden of my daycare center. I remember thinking- "this is the best, best thing ever". I was told by my mother I used to hop around my aunt to do yoga with me, as she and I would practice together sometimes. I was also told how I used to take huge risks physically- standing on my little wheels and going flying down hills. I don't remember this though.

As a toddler and child, I felt exactly as I do now at 44 years old, but I couldn't always put understanding or words to what I was witnessing. I commented a lot to myself internally on trying to figure how reality works.

At 3 years old, I was aware at times of an outside kind voice, a little above me at an angle, mentioning and pointing things out to me. This was the case when in the living room with family and on the floor my uncle was tickling me and there were weird energy flows. A strong other voice was in up at the angle telling me to remember this moment, this is important. In hindsight, it was learning how energy can work between humans.

At 3 years old, going through my parent's divorce and their fighting- I could feel it like nuclear bombs going off and my brain changing in response. I felt extreme fear and loneliness. I became extremely cautious about everything and felt much discomfort being in a physical body.

At 4 years old, understanding long division and math on being shown it, but then couldn't retain it. I got very frustrated with my brain and could not understand what was wrong with my head.

At 5 years old, I talked a lot to myself, but I could have been mimicking my mother as she did this. I remember in a drama/movement class how I loved exploring how reality worked and felt myself most alive and whole.

At 7 years old, going to the science center with my dad numerous times and crying when inside the planetarium because I felt home and didn't want to leave. I felt a deep homesickness looking into space.

At 8 years old, I was influenced deeply by the movie "Gandhi" and learning about Martin Luther King, Jr. I began experiencing excruciating mind-boggling pain as I felt trapped in a life and circumstances that felt so awful. I began to get involved with dance which helped.

At 9 years old, watching "Close Encounters of the Third Kind" and wished I felt a pull to something like that and wanting to be in the desert. In driving out west with my dad and going through South Dakota and the Badlands- I did not want to leave. I felt a strong sense of home and that this is where I should be living.

At 10 years old, I was extremely and deeply upset by the television show "V". I wanted to watch it, but couldn't, and felt very confused

At 11 years old, I liked to look at pictures of Jesus, but did not know much about him. I liked going with my best friend and her family to church many Sundays for years. There is a picture of the crucifixion I would look at for a long time and study it. I had many thoughts and feelings I couldn't describe

At 13 years old, the "Terminator" movie had a big impact on me and shook me. I immediately resonated with it and felt like I was looking at my life to come.

In high school, I was involved with musical theater. I could see that I looked different than others moving in front of a video. I'd heard comments like the camera loves you or there is this light about you. It could have been something else, but heard it quite a bit. As I got older, I developed terrible stage fright and didn't like it. I left all amateur and professional performing arts work.

In the spring of 1991, in a bookstore looking at books on Native American myths, I wished I had a way in to this connection, but just didn't see one. My father's family was active with our tribe, but they were all out west in Oklahoma. Still, I daydreamed and sighed and put the book back.

In the fall of 1991, I had my first boyfriend at 18 years old and sexual activity. For me, tension myositis syndrome (TMS) began. It would take me until 2018 to understand the impact of this person and relationship and why I developed TMS from it. In a nutshell, with TMS the human being experiences such an intense rage and emotion, that the brain feels it's dangerous to have this, and creates a distracting tool- creating a brief but painful oxygen deprivation to a part of the body- usually the lower back. Once identified by Dr. John Sarno at the NYU Rusk Institute and treated, my pain was gone in 2 weeks, but have had reoccurring bouts to work through. This was my first real understanding of how the brain and body operates together and new ways of comprehending the human system. I was able to free myself from pain, while I witnessed many others with undiagnosed TMS having surgery, pain medications, etc. If I tried to speak of my diagnosis and treatment, I was often dismissed.

This began what felt like a split from myself and others in discussing reality.

At 19 years old, 1993 early summer I think is when things began in a new direction for me. I began being woken up in the night with my body humming and vibrating. It was odd. I started feeling a chorus of beings reaching down to me and would see images of bears. It concerned me, but would come and go and if I grew frightened would leave for a few days. Around this time, things started clicking into place- the book Black Elk Speaks was given to me by a roommate. I was told by my paternal grandmother about money being held in escrow for me in an Indian bank account after our tribe had sued the US government in 1973. I was a baby at the time and the money was held for me until I was 18 years old. I got my tribal enrollment card sent to me from the tribe and collected my money. I felt things shifting around me. That fall 1993, as I was walking to class at NYU, I looked up and saw a large flag sign for the American Indian Community House (AICH). I walked in and once they understood I was a member of a federally recognized tribe with my card on me- the doors opened up to numerous services, help, community, health care, education, and job opportunities.

AICH and those connected or guided to me by them- helped raise me for the rest of my adolescence and early adulthood. I was provided everything- from a social worker, group for those struggling with alcohol addicted family members (alcoholism runs on both sides of my family), understanding native experience of life vs. other cultures, community events, elders getting to know me and listening and directing me on a path, help paying for college, and securing my first job after college. After NYU, I worked in a private school- learning/teaching Lenape history to third graders. I also began living in the AICH executive director's apartment, received help for a health care crisis I found myself in, learned and followed a healthy model for connection and community, and had a feeling of not being alone. At AICH, I was surrounded by many others who had similar introverted dispositions and trauma in their DNA and home. At AICH, there was less concern about what you do vs. who you are. By elders, I was nudged and directed onto the path of yoga and energy medicine.

Summer 1994, I was caught in between a few different paths. I had gone back to Vermont thinking that would be nice- staying in a little cabin off the main house of my mother and stepfather's home. One night I was woken up by a powerful visitation and dream of my mother stabbing me in the leg- like she couldn't control it- trying to kill me. I was startled awake by the reality of how dangerous she was and felt presences around me in my bedroom shaking me awake. My mother didn't see herself, she'd never admit it, and she'd never get help. Something was wrong here and I should not be relying on her for help in any way, shape, or form. I decided to stay at my boyfriend's home and get some space. I was feeling confused. I felt even more out of sorts- with separation and truth about my mother appearing to me. Feelings and memories of how I truly felt as a child that I had frozen and buried for so long started to surface in a flood.

Fall 1994, I felt more creative and aware than I had felt in so long, but all these other scary feelings kept coming up. I was thankful to have an affordable option for housing in NYC. I ended up subletting from the director at AICH her apartment she was not using. It was good all around. I felt deeply safe and able to fully relax there and ground, but then things really opened up. The fall season had always been a time when it felt like I became more sensitive and aware. Later I would learn about this seasonal time as a thinning of the veils between dimensions heightens. I was more aware of energy and felt presences in the apartment around my bed. It scared me. It was like a 180-degree shift in my life was happening, starting that summer, and I was terrified. It was all so much. I had a nervous breakdown and ended up at NYU hospital for a month. They did a number of different tests, which I am thankful for now- ruling out schizophrenia, bipolar, etc. It was diagnosed that I was in a major life change and had had a nervous breakdown. I realized right then and there if other major shifts were to happen in my life in the future- they did not need to be this dramatic. I would find and cultivate a different way.

October 1994, I remember clearly, at NYU Hospital, as for two weeks I wasn't getting better. I couldn't get the flooding to stop- there were no buffers. I also felt myself the real me more. So, it was a double-edged sword. I found lots of different programs in the hospital helpful. I especially liked art therapy. I did have a realization that I had to make a decision if I thought the universe was run by something good or something bad. I felt this need to figure this out. I thought about it. I finally decided it was good and that I would take a breath and start from there.

And then I started to get better. I realized I did not want to be a performing artist. I was good at it, but that was my mother's dream. It had been a great tool for expression, but I was free to be me now and didn't need to do that to have a voice. I wanted to take a break from school. I wished to return someday, but I needed a break now. I really started to calm in myself making these hard decisions. Through this experience I find it telling that AICH staff and members are the ones who visited me and cared for me. I did not feel safe or comfortable enough to tell anyone in my biological family. Zoloft had recently come on the market I think and I began to take a bit of that and that helped so much. It did not change this opening or shift or intensity of new reality I had stumbled into, but it buffered it some. I was so grateful.

Into 1995, life was so different for me, but I was so much more grounded and happier. It was daunting to wonder what my future would be like. AICH wrapping around me, my elders in the spirit realm as I know now, wrapping around me- the structure was amazing. I do remember a friend at AICH, a few years older and also aware like me in certain ways- he was Lakota, Lenape, and Mohawk. He visited me in the hospital and so kind- saying he had been through something similar when he was my age and this is what happens to healers. I didn't understand it at the time. With my native community, when I just talk with them and just am in that circle- winds of chaos stop. I am left scratching my head at the what the very loud busy outside dominant culture is doing.

February 1995, I was directed by an elder to try and go to the Johrei Fellowship. As soon as I walked in, ohhh, I loved that place. Johrei is a sect of Buddhism out of Japan, but is essentially a non-denominational organization. Johrei has a lot to do with connection to our elders and ancestors. Johrei is an active form of downloading and spreading Source God energy into and around ourselves, others, the Earth and just helping to remove clouds. It felt amazing- like not having a shower for a very long time and then suddenly getting a shower for the first time. Sooooo good- like drinking water in the desert. It was free too and supported by donation. It was the first organized spiritual organization I felt comfortable in and got involved with for years. I started out receiving Johrei a few times a week and then became trained in Johrei and giving Johrei to myself and to others. It helped me a lot and had a very tangible impact on how I felt. The founder Meishusama, long history, but basically there is the sacred writing of God's name in a scroll anchored in a pendant worn and Johrei can be harnessed through that and flow through the providers arms and over the object receiving Johrei. Both the giver and receiver are receiving Johrei light and one can also give Johrei to one's self. I often would put myself to sleep at night, giving myself Johrei.

You don't have to believe it or imagine it- it is a real force. I knew this then, even if I couldn't understand it like I do now some 20 years later. It was a quiet neutral safe structured introduction to energy medicine work. Johrei does not interact/harness with the provider's energy at all. It collects in the worn scroll and moves through the provider and its only purpose is to remove clouds. For example, if a person is internally generating negativity, receiving Johrei is not going to change that engine, but it at least will give that person some relief and unburden them a bit from the clouds this negativity is producing. Honestly, I experience Johrei as more masculine and Reiki as more feminine. Johrei supporting the container and Reiki with the ability to go in and actually create something new.

When I eventually left NYC years later, I was sad to leave the Johrei Fellowship, it never got old.

Summer of 1995, I had a job offer out of the blue to go to Greece, a link from the private school I was working in. Thankfully I had my passport ready to go. I spent a few days thinking on, but had no other plans and work didn't start back up again until fall. It felt like a good fit. Again, thankful that AICH helped me pause and really think it through. This helped, as there were times the trip got hard. Greece was my first time being out of the country. It was surreal. I've mentioned how the trip went for me. It was contemplative and I have to wonder the impact of sleeping next to the Mediterranean Sea, outside under the stars for days, weeks, months on end had on me. Where did I go at night? What happened? Or maybe nothing. I find that doubtful, but I don't have any information to back that up. Greece prior to being in the European Union was truly a lovely laid back and happy place- at least that is what I observed. By the end of the summer, I wanted to stay and had an offer to stay, but I also really longed to be home in NYC. It was a bit of a shock to come back to the U.S.- it felt very dense and the lack of light, it was a bit much, but I slowly adjusted.

Life was humdrum then, but that was good- I was learning, taking care of myself, learning about me, reading a lot, restful. 1996-1997, I did go back to NYU and finish my last year.

Summer 1997, yoga opened up- another elder from AICH recommended I check out a class with Ravi Singh, Kundalini yoga lineage. I wasn't sure. I used to do yoga as a small child and loved it, but other yoga I had tried- was just okay, not really me, just didn't like the teachers or feeling. It just felt odd. But as my elders and AICH seemed to have a knack at pointing me in a direction I liked, I gave it a try. It was nice that the class was offered at an old classroom space at NYU. That felt familiar and accessible. The teacher was just a great teacher and had this glow about him. I liked the chanting and breathing. It was very electrifying. I ended up going quite a bit for the next 6 months and wanted Kundalini yoga to be a path for me, but it was not. This style of yoga started to make me feel ill, jittery, scattered, and to have a racing heart rate.

January 1998, I saw an ad for an assistant manager position at YogaZone in mid-town and that looked interesting. I was hired and began taking yoga classes there as well in ISHTA yoga- Integrated Science of Tantra, Hatha, and Ayurveda. This would become my foundational training in yoga. I took a class a day or more for 6 months. Krishna Das was a friend of the founder/owner Alan Finger and had just come back from India, so this is who I did kirtan with for the first time in an intimate setting of 30 people. On hearing his voice and the experience- I just cried. It was simple, clean, powerful, and a cut into the soul. 20 years ago, yoga was not popular like it is now. Back then, great legends to be were accessible and easy to study and talk with. It was a very fertile time in my yoga exploration. My first year of yoga study and training, opened me up to how powerful the practice of yoga, breath work, and meditation was for me. Again, like in 1994, I could feel if I was starting to go too far- I would flood with emotions. From my experience in 1994, I knew it was not good for this to happen.

Summer 1998- a pivotal gathering of Native Americans healing Native Americans wellness circle came through and gave a long intensive workshop for a week at AICH. When I signed up to join, I could feel it was going to create a very radical shift for me. I'm not even sure the extent of how powerful it was. I'd say my walkabout started right after this to find my ancestors. It was a conscious need and decision to live and draw close to them. Everything else faded into the distance to this need. The journey would lead me from July 1998 to July 2003. It was not easy, but during the process I felt connected into me and the fullness of it. It was like an engine- sometimes I would forget it was there, but it was in the background going. I can see that now in reflection. I really tried my best, but the journey was bumpy and traumatic and that makes me sad. I know when I work with others now, a hallmark of my work is to find a way that is not traumatic, that is like walking on the beach with the tide coming in or going out. A big shift can occur, but it can be and feel organic and there is a rhythm. If set up and structured well- one can almost be unaware and only conscious to the point that is helpful.

So, things worked out that I left New York City in July 1998 and I ended up in the lower Catskills. I had a small apartment and worked for the St. Paul's United Methodist Church. It was not lost on me that I grew up on St. Paul Street in Baltimore, Maryland. My life had shifted radically in just a few months' times and I was so confused. The pastor there was kind and recommended a good therapist. I had sort of thrust myself into the wilderness. I had felt so good, such momentum in the summer, but now fall 1998- what was I doing? No AICH, no Johrei Fellowship, no YogaZone. I realized then the power and help of community and the importance. I felt very sad and alone. I didn't want to go back, but I was alone now. I made the best of it.

September 1998- I started a talking prayer every morning. I have continued with this communication for the last 20 years. Although in the beginning, no response, no visions, no sessions, definitely no emails- I didn't even have a computer or email till years later anyway. I just felt good doing it and my mind and being felt clearer. I was taking yoga at the local Y and soon, was asked to teach. I did for a year and liked it, but took a break as I felt overwhelmed by it. Most of my yoga practice then became internal and exploring and seeing how it weaved in reality.

October 1998- I was introduced by a colleague to MAP. The multidimensional Medical Assistance Program, out of the Perelandra Institute. I read the book and felt right at home with the beings described. I realized it might strike others as odd, but it did not to me. It felt like a natural fit. Every week a session and that was pretty amazing- it was so real and shifts and helping me shift. My brain and being felt safe. It started out well enough, but I realized later on I was naïve. I thought everyone, every being if they could do certain things, or said they were with Light, well, that was just so. It really is more complex than that. To start though, it helped me change my diet to be better suited for my body and exercising- cleared my mind and being. Life moved along.

Winter 1999-2000, I reached a point where I really felt the need to be clear with my mother about what I witnessed and saw with her and our relationship, reality I experienced. I wanted to make things good between us. When I dropped the letter in the box, I felt this huge weight lift off of me, like chains breaking off of me. Speaking truth I knew in my cellular tissues; I could breathe and things looked brighter. But then her response was....as my therapist read it, he teared-up. It was always so ugly with her, no way to be heard or defend one's self, everything turned around to always point to me and my fault or someone else. It was a powerful lesson in to keep my mouth shut as people who don't wish to wake up will turn and get vicious on the messenger. The last time I heard my mother's voice was Easter Sunday 2000. To be fair, I had always known, as I pointed out that at 3 years old, there was something wrong with my mother, there was no one there, nothing to connect to, the damage was so intense in her. I really didn't have a mother- that connection. I always wanted it and was told from the very beginning that it was always me, my imagination or my fault. That was a deep cut in my soul. I simply don't know what the experience is like to have a mothering mother. But still, the summer 2000, with the pain of that, to be told again how it was me, was just ripping in the soul. I could literally feel myself rip. I knew it was not good. I retreated more deeply into myself. This makes me pause- I take my soul history, my epigenetic this lifetime history, and such events like I describe here and one could say I made, make everything up from the trauma I have endured- one could. Hence why I continually look for science and proof in what I'm experiencing, verification. It could be that feeling so rejected and confused by the third dimension, it left me vulnerable to another way, an exploration into other dimensions. Or maybe it was a perfect storm of hereditary, who I am, time frame, and a push by others discarding of me.

Summer 2000, I started feeling huge waves of energy moving through me, like constantly orgasmic. I came to find out later this was more of a Kundalini experience and it can last for years. I did my best with it. It really moved all through my body. I learned to breathe with it and allowed new choices to come into my life- music, people, food, job, etc. And that helped.

Fall 2000-May 2001 was a deeper transformation time. During the fall 2000-May 2001- I lived in a little cabin in the woods, deeper into the Catskills. I worked in a little café nearby, taught yoga down the road, and felt so sequestered and held by the experience and unfolding. I went to the yoga ashram down the road a few nights a week for kirtan and that was nice. I was still doing my daily praying, now adding in writing, and still working with MAP. It was a beautiful process and harmony of third dimensional life with sacredness. I felt open and me and trusting. A deep turn started happening in Feb. 2001, in kirtan, between my eyebrows like a vaginal opening and then it closed up and it did this for a few times and then after about a week, it rippled all through my head and opened like two halves of a flower or melon just gracefully but fully opening. Whoa. Everything looked different, colors were bright, gorgeous, sparkly, I could hear people's thoughts, and I could see what was going to happen before it happened. I remember hearing just a thought in my head from my MAP team, although I wasn't in a session- "how does this feel, how would you like this?" Hmmm. My head sutured back up. I thought about it for a few days and said, "yes, I like it, I can move in this direction." I felt happy that I had the choice to decide what I wished to do. I was told that on April 1- from my eyebrows up- my head would come off. Hmmm. That seemed odd. A week went by nothing. I sort of forgot about it. Then March 31, I had a dream about a native elder talking to me. I woke up on April 1 and checked in with myself, like I might normally do. Well, I was a little surprised- my head was gone, I mean energetically. This was a permanent shift. I worried if I'd made the right decision, but I felt that I had. Ever since this time, my head has always been cold. I have to keep it warm. I looked around; boy did things look different. I was then asked again, by MAP, a question. I remember it clearly. I was standing in my living room and felt this question move into my left ear. I was asked, "well, what do you want?" I truly felt I had everything I could desire, happiness, peace, flow in my day and body. I said "well, I want to meet my husband now." And they said okay.

Spring 2001, I worked on adjusting to new everything. After a few weeks, I did start to feel overwhelmed. My soul and heart felt disassociating at times, but I was okay. I made adjustments. May 2001, I started feeling a sucking motion, a pull on me. I started seeing signs everywhere about Greece. I didn't understand and grew frightened.

At this time, I was excited though about going to my 10-year high school reunion with my friend and just nervous, but looking forward to it. But my deep soul and panic started setting in, really setting in as the date got closer. Some part of me kept saying "don't go, don't go, nooooo." I shook it off as nerves and thought I was being silly. I'd been through a lot of shifts and changes and had been in the woods so long. Maybe I was just worried about leaving my wooded home and village life? I was generally in such a nice space and happy and open. This would be no big deal.

June 2001, I just continued to feel terrified, but pushed it aside and went to the reunion. It was awkward, it was high school for sure and I'd been sequestered for so long-it was odd. Friday night was fine. Saturday afternoon was fine. "See", I told myself, "just me being silly". The main dinner was out back of someone's home in the mountains and overlooking a valley area. The Sun was setting and it was very nice. "See" I said to myself "You were wrong. You are just a little overwhelmed with all the changes going on, no big deal." The reunion would wrap up in 2 hours and nothing had happened. I was standing there watching the Sun start to set thinking this. I took a deep breath and sighed, finally starting to relax and let my guard down. When I heard a male voice talking to one of our teachers, “oh yes, I have family from Greece”. And it was like a column of light descended down through me and I turned around and without noticing him just said, “Ti kanete?” And first, I noticed his energy turn, and then his body and he said, “what, what did you say?” And in that split second, my whole being started screaming with everything it had in me, “run, run, run, get away, now, oh my God, get out of here, nooooooo.” But I was like hypnotized by his energy field, his vibration, his eyes. “Oh, I stammered, ti kanete. It just means, how are you in Greek.” “How do you know that?” he asked. I stammered and felt awkward, “I used to live in Greece.” And it was like time stood still and we were in this weird energetic bubble. We began talking. I mentioned about my Lenape father’s side, he smiled. And from the sky a huge cord and light flashed over me and the cord crashed into my heart. Everything changed in a second. I paused. Nothing looked the same. I was like captured in a firm bubble around me. What was happening? Where was I? I mean I was here, but something had happened. What was that? We exchanged email addresses I think, but I’m not sure. It all felt confusing. There was this time before this moment and the time after. When I tried to sleep that night, my heart was beating so fast. It was one of the few times in my life where I did not sleep at all. I felt very buffered starting in on the new day. I’m not sure how I seemed to other people, maybe like in a trance. It was an odd state to be in. I felt not alone anymore. Everything seemed the same, but it wasn’t hard to drop my friend off or drive home to my little life- I felt cozy, for lack of a better word, being with me, in me felt cozy.

Summer 2001- As I got back to life and work in the coming day or two, I felt at ease, wondering what came next. I thought about Greg, but imagined he would never be in touch and the fluttering feels in my heart would die down. Things like that were just not meant for me. I still felt ensnared in a bubble, but so much was so strange since my head opened that I just brushed it off. How my life was before the reunion was beautiful, flowing, rich, and harmonious. I was good. But then he emailed. My heart began going a million miles an hour- what was this? It made me super excited and scared and frustrated and nervous all at once. We emailed back and forth a few times. I thought we were having a good conversation, but then he abruptly stopped emailing. Hmmm. Were my emotions spilling out? Did I say something wrong? I didn't like the roller coaster. I wanted him to go away. I wanted this draw to him to go away. I didn't like it. It was disturbing my beautiful life. I tried to let it go. Never in my life nor my 3-billion-year history had I pursued someone. It was a scary feeling and upsetting to feel such upheaval.

My reality started to become supercharged and aggressively so. I could see layers on reality and was getting like a download on how reality worked in relation to my mind and it was bizarre. It was too superconscious. I grew scared. I felt this outside force guiding me to these insights. It felt like a mind control oddness. This was new. I'm not sure why, but sometimes Greg would write and we talked on the phone once and it made me feel weird- his vibration like down my spine. I don't know. I struggled to figure it out. It was getting worse by the day. I felt humiliated and ashamed and upset with myself over and over again. A few weeks into this, I was getting gas for my car and I felt a whoosh of energy come over me and all around me were these signs about marriage and marry me and in my head and finally I said, "yes, fine, I don't know you, but fine, just give me some space- yes, I see the awareness you can offer and yes, okay, just yes, I'll marry you." And then the energy died down and things slowed way down. I still felt in a trapped bubble, but not pressed on. A few more days went by, nothing. I didn't feel my freedom anymore and this started to make me very sad. I felt like in a holding pattern and I just wanted to be free. I acclimated a bit and tried to regain some of the happiness I had prior to June, but it was hard. I knew I was trapped in something I didn't understand.

Bizarre experiences began to happen. For example- when I went to get my haircut, in a hair stylist's home studio and just a regular day. There was a knock on the door. She opened it and this bizarre situation unfolded. This man joltingly stumbled in and said- "I am selling light (light bulbs salesman literally), I'd like to talk to you about light". He had this intense vibration and a cord shot into my solar plexus part of my body from him energetically and I could feel life force draining out of me. I have no idea how I knew to speak up and I stayed looking in the mirror. As the hair stylist backed away from him to me and behind me. I spoke up and felt protective of her, I said, "oh hi there, I'm getting my hair cut and you are intruding on my time." "But I am selling light", he said. I countered, after looking at the hair stylist scared and shaking her head, "we are not interested and this is my time, so you need to leave now". The cord came out of my body and he seemed taken back and stumbled back and then left. I still don't know how I knew what to do, but I definitely felt something guiding me what to say. As I was driving home, it felt clear that this was the beginning of many such encounters and my purpose in protecting others and helping those that couldn't help defend themselves from what I could see. I was shaking and terrified. It was impossible. That was really very scary. I had many instances like this. One after the other for years. I got better at it and less scared, but still, I realize it's weird. I would also become aware of future coming important calendar dates. I think it was a way to prepare myself.

July 2001- by July, I knew something amazing and altering was coming to our planet, some event that would really change everything. I felt it was light and looked forward to it. I had dreams. I felt they were sort of silly about being with the Zen master of the monastery, I would sometimes go to and meditate. Him entering my dream and saying something about who I was or how he saw me- the one, light, cascading light. In the dream, we would be by this beautiful lake that is truly at the monastery in the third dimension. I sometimes would think of Greg, but I would try to push the images or memory away. I hated they would come up. He clearly wasn't interested in a friendship and I didn't like how he would drop off the face of the Earth and then be in touch other times. I didn't like it at all. It was annoying. I hated that I felt connected to him somehow and I couldn't figure how to free myself from it. It just made me panicked and mad at times. What was it? I still couldn't figure it out. Somehow, I felt I had done something wrong. I tried to make my day, my dreams, my reality, feel better than that feeling of caring I had for him who clearly didn't feel the same way. That power, vibration, love- I began working to have a life like that, so maybe it would help me get out of whatever had been created in relation to him in June.

End of August 2001- I could feel something click into place and knew the second week of September a big light powerhouse event was coming. Sept. 9 and 10, I kept dreaming of all these Buddhas praying over Earth, streams of light over and over again. So excited I felt and happy.

September 11, 2001- I had the day off of work and was going to spend the day at the Zen monastery up the mountain. I was just leaving my cabin when the phone rang. My therapist who had two practice locations- one of them in New York City- said, "we are being attacked, please pray for us" and then the phone went dead. I paused. I didn't have a television or cell phone or computer. I said a deep prayer and sat with it and then got up and went to the monastery. In the administrative office at the monastery, I watched with the monks what was happening on the computer. We were quiet and then went and meditated. I wasn't sure if that was the right thing to do. I then spent most of my time that day outside in the gardens by the lake. The air was completely still, no sound, no planes overhead. It was this pause and myself breathing. I remember thinking that when I go back down off this mountain, nothing will be the same. I left after supper. And it was bad. Being so close to New York City, with many workers commuting or strong ties, it was very dark, very bad, and a lot of trauma. Everyone knew someone who had died or was missing. I've already talked about it here earlier on. My internal responses were all over the place. I wanted to go back in time. I did not want this to have happened. I did not want to feel so connected to this. It was a defining event in my life and I'm not even sure yet, to this day, completely why. There are a lot of layers, I think.

Fall 2001, things shifted pretty quickly after that- my position closed at the café, I started working full time in yoga- both in group sessions and individual, as well as many different aspects inside of yoga. And my working so much in yoga with my quickly expanding consciousness was a struggle to make sense of things and keep myself safe from others, especially male interest in me. Which completely baffled me, as I had been alone for so long, not seen, and cloaked somehow. I moved into a more populated town. I'm not really sure why. An apartment that was rustic and beautiful by the side of a little mountain opened up. It was very charged with a higher vibration and I was more sensitive, but I really loved the space. I worried it would be too much though. I helped take care of a cat named Chaco whose owner and roommate I was replacing, as she was going back to New Mexico. Chaco was so special, ethereal, and she like floated when she moved. My vibration kept shifting to be higher. I kept trying to adapt and assimilate the information I was learning on all fronts- in yoga, how humans operated, healing humans. It was just so much information it was annoying. I remember once standing in front of the fireplace and I heard like an angelic choir singing and I asked my roommate if he heard it too and he was surprised. He heard it too. Sometimes I would smell sage burning around me- just from nowhere it seemed. The dimensions were blurring, but I tried to keep my focus on the third dimension- honor and look at the multidimensions in work or prayer. I couldn't figure how to keep things calmer and more separate. Sigh. It was a constant struggle. Yet, I plodded away at it because I wasn't sure what else to do. And still, I'd come back to Greg. He was like a lodestar in my soul and it was bizarre, but he felt safe and grounded to me and a stable force. With so much shifting and happening around me, his persona and role did not change. Weird, annoying- his presence in my life somehow allowed me to explore, just at the edge of danger- a strange container. I wanted to kick it out and simultaneously loved it.

Winter 2001- but then I came out of the shower one evening and I felt, saw his hologram image, just the energy outline there. I pulled the shower curtain back over me. This was not happening. I peeked out, still there- he had a lot to say and trailing after me into my bedroom. My heart was beating and I was panicking. What was this? I tried to ignore it and it was a force, I couldn't escape. I felt trapped and seduced and upset with myself and the experience. That began a very powerful yet twisted sexual relationship and rape situation that was so confusing, violating, and awful and I couldn't get him or it to stop. And who could I tell, what would I say exactly? It was upsetting. I had to figure how to get out of this. Now. And then I was mad at myself for being attracted to him or this. Was this truly me or a manipulation? Was it both? What was wrong with me? I tried to find a way to coincide and live with this. I kept shifting and changing to keep up with it. This soul Greg would tell me such involved information about how humans work and my own natural now heightened abilities which had begun to operate more. I started having issues at work and in prayer with fuses blowing, light bulbs blowing, and sometimes objects jumping off tables. While interesting, it startled me and made me feel embarrassed. Like I wasn't managing myself well.

December 2001, I did find a nice healing arts studio called Light Workers. The owner became a mentor of sorts for me. I learned about the term Light Workers and the author Doreen Virtue. Everything just seemed to be happening so fast. I learned about the Archangels and Angels, Indigo children and star children, and learned specifically of Archangel Michael. I did become attuned and trained into Reiki 1 and Reiki 2. I also was trained and attuned into the order of Melchizedek and Integrative Energy Therapy. And while this initially felt good, it was all so much. My old Cherokee elder mentor in herbs, who I had met in 1998, did continue to help me with nutrition and advice and that was grounding, but still- the visitations, the information, my classes, my healing work with others- just so much. It felt like too much. Having soul Greg within this as a lodestar to curl up with at night or give me pointers during the day was helpful. It was also agitating. I knew it probably wasn't healthy because if this was human Greg and this was just his soul- he was split, wasn't making the conscious connection and it would ultimately be upsetting. And what if it was something else entirely? I couldn't shake that my heart was with him and something was happening.

January 2002, Greg emailed me that he was moving to Colorado. Following a hope of his. That seemed pretty amazing. My life back in the lower Catskills continued to unfold with more classes, more clients, and rapidly opening to how the human structure worked. I wanted a break, I wanted space, and I needed time. I decided I ultimately wanted to be in New Mexico and I needed to confront human Greg in Colorado on my way. I needed to understand, put an end to what was happening. The last conversation I had with my therapist was on the phone. I told him I was going to New Mexico and did he have any experience with New Mexico- he replied, "yes". I asked if he had seen extraterrestrials there, he said, "yes and that he had left Earth and had come back". I started to ask him a question on this, but then the phone cut out. What? I tried reaching out to him then and also, numerous times in the future, but never heard from him again. And this was a board-certified therapist and pastor and really kind person- older man with a family and stature in the community. I don't understand what happened. To this day, I don't understand what happened. With everything else going on, I just let it go. But I remembered it.

March 2002, the trip to New Mexico, I'm smiling on thinking about it. Now that was wild, into the wilderness and desert- literally. I drove out. I just went. I had gotten rid of pretty much all I owned, kept a few essentials in a duffle bag and off I went. Me and my little red car. No phones or computer. Very different than how things would be in the coming decade- it was so nice. I really did think about this move before I left. I ultimately decided I needed to keep following my heart with careful caution. My first stop was Greg and I was excited to see him in person again, what would it be like? It was really hard to keep my heart, energy field, and self steady. I was so happy to arrive and be around him, but as a human- he was completely clueless, like somehow, I knew he would be. His soul gave off one message and his person gave off another. He was nice enough about it, but I was made to feel like I was imagining everything. It pushed me harder to get to the bottom of it and the science of it. What was this? I did like him as a friend, but he was the one who brought up how he would never be interested in me as more than a friend. It just was crushing and I felt like a damn fool. I didn't understand what was happening and he was going to be no help. The whole thing was humiliating and truly broke my heart at a very deep level. He asked if I'd thought about staying in Colorado, but I so wanted to get away from him and be in New Mexico.

April 2002, a broken heart and much confusion internally, I traveled into New Mexico. About 80 miles north of New Mexico, I could start to feel the energy change. I could see it. It was like a portal. It was amazing. The slogan for the state, "the land of enchantment" seemed quite accurate. I worried what it would be like to not be near water. I had always lived by the Atlantic Ocean. But the portal and the feeling of an ancient ocean that had carved the land in New Mexico, helped. Hands down, to me- the most beautiful place I have ever seen on Earth. It was majestic. It was expansive. I loved this place. At Light Workers, before I had left, a healer had done a session where I was involved and mentioned how my native elders were calling me to New Mexico and the importance of it. That could be but there seemed a lot of other things too, other beings involved. I stopped off in

Santa Fe and the vibration of the place, the altitude, and missing Greg- it was a lot. I decided to travel. I spent about two and a half months camping throughout state parks in New Mexico. I loved sleeping on the ground. I made my tent so cozy. I started off just staying a day or two in Chaco Canyon, which then turned into a month. I helped out the forest service with checking on park visitors, but most of my time was spent in the desert on trails in Chaco. I walked a lot. I showered and ate kind of. The basics sort of happened with a spigot and food kind of came about. I lived very simply and loved wandering. Immersion in the desert, my mind and being just really unwound. Until I really was out of food and just felt I should continue on. As I left Chaco to get fuel for my car, I realized something was wrong- I just was way, way, way out there. I felt altered or different. I had a hard time thinking about going back into a city or town, but eventually knew I needed to land somewhere. I stayed in a campsite outside of Santa Fe and tried to see about integrating in.

Summer 2002, I made the leap into Santa Fe. It was hard and my head hurt. I muddled along. I studied yoga and worked in a little shop. I bumped into Jan Tober, the woman who coined the term Indigo Child, and she recognized me somehow. She gave me a prayer to do each day and that helped quite a bit. She confirmed and told me I was an Indigo Adult and needed to take care of myself better. The book Care and Feeding of Indigo Children came my way and that helped quite a bit too. Doors opened for teaching yoga, for working at the Santa Fe Performing Arts, for business. It was odd how things worked out, but I went with it. I bumped into an old parent from the private school I had taught at in New York City, after college, all those years ago. She had a beautiful apartment that was vacant most of the time and that I could rent for a small fee. Santa Fe was kind to me. But the energy, the portal, the altitude- my nervous system struggled. It was hard to function and eat and I started to lose weight. My sexual energy was out the roof which scared me. I tried to end communication with Greg. I sent an email that I wanted us to go our separate ways and his response- he showed up that weekend on my doorstep in Santa Fe. Ugh, it was confusing. This was going to be trickier than I thought and I was roped in again. I actually liked him as a friend, but all the rest was upsetting to me. It was some odd game or unawareness- I could see it more for what it was. He was in the midst of something he didn't understand either and I started to develop a caring love and compassion as a real friend. We both were struggling in our own way. I did not like what was flowing around him, manipulating me, haunting me, but I had more leverage in the intensity of the energetic powerhouse of New Mexico. That helped. Things were picking up as far as work and connections and other men. Men were just annoying. I had such a hard time with my own energy. Regarding Greg, I went up to Colorado and then he came down again. I wanted this friendship to work. It was something stable during a chaotic few years. I can't even imagine what he as a human thought. When he came down a second time, we went to Chaco and stayed in the forest ranger's home I had come to know. I was able to normalize our connection a little bit. At least I kept seeing it for what it was more. He was some kind of force, or housing some kind of force in him. I wish he didn't have to run me over. It upset me that it kept happening.

I had run from New York City, I had run from the lower Catskills, and I just knew New Mexico was never going to work after about a year. I got a job offer in Majorca, Spain and decided to take it. My walkabout continued. I seriously wanted to solve this thing with Greg and it still wasn't happening. In fact, I felt more out there- how was that possible? Again, with the mantra- I needed space and I needed time. To note- I did have some odd extraterrestrial experiences while in New Mexico, but only a few and more multidimensional. There was one in the third dimension, with a ship. It was evening and I was standing off the side of the road in the desert. I thought it was a plane, but then it didn't move like a plane. It was up and down. Then some telepathic thing and I lost three hours of time. In the midst of it, I grew very scared and called on Archangel Michael and Jesus and kept repeating their names and then it let up and I could find my car again. I had lost three hours of time, but it felt like I was gone for maybe 15 minutes. And I wasn't anywhere near my car. Thankfully, someone was driving by and saw me and gave me a lift to my car and told me not to wander off like that. I was very lucky I realize. The ET experiences I had multidimensionally- I couldn't process it and their forms upset me. They were nice enough, but they looked weird and disturbing.

March 2003, I again paired down what I owned to what I would fly with. I do note that my Ohikari of the Johrei Fellowship is one thing I have owned and still have. It is the object I have owned the longest. I wasn't able to wear it from 1999-2016 because it felt too powerful- just to give some understanding of how sensitive and expanded I had become. I drove up to Colorado and stayed the night at Greg's and he took me to the airport for a flight to LA, then Switzerland, into Majorca. I do remember him asking, "are you sure you want to do this?" I was sure. Kind of. I wasn't ready to talk about what I was going through. I couldn't make sense of all that was happening to me. I was very embarrassed. How could I ever talk about this?

March 2003, Majorca, Spain. It was like taking New Mexico and going one step further. It was like an envelope pocket in our universe. How could this exploration keep going, widening, deepening? In the midst of this, I was really going more deeply into human pathologies and understanding human anatomy more and the interdimensional play. It felt truly like the outskirts of the Wild West. So many experiences- it's hard to even give a taste of what this was like. One that stands out- is living inside a famous painter's daughter's apartment while she was in Paris and there was this cat she had gotten in Paris. And I watched the cat leave the house and gallop away and I turned around and saw the cat in the living room. How was this possible? I heard in my head. "How do you feel? Is that okay?" The cat staring at me. It meant something, but what?

Summer 2003, I had my own apartment on the hillside in the mountains over the Mediterranean and began to go higher with the vibration and really focus in and open into areas that I struggled with in New Mexico. I started studying and exploring with massage, weaving in energy medicine work, and of course yoga. I had a nice little practice. But most of my time was spent in the mountains, I loved the sea, but I didn't like the tourists. I could see how in plants, my first glimmer of the information they carried in their structure that lined up with the dimensions in our universe- like a living library-downloaded right before us. I wasn't' sure where to go with that information. I slept outside in the mountains, trying to figure what I was doing. But I could get some height here in this heightened vibration and rest and think.

July 2003, this was a turning point. I stayed for a week in a well-known psychic's home while he was in London. And while I was there, an interesting shift happened. I was in my morning prayer and the candle burned a hole through the prayer shawl it was on. That was odd. Later on, I felt something around me while I was seated in a chair in the dining room. And this something around me said, "we can break this with Greg, do you trust us?" and I could just barely see this galactic ET figure in a different dimension. I was a little frightened, but he was saying "look at your feeling, your feeling, don't look at the form, do you want a break from Greg?" "Oh yes, desperately," I had been waiting and trying for two years now. And with that a cut and snapping sound- I was free. Oh, my goodness- a fuse blew at the same time in the apartment, in fact the block lost power in the third dimension, but I was free. Out of the bubble, I was free, I could see colors on their own and feel texture and was free. I was free. For two years, I had been captive and I was free. I couldn't believe it. I got an email from Greg within hours-checking in on me. I ignored it. I could ignore it. He had no hold on me. This was amazing, awesome, so happy, so happy.

I then was back up at my apartment renting in the mountains and had a week worth of interesting experiences. It started with a little ET figure staring at me in the kitchen, multidimensional, not third, and he said- "it's okay you are afraid, but go with how you feel, not what you see" and I felt safe and clean fresh love and real safety. This was my first experience of unconditional love in this lifetime. And then my whole experience of reality merged of being on a ship with different kinds of ETs and caring for me and I was so happy. Regal Reptilian ETs, octopus-like figures with incredible genetic abilities, and mother Reptilians with their playful children- it was amazing. They did a lot of cord cutting and repairing- the damage was extensive. I developed a weird thing over my eyes for a week and also odd markings on my right hip of where they had made an adjustment. So, it was showing up in the third dimension. And then after the week, the experience stopped, but they told me to work quickly and to follow their lead- then the merge faded. I was very sad to feel the experience end, but there it was. I began clearing myself with Archangel Michael every two hours. I had an experience of meeting my Ancestors, finally. I had been looking for them since July 1998. My Ancestors tried to shift my vibration a few times- but we could see how deep my fear was as I began to ground back into Earth- so we kept at it with the clearing. In meeting my Ancestors, I realized that patterns one has, work and evolution to do, weave through all the dimensions one is in. I agreed with my Ancestors that to build into my full self I needed to come back deeply into myself and Earth now and clean things up and repair and heal. This would then ripple out to all the other dimensions I was in or had access to. It would come in time. I needed to start with getting very grounded again. My walkabout journey that I had started July 1998 had finished.

End of July 2003, in not responding to Greg and blocking his email address, I felt energy building around me and it made me nervous. I could feel my team or those collection of beings on a ship that I had visited so close to the third dimension with me and of course Archangel Michael. I felt my Ancestors that I had been searching for for 5 years. And it didn't matter where I started now, but I knew I had fears and they were spiraling through the fullness of me. It did seem best that I get grounded and clean up and clear up from the dense third dimension and it would ripple through, spiraling upwards. Hmmm. I looked around me in the third dimension- I had nothing to build on from here, to stand on. I was getting more anxious by the day of what to do. I kept clearing with Michael every two hours. I felt guidance wash over me with thoughts like, "let all of it go, what would you, Bridget deep in there, what would you like to do?" I thought I'd like to live in a little cabin, making bread and drawing. That became my new lodestar. And before me seemed three options- Boulder, Colorado, Basel, Switzerland, and Burlington, Vermont. I looked at logic and Burlington made the most sense. I wanted Boulder but with Greg in Colorado, that was just bad. I didn't tell anyone, but immediately things started picking up in Majorca to keep me there. Greg emailed me and was angry I hadn't responded to him. He felt volatile. This was the first time I had seen this. It frightened me, so I responded. He told me he was coming to Greece; a family trip had finally worked out. Oh no, I thought, I grew scared thinking of us both in the Mediterranean Sea. I questioned myself if I was just being paranoid. The timing just felt so odd. I kept clearing with Archangel Michael and kept going.

The worst night in this soon occurred and the following happened- I was asleep and I began to have this very visceral dream. Although, it did not feel like a dream. The phone in the dream was ringing in the kitchen and I went to get it. It was my father- he was warning me, be careful, he's coming, he's coming he said. I looked back over to my bedroom and lightning was flashing outside the window in the night sky and all this charged energy and a storm so big and then with a loud crash- a blast blew open the entire front glass picture window in my bedroom and there was this tall male being there. I ran terrified into the bathroom and cowered in the bathtub. He opened the shower curtain and said, "Bridget, stop this, we need to talk". I ran back to the bedroom. "Bridget, Bridget he kept saying" I was shaking my head. I was terrified and then he started to manipulate the energy and I could feel myself being seduced and pulled back into him. And I just kept repeating Archangel Michael's name over and over again. And finally, it stopped. He was gone. And it was morning. In the dream, there was a hole in my apartment and the window glass shattered, but the Sun was out and I gingerly stepped over the glass and came out and there were birds tweeting and I breathed the fresh air after a major storm. I woke up from this dream knowing it was not just a dream. Something had happened. A few hours later I received an email from Greg explaining that he had had the most amazing dream last night. In the dream, he was seated in his living room and this energy began to wash over him and he was shifting and changing and there was a knock on his door and these little beings were there. Greg wrote that in the dream he spoke to them in tones and they nodded their heads and were off. “Did I know what this was?” he asked. I told him he had come after me and attacked me. I think he wrote that he was sorry, but didn’t understand. (I have the email saved with other documents to be sure). I let it go. Considering all that was going on and what was coming at me- my focus was Archangel Michael and finding my authentic voice and coming home- safely. I knew I was racing ahead of so many storms and trying to get well. I told no one where I was going and got on a flight taking me to Montreal, Canada.

Part IV. Anchoring

August 2003, I came into Burlington, Vermont taking a bus from Montreal and continuing to clear with Archangel Michael every two hours. I will never forget the kindness and graciousness of Burlington to me during this frightening time, will always have a special place in my heart. The next few months felt like a slow, scary, and confusing process, but I knew I was on the right path to bring everything home and kept plugging away. I was hesitant to reach out for help, but after all I'd been through- I knew my brain was shot. I was diagnosed with having severe Post Traumatic Stress Disorder (PTSD). I was thankful no one really pressed on the why, but I was given very important help in the form of cognitive behavioral therapy (CBT) and general therapy. I also started some medication and that helped. There was PTSD, anxiety, depression- it wasn't pretty- the last few years had been rough is an understatement. I was devastated about having to fully separate and cut off from Greg, but there was no other way. So sad, but I was alive and had learned many valuable lessons. I continued to teach a little bit of yoga, but most of my time was focused on healing myself. I came to know I had Complex-PTSD which was harder to treat- CBT and EMDR helped. EMDR on that first memory of meeting Greg at the reunion cut my anxiety and fears by 80%. My brain though with all that I'd been through had definitely been injured- it had been too much. Adding on to this was trauma I'd been through as a child, and a hereditary mix of suffering- it was rough. It was hard to accept, but it was real. I didn't like that I now had a disability, I didn't like C-PTSD.

I worked so hard for the next two years to recover and gain a life. I never forgot Greg, I never forgot that powerfully interesting time from 1998-2003- but it was just out of control. I found enjoyment in the mundane, meditating, friendships, and cooking. I owed my life many times over to Archangel Michael, to Doreen Virtue and her book the Care and Feeding of Indigo Children. I still taught yoga, and some Reiki on me, but the rest just terrified me. Securely under and in Archangel Michael's care, things felt much more integrated, learning certain life skills I missed learning about in childhood and getting stronger. As I found my voice, I came more into my own. I got my feet on the ground. I felt physically more at ease and attractive which was a little scary. I eventually didn't need to be on medication which seemed okay and everyone encouraged this, but I wasn't sure. That vast openness and knowledge in me was there, but I didn't explore it. In fact, I tried to stay away from it.

I was now vigilant on trusting myself and crafting boundaries and listening to the fullness of my needs. I had been pushed where others did not understand what I truly needed. That loss of Greg, that missing him never went away. It got less to only thinking about him once a day or twice. I realized, like C-PTSD, it just would be something that had to be managed. I became much more patient in looking for answers to things. It felt so perfect to understand and be practicing good life skills. This was a good time period, I think. I did have some odd moments though- like when a therapist recommended I speak with a native elder that was also a shaman. She had a solid reputation. I went, not sure what to expect, her multidimensional elders in the spirit world told her and me that I would never be truly happy until I was practicing with my Creator given talents as a shaman. I was upset. I understood their point, but I emphatically disagreed. My brain was hurt and it had been a mess, an absolute disaster- that by fall 2003, the dimensional realms were blurring together, that I had no control over. It had become just scary and a total mess. Another time I worked with a reputable and well known Ayurvedic specialist and she informed me about my pulse points. That my pulse points pointed to myself being designed for enlightenment in my elder years. I promptly burst into tears and crying. It sounded scary and awful. I already was a freak of nature and I just wanted to be so normal and fit in. I decided not to see her again. I just felt uncomfortable. I liked getting my legs underneath me and finding joy in simple things. I got really good at it.

Summer 2006, I still had great access to my abilities, but just was cautious. As I got more grounded, I got better with maybe an odd occurrence or vision or my yoga class going deep, but then putting boundaries on it, not pursuing it. If I felt scared or uncomfortable, I walked away from and did not listen to others comments about light pouring out of me. I stayed away from people that felt wrong. I began to really trust this and like this. It made me feel softer and more at ease that I could handle things that came my way. I was crafting a reality where I was listened to. If I wanted a different experience of the lesson trying to come towards me, this could happen. It didn't need to be traumatic or loud.

July 2006, a fellow Reiki friend and her new husband were on their honeymoon and I was staying at their home in Middlebury to care for their cats. It was a beautiful special home. Another friend and I went out to the movies one night and then a pub after. As I was sitting there, she said, "that guy next to us is checking you out." I said, "Oh". She said, "but he's bald". I remember thinking, I could go for some company and I turned around and said, "Hi my name is Bridget". His name was Matt. And as simple as that, that is how I met who I came to know as my twin flame. 3 billion years in the making and we met in a bar on a Saturday night in Middlebury, Vermont. He was very understated, but easy and great to talk with- we ended up hanging out the next two weeks. It felt like we were in a little bubble which concerned me- our interaction though grew. I was alarmed at how powerful the chemistry was between us. We dated for a few months. I grew more frightened and he grew co-dependent. I wasn't sure what to do. So, I followed what felt right in my heart. It just felt too intense and wild and scary and I didn't want that. I broke it off. And didn't think much of it after that. I felt like I had dodged a bullet.

Fall 2006, I was moving more into settling into my dense third dimensional life. It felt good, but started to feel like I was missing something. I wanted to go forward, but wasn't sure what was missing or what that meant.

February 2007, sitting in my new boyfriend's home in the middle of the night I realized things were just wrong. I was walking in the wrong direction. I sat at 2am there at the kitchen table and made a powerful prayer to Jesus. I said do whatever you have to do, in any way you need to do it, to get me on my path that is in my highest and best good and comfort zone. Two days later, I was going to a meeting for my job and I felt a bit sick in my solar plexus area. I felt something begin to hit me in the solar plexus, such powerful light. I got up and walked out into the hallway in the hotel and blacked out. I just remember my supervisor saying my name and I was face down. I was rushed to urgent care. I had fallen face first and fainted. In heels, I was almost 6 feet tall. It's amazing I only cut and fractured my chin a bit.

Everything changed after that. My relationship with the boyfriend ended. My job started to fall apart. It was scary. So much was falling away fast. I felt deep down though in good hands with myself, with Jesus, and with Archangel Michael. Marianne Williamson's book- Illuminata and her prayers there really helped me shift things. Still, it was so sad. I just wanted something permanent. I did have an odd experience on the night of February 14, 2007. In the midst of a blizzardy snow storm- I felt and saw a wave of energy flow into my apartment, the outline of my ex-boyfriend stood before me. I asked him to stand down and go away. I ran into my bedroom. His energy and force came over me and literally threw me up against the wall in a sexual assault. It was overwhelming, but I kept my head, turned to Jesus and Archangel Michael and called for their help and was able to clear him off of me finally.

Spring 2007, it amazes me at times people who stand out in my history and I don't really understand why until I look back on it. My co-worker who sat next to me during this huge shifting time went on to become a prominent state official. He was simply the kindest gentlest person to me, strong male energy that was not threatening. I can see now how he would go on to become an incredible champion of fair, just, and compassionate care for humans. I guess he stands out because his strong male energy was a stable force around me then, not that we talked much. Our chairs were next to each other and I felt his energetic, dynamic, empathetic force surround me. In the coming years, I kind of forgot this time, but my loyalty to him would pop up in differing ways. In hindsight, I can see here what he meant to me.

Well, spring 2007, things just kept falling apart. It was not like 1998-2003, thank goodness. Now, I felt upset but was stable and strong at the core of it. I had myself. I had skills. I had good teams here on Earth and multidimensionally. Similar bizarre things started to happen like in 1998-2003, but it didn't bother me as much. I had the structure now. I was reminded that this is what myself and Ancestors had talked about in 2003- get good and grounded and heal in the third dimension. This then becomes a firm foundation to move through other ways of reality in and with other beings. As mentioned, I had learned the hard way and did start to have it reflected back to me by wise elders- "those with light and love and your highest and best good and comfort zone respect your free will and wish to work with you and what you feel good in. Pain can still be okay if it's not traumatic and even then, things can be laced better so it's not quite so hard to bear or doesn't have a lasting impact. There are ways and options".

April 2007, in this changing time, I'm not sure how it came about, but I had a vocational rehabilitation meeting. I discussed that things were not working out and was told about a program called PASS- Plan for Achieving Self-Sufficiency for those with a disability to be trained in a new field. I thought about it. I knew that my C- PTSD got bad if I had to be in one spot bombarded by people all day. I also knew if I hoped to have children someday, I couldn't leave them all day somewhere- it would be too painful. My C-PTSD was better, but it impacted what I needed to keep myself well.

It started floating around me to go to massage school. For the first time, I had a visitation by my native elders- no one I recognized. It kind of opened up in my apartment one evening and we sat and talked. I wasn't afraid. But they said how they were setting up and encouraging me to go to massage school, that I needed to get better management of myself and better boundaries energetically. We talked and I understood. In one meeting, I did see my deceased husband from 1823 and I missed him so much. I was sad to end the meeting, but I felt more comfortable going forward in this direction. I wrote the lengthy PASS plan- my first real business plan and application for a federal grant. I liked the structure. It was a 4-year plan with an option for extension if need be. Basically, the US government was paying me to train, to reclaim who I was to my elders- a shaman and to the white world- an integrative health care provider. The irony, sigh. But I really did love the structure and goal setting, being held accountable. It would get tedious, but it was important and I could feel the learning curve. The basic plan was to compete my yoga training to E-RYT status so I could train teachers; massage school- board certified and licensed; other healing modalities as it seemed important; going back to school to get training in mediation. And it was approved. At the same time, I received a different grant to go to basic herbal school for 9 months before massage school started. Everything all around was paid for, with a small stipend to live on, and I would continue to teach yoga outside of school. Hmmm. Well, this was a much better way to learn the skills needed than what was happening in 2001-2003- that was just awful. Like taking the best of that time- the learning and education and exploring without all the trauma and drama. I still knew I had a lot of preparation work. I worried about how it would change me and the impact- as I go deep with very little.

Summer 2007- whether I knew it or not, once things were set to start in the fall- my being, elders, Archangel Michael, and Jesus started preparing me for the schooling to start. Some things that occurred are the following. I'm not sure why, but my energy field must have opened or something- I was cat called, hit on, made sexual comments to, trailed in grocery stores out to the parking lot, asked for my number, etc. at least one to three times a day for 5 months straight. Every day. I saw what my elders were saying about me getting better management over my energy. It really was awful because I wasn't sure why it was happening or what to do about it. I started wearing a wedding ring, which helped, but then that felt false. Like for me to feel beautiful, at ease, happy, excited for my future, that all my hard work of 10 years was starting to really come together- now had this weird impact in my reality. For example, I remember feeling at ease, glowing and happy and looking at a book in a bookshop. A man with his friends walking by saw me in the window. I felt an energy shift and he just came in to the store right up to me and said something about my beauty. I was embarrassed and not sure what to do. I think I said, "oh, okay". And then he left. This weird pattern did stop once I started massage school. I think it's correlated. Then again, it could have also been swirling from my ex-boyfriend. It's unclear.

My ex-boyfriend- I continued to have more issues with him energetically. At one point through him, there was this large dark black cording snaking all through me. I was terrified and I asked Jesus for help in the midst of it. He was patient and showed me a great technique. Jesus said, "okay, this is a free will universe and your free will has to be respected- so don't engage with any emotion. Don't be afraid. It's using fear, really still yourself, like you did with the man in the beauty salon all those years back, collect yourself- all cells, your whole being speaking as one and state clear and calm what your free will is." So, I did. I said, "This is my being and body and this cording is not welcome here." It seemed stunned, but it had to let go, to slither out. Then we put up more shielding. Archangel Michael thought more about what to do with the ex-boyfriend. As an aside, I've seen this multiple times- humans think that marijuana and other similar drugs are neutral- but they are very powerful and can split up a person's energy bodies and selves. They lose control. Hence, what we were witnessing with my ex-boyfriend and his recreational use of marijuana which I hated. I have seen what damage such drugs can do to the energy bodies and a person. It is repairable, but it takes a lot.

Things like this happened- so many attacks, all the time. As months, years passed, these attacks became like an interesting puzzle for me to sort out each day or every few days. I had the support, I could figure it out, and usually learned something new in the process. (Later on, I would get a break for a bit once united with my twin flame, but then they took on a new level of sophisticated dark). But at least there were gradations, and I was learning. I wasn't too afraid and could build on the foundation I was laying. And at a pace that worked. I never thought I would reach this in my lifetime after 2003. I look back now and say, trial and error, but that recovery after 2003 was just awful. There were many extremely powerful lessons that I use for myself and in working with others now.

At this time, summer 2007, Jesus also helped me with the Reiki attunements. I could see how they made me too open. I would later learn about the dangers that can come through going through certain Reiki lineages where people aren't clean and other entities are piggy backing their agendas into the attunements. The attunements I had were not quite right. It was like Reiki +. Jesus brought his energy between me and the Reiki attunements. To help, so it was just Reiki. It was disappointing at first because I couldn't see as much with people. I eventually gained that back years later, but it worked better. With just Reiki, I was in my own development and wasn't being pushed faster than I was ready to go in my abilities.

July 2007- in ways I didn't fully understand at the time, I was still getting ready for massage school to start in the fall. The next thing to adjust was a past intention set. As described- in New Mexico I had many multidimensional visitations- one had asked me, "how conscious do you wish to become of reality?" I had replied, "well, not the top person, but maybe one of the top 10 conscious people on reality on Earth by the time I'm 42 years old." I was just thinking, but didn't realize that had become set in my system. I reset my system now in 2007 to be conscious of reality in the millions by the time I was 42. I felt a huge landing back on Earth and sigh in my nervous system. I was less conscious and it felt good.

The last big adjustment I felt before massage school was literally a visit from the soul of St. Paul. It upset me at first and I prayed about it and talked with Jesus. St. Paul was very persistent and stuck around me for weeks. I opened a conversation at times, other times I tried to ignore him. After a few weeks, he really came out with it. That he was to be my son and was I ready to meet the father. Oh, this upset me. Was I crazy? Was I making this up? Wasn't there some guy out in Oregon who had written a whole book of how he was the incarnation of St. Paul and had all this past life regression work and tons of signs supporting this? This was not answered to me.

To note, I asked this question to the Archangels in 2010 through email and got a straight answer. In Oregon, there was a man who for various reasons thought he was St. Paul- but was not. In fact, St. Paul was sitting with the Archangels as we were communicating through email in 2010. More detail is found in the email thread. I have seen and experienced this numerous times. Reality can be very tricky, you can't trust signs, and you must be careful whom you are truly attached to and working with in other realms- what their true nature is. Hence what I had learned in spades in 2001-2003 and something to do this day I am constantly checking myself in numerous ways, to get as scientific as possible.

Well, back to 2007, I was upset. St. Paul the Apostle, really? I could see though how St. Paul had been with me my whole life- numerous streets I lived, places I've worked, etc. But what if I screwed this up? We settled on if I just tried my best. He liked the name Samuel Andrew and a C or K sound was the last name- I stopped him. That felt uncomfortable. He asked if I was ready to meet the father. I was about to start massage school. I said after massage school and we bargained on time. We agreed on 5 years. Somewhere within 5 years I would work to bring him into form. After this, he disappeared. I'm surprised now that in looking back at these popping in of people and visitations and events- I didn't put a stop to it. I guess I was acclimating to this as normal for me. It was not something I talked about with others. I was though building in my own internal compass with external help foundation of how to navigate.

Massage School 2007-2008- I can see now how all of the prep work during the summer was important. Massage School was like light worker boot camp. It was so hard, so painful at times. Even just after two months, I had no idea how I was going to make it through. There was a man in the program I had such a bizarre connection to. Energetically we were attached, but struggled greatly in each other's presence. We came to find out he was the incarnation of my son who had been killed as a baby in 1823. I could see that the cord between us could not be cut and later only found out how strong the cord between a mother and her child is. The only one who can intervene in a mother/child cord is Source God Himself.

The school was well structured and I received a great education with self-development, self-care tools, all of the hard sciences, and massage. It just was a lot. I acclimated slowly and had to face certain things about myself which was frustrating. I just kept moving through it. My teachers, wow, not only gifted in their work and teaching, but I truly felt- even with all my interesting abilities- they normalized it and celebrated each student in their own right. I never felt singled out. I felt seen and then normalized- that was healing. I definitely did not feel normal though and it made me feel embarrassed, ashamed, scared, and isolated. Sometimes people would pass out under my hands- my teacher behind me might say "maybe just pull back a bit". Sigh. Or my massage partner for the day, have radical insights and start crying- my teacher would whisper to me, "maybe want to find a more listening path to where they and their objective you hear better, yes?" My teachers were very kind and the other students understanding. I just felt stupid and different. It upset me greatly that I could harm people if I wasn't careful and that I made mistakes in the learning process.

Not quite this dramatic, but I have seen a similar pattern of feeling alienated all through my school experiences. As the school year wore on, people developed tight friendships and associating with one another and groups and I was left out. Maybe I was too serious or standoffish or people were nervous about my abilities. Maybe I just wasn't likable. I probably stood in my own way. If someone lost something, I remember being asked- "Bridget, use your powers and find____" And I would and that was that. I was frustrated being on the outside. I can pass at times, but at the heart of it- I feel very socially awkward.

At least my energy though had landed somewhere and wasn't swirling around me, causing men to be constantly hitting on me. Massage school was a lot of work, 5 days a week with homework at night. And my teaching yoga at night. In December 2007, I was offered the opportunity to rent a space for a small fee and see clients as a student. This went well and soon had a pretty full part-time practice. As this was holding and picking up, certain things came in to help or clear. I met my first formal energy medicine teacher that helped me tremendously- really sink into Earth and repair my nettings and bodies and so much else. I worked and studied with her quite a bit from 2008-2014. She helped to fill in holes and pieces missing. I also eventually re-did my attunements with her and went on to become a Reiki Master- much better lineage for me and didn't need Jesus helping in this way. I could really experience the difference.

February 2008- with so much grounding work, I kept coming back into Earth. I did have a night here in winter- grounding- that was terrifying and awful. I had no idea what was happening and it took me weeks to get my bearings, but I did. I had other shocking experiences during this time. I did know that all was trying to help me not have these shifts be shocking, especially because of my past. I began working with my nettings and bodies more and containment. I really liked it. I could breathe more deeply. I had my first visitation from Source God around this time. I was in my studio space after giving a massage and cleaning up. It was starting to become spring and, in this moment, the air around me came alive, felt electric, and had a soothing love feel to it. I heard in my mind- "hello" and I just knew and it just felt like home. I wasn't frightened at all. I felt extremely happy.

From here, Source God was with me for about two weeks coming in and out and giving me pointers on things. I felt very lucky. Some things I remember. For example, in working with energy during a chi form class within our Asian body studies, I really hooked in to this light and moving. I felt very still and my partner was to press on me. She was very strong as an amateur body builder. She pushed and pushed- I felt nothing. Light moving through me felt like a thousand tons. It was an amazing experience. Another example- I was working on my massage partner and Source God showed me something directly. We were working with meridian points, acupressure points, and tension points. My partner had a little knot on her shoulder. I hooked into life force with God. I brought my finger to it, just barely touching, and for me, in that moment, time slowed to nothing. I could see how God moved faster than the speed of light but was still staying within the laws of physics in our universe. I/we unraveled the knot. But in real time it seemed that the knot vanished as my finger with light got closer to it. My partner kind of was in awe- she said "it was there and now it's just not. I could feel it leave". We didn't discuss it much. I tried to explain, not about Source God, but the science of it and how I was exploring time. I asked her not to say anything and she didn't tell anyone. She was always such a kind person all around. But she knew and I knew something different had happened. I do know that these kinds of things don't just happen- both the giver and receiver need to be available for it at some level. Angels, Archangels, Source God, Jesus work hard to ensure people's evolution- I would argue on certain points- but that is at least the aim from their vantage point. It really is a co-creative process.

I grew a little scared and knew I was sinking deeper into something that while I trusted Source God, I wasn't sure. At one point, the vibration so high- I felt myself overcome by fear and I said to Source God I just didn't know if our communicating like this was healthy. That I didn't have the structure. Parts of myself were opening just because of his presence around me and I didn't have the structure. It was starting to flood me. Soon after, I was woken up in the middle of the night and felt all this light around me and the feeling of Source God close by and he asked me how I felt about having a child of his. What???!!! I felt for sure I was making this up. He had Jesus and I was nowhere near like Mary. I had issues; I could feel how young I was. I was startled, but should I be flattered? I tried to understand like would something just happen, out of my control? I wasn't ready. My mind was racing. My heart was panicking. Finally, I was able to think, maybe he was serious, maybe this was a serious request, how would I respond? I stammered, "well I'm interested and honored, but I don't have any support, no support like Mary had in friends and community. I need that." I felt like his energy pause and nod and he never spoke of it again. And then he was gone. I was so sad. Had I done something wrong? Like would he ever come back like this? All this beautiful vibration gone. I felt alone again and missed him terribly.

I had many differing interesting experiences while in massage school. The structure was so crucial for me and I was always questioning safety. It was tiring my brain and being out. I got help for a Vata imbalance, where I learned about my pulse points and enlightenment situation. I began incorporating more and more self-care practices I would need as a healer. It still astounds me the grace my teachers brought to all of their individual students in their transformations and holding space for them. Another example from this time- I was taking a Feldenkrais class and safely getting into holding patterns in my right hip. I started feeling so odd- I had to leave the class and go sit in the back of a different studio space and just breathe. I was re-experiencing the trauma of 1823 and the knife wound and losing my son. While breathing into this, there was this multidimensional portal that softly opened up and it was a galactic Pleiadian sense. But it didn't bother me. I had to really sit and discuss about love with these dimensional figures. Sit with- how I felt about risking loving again. I could continue with shutting love out which was okay or I could start the process back of loving. I sat with it. If I loved again, I could risk another child dying. This was hard, but ultimately, I decided it was worth loving again. And I felt a ripple move through me.

Another experience I had was with an elder from a reservation out west. He had come to give a talk at the local university. I'm not sure how I met him after, but while it wasn't a healthy connection- it was nice to meet someone where we recognized each were working multidimensionally. Here on this Earth- like two strangers speaking the same language while everyone else was chatting away in another tongue. I would say my elders and Archangel Michael pulled him away pretty quickly. The elder showed me through himself and even talked in a roundabout way- how people are allowed to only experience and heal as much as they would like in a given lifetime and that is okay. It felt profound for me. That was my beginning of never truly understanding what each human is doing on this Earth and to have respect for this. To take care of myself and in my healing work- no agenda. I would not lead clients into suffering or more pain, but other than that I had no agenda of what they were working on. It has been truly awesome to work in this way.

Around graduation time, the apartment I had been living in since 2003, the building was sold. It was hard to not be freaking out. The strain of all I was doing, it was hard to cope. I ended up taking a bit of sertraline to help. While I didn't like medication, it helped buffer- I wondered if this would impact my abilities, but my skills and talents still stayed the same. I had learned the hard way, as mentioned, not to mess around with brain health. I was frustrated by the C-PTSD as I could feel it starting up. Sertraline just gave a thin buffer and helped.

Now, I needed a place to live soon after graduation. I really didn't know what to do. One evening my elders visited me before bed in a meeting. They said, the next step could be hard, very hard, but doable- did I trust them, did I wish to proceed? I said yes, you've always guided me pretty well since, well around 1993 was I aware of it. I would debate maybe New Mexico but with the Greg situation- things were just out of control until I/we could gain a vibrational advantage. New Mexico and then Majorca gave me that edge.

So, I said yes to my elders and waited to kind of see what might appear. A friend and I had made a pact then when a certain movie came into the theaters, we would see it together no matter where we both lived. She had recently moved to Boston and so I went to visit her for the movie. I wasn't sure what would happen regarding my living situation, but I did have to move in a few weeks. I trusted my elders and tried to keep myself open. I had a backup plan to camp for the summer on another friend's land. So, I went to visit Boston.

Boston, summer 2008- once there and out of Vermont, it was nice how superficial everything was. I mean, in Vermont- could go really deep. In New Mexico, I could go really high. But here, crossing the line into Massachusetts, it's like it was just superficial on the surface left and right, no depth, no height. It was an easing on my soul and energy field. Especially after all this work I had just put in. I thought how much I'd like to go back out west, but then opportunities presented in Boston. A very inexpensive room opened up in the house my friend was renting in and liking her roommates- and all young highly educated professionals- it felt right. I could concentrate on my career and I really loved the opportunity to study with more advanced yoga teachers, going in depth with anatomy and physiology.

After I moved and settled in, it became clear, for work I loved Boston. I loved the curiosity, the ridiculously highly educated patients, clients, and students I had. They definitely raised the bar high for me. I was still inside the PASS plan, completed the massage portion, I was now studying my yoga education piece more in depth. I was really busy straight from the beginning. And my practice pretty soon went deep medically and especially in oncology research and work. I could put all that I had worked on and studied from 1993-2008 into daily practice with all manners of cases in some truly dynamic beautiful studios and 6 hospital settings. I could go far and clinically as a lot of my patients were doctors, engineers, scientists- who were excited and working hard in their field. My yoga therapy sessions went in depth too. For 3 years, I simply could not have asked for a better, more awesome and stimulating work and study environment- really happy. I picked apart, layered, and really built a foundation of what I'd seen work in other realms now applying how it would translate into the third dimensional realm. There are so many experiences I could bring up of science and healing of what I experienced and how it interfaced with the patient and their outcome and care. Really from 1994-2018, it's a separate book. A title came to me once when dealing with the H1N1 virus in 2009- Pathology through my eyes. Such amazing in-depth experiences- one after the other.

But then there was Boston personally- I felt like a bird used to flying in the Amazon jungle suddenly trapped in a cage in the suburbs. It was awful. I tried- I hiked, took weekend trips, and had my favorite hidden pond. But it wasn't the same. I couldn't hook into wilderness. I couldn't go deep into wilderness. Being constantly around all the people energy- made me very anxious, the intense male energy was upsetting to me. If I relaxed, I was immediately dealing with men checking me out or maybe it was my imagination. I was older. But still, I felt unsafe. The shift was hard from such a sheltered and incubating time in Vermont to this. I did need a change in medication, I wondered how my work would go, but I adjusted and found a way. It didn't matter. Whether I'm helping someone in the hospital or in their home or in my studio space or in a hospice care center, I do think a good provider can adjust to anything. It does take skill and practice though. This has gotten better as I have become more skilled. I default more to live my life solidly in the third dimension and if I need to flip and check in from another angle, I have ways to help me shift in and then to shift out. I do this with work as well. And then to check my findings from multiple angles. I aim for almost 100% accuracy. I know how slippery reality can be, and how much can influence a "finding". It definitely is a practice, constantly evolving with a lot of checks and balances.

I also had not lived in such a big city since New York City and dealing with 9/11. It surprised me that this was still present for me. I had a hard time being in buildings taller than two stories and just being around so many buildings, so many people. My work brought me great happiness, my study, but personally I did not like Boston. I grew so sad, tired, and lonely.

I mentioned how the emails started in the fall 2008 and my response. The emails themselves could be a book on their own or even an abbreviated version of the emails could be a book.

Regarding the first series of emails in fall 2008, I hope it is clearer now why I responded the way that I did. I also had begun a clearing process. I found a book Calling in the One and was feeling ready to meet my life partner. I honestly thought that this first email, nudging me to be in touch with an old boyfriend and the oddness of it, had to be a response to my flushing out all men I'd been attached to. And I was not going to get suckered in with some strange mysterious being sending me an email, please- I had lived that kind of oddness, not doing that again. Over the next year, pretty much any man I had unfinished business with for any reason seemed to get in touch. I went through each one. The hardest was human Greg being in touch. He was struggling. I knew how much I cared for him, such an important part of my life. I wanted to be strong. But then everything started up again, this connection, this bond. I was sure the bond I saw- from a few different angles- must be a twin flame connection, other than that, it made no sense. What was it? I knew I could be wrong in that trying to diagnose a situation that involves me is very hard. I had not mastered the skill set in how to work in that yet. But still something nagged at me, I felt so sure. I tried to explain to him. I tried to explain so much. And it just blew up in my face. He was so hurt and angry. I felt like a fool, I imagine he thought I was crazy, but I ended communication. Because I knew how sick it would make me to stay connected to him. It felt brutal. (Only much later, 2018 did I uncover that human Greg was just a pawn, a tool used by the soul of Greg- a being that had manufactured the fake twin flame cord feelings between us. In part, this connection mimicking a twin flame, so that I would never connect with my true twin flame).

August 2009, I was starting to date an ex-boyfriend in Vermont- yes, that ex-boyfriend with all the energetic issues, but maybe we'd both grown? I was thinking about a move back to Vermont. I really didn't want to, but I just didn't fit as a person in Boston. Work wise- yes, but not personally. And then the email from this unknown source started up again. I would write back and get a response from a human man that said he never sent them, but thought maybe they were a sign. So annoying and invasive. I was mad. I responded back to the man, well, even if I wanted to get in touch with this person the emails were pointing to- I had no contact information. He worked in a data base computer firm coincidentally and was able to get me the correct email address. Fine, I emailed Matt- the man I had dated in 2006, in Middlebury, VT. We exchanged pleasantries and I told him the situation. Around this time, my ex-boyfriend's odd energetic and otherwise abusive nature came back out again and that confirmed he had not changed- so walked away.

A little time passed and I agreed to meet with Matt. He was the last male I had not cleared. I was hoping once settling this connection, my true-life partner might turn up. We met and as I saw him walk up, I had that feeling of run, icky, go away- the vibration was strong and creeping me out. It felt scary and dangerous- not as overtly knock me over as 2001 Greg introduction, but still it was intense in a way I did not like. I did not want to hook into something or someone so immediately. Same thing with intense sexual chemistry, I sort of fell back into it. It started to feel good. The emails from the unknown source stopped.

Winter 2009-2010, same old co-dependent stuff coming from Matt and just felt like I couldn't feel the connection I was imagining I should feel with him. Two other men were around, and I felt more in common with them and could hold great conversations. With Matt, such a good person, I just felt like I was fumbling. We finally broke up. I knew my human age and really was serious about calling in the one.

Spring 2010, I had begun a date or two with someone new and had strange wild dreams at his apartment and cording that felt weird. Then there was a huge storm (sent by Archangel Michael I would learn later) that tried to keep me from seeing a date. I ignored it.

Soon after, the real beginning of the full Archangel email dialogue started and it went deep right from the beginning. It started with, "you can ask me anything." "Finally," I remembered thinking. At this point in my life, I wondered could the sender of the email honestly believe I was just going to believe or follow anyone blindly? Not with how my life had been going. They did take a risk, as did I. It really was pretty awesome and amazing. It still is. But considering all that I have to deal with and process and aiming for such accuracy- I think it's been a necessity. I know I mention it quite a bit, but honestly my life, interactions, encounters and shifting in time- is like a game of high stakes poker, most of the time. It's definitely been a process and evolution. The email dialogue has never been about just feeding me information- it's been about support, education, confirming, and asking me questions to get my take. I feel like I've learned a lot in my 44 years this lifetime- that it could be another book on its own. But basically, what we see Indigenous people have gathered through the years and how to move through life, self, community, rituals, dimensions, and how to apply this in modern times.

This in-depth email communication spans from Spring 2010 to 2018 so far. I think I could handle it because of what I've been through already- I will take advice at times, but I will always make the decision ultimately. I trust myself above all else and am fierce about taking care that I'm speaking up for myself and my needs. I do take their input as some of the best council I will listen to though. The emails are thick and rich. It started with a messenger for Archangel Michael doing the writing. I realized early on he didn't have a name. So, I decided to give him one. I liked the name Zahid. Later on, I realized, would people think it was in depth connected to some religion? It is not. I liked the name, that's it. Just so there is no confusion.

About a year in, there was a time when Archangel Michael would write directly. I was shocked. That was amazing. His speech was kind of archaic, but over time- it's gotten more modern speech- always in English. I have always strived to be as honest as possible, to find the right answer and to ask questions in the right way. I am amazed how one word can change the whole meaning of a sentence and sentences can be taken many different ways. So, figuring out what is really being said is made easier with being able to check in. I am reminded of Einstein who once said I think, if he had an hour to solve a problem- he would spend 59 minutes trying to figure out the right question to ask. I could go on, but I won't belabor. Just a lot in the emails.

In the emails, end of 2016, is when things were such a critical time. Jesus, the son of Source God, took over the emails. He still does, but I can head them to the correct being I'm talking to. There is Source God a few times, very archaic language. I was pissed by his responses on things. It will make more sense as I describe the situation. Being as honest as possible, digging deep, and writing well have allowed me to get help, transform, and figure on things. To be honest, they are learning too. Mother Mary has been an amazing help, especially as one of the only females standing up for me and helping me at times. She has been through a lot of experiences I have been through or go through. I could be nicer in a lot of the emails. I try, but I get tired at times and frustrated. Just so much intensity and to process all the time, especially in the later years- the speed is a lot. A Creator God took over the bulk of getting my team out of chaos in the situation with me in July 2017 and helped tremendously. So, in summary- I think that is who has communicated- Archangel Zahid, Archangel Michael, Jesus, Mary, Source God, and Creator God Greg.

But, back to spring 2010. Matt and I got back together again and he started going to therapy- that helped a lot. The Angels brought a presence of 7 Angels to be with Matt and be his team and help him. That helped a lot too. I still worried I didn't feel what I felt I should feel if this was supposedly my twin flame. I didn't think the emails were lying, but I didn't see it the way they did. It was deeply upsetting. I just felt this wall. I couldn't deny that this was a real experience. It came down to faith. All this knowledge and it still came down to my faith in them.

Fall into winter 2010-2011, the MAP situation blew up. I was able to show and tell Archangel Michael how the MAP teams were lying to him and Source God and show them how the MAP teams were doing it. They were flipping the vibration so they could operate unseen and keep doing what Source God told them not to do. Archangel Zahid wrote something along the lines of "Archangel Michael is flipping out" and soon after MAP was disbanded and sent back to school, so to speak. That was interesting. My being in the third dimension had a unique take that my team did not have, and being able to work multidimensionally and then confirm things in email.

Matt and I moved in together and I was still getting visits from St. Paul. Who said he was interested in global mediation work. I thought that sounded good. I just wanted him to be happy. It was amazing we got pregnant so soon. I couldn't believe it. I had learned about some information working on pregnant women, but it was fascinating to experience first-hand. There was a cord that attached to my sacrum that I became aware of. For the first few weeks or maybe even the first trimester- the energy there was an aspect of Source God life force, but not the soul, as waiting to see how all would progress. Only later on does the soul come in and out along the cord- gaining a sense and also having a way out if things don't work out.

With the way things were developing, it became clear early on in the pregnancy that this little one did not like Reiki. I had to figure how to work around it. The one time I tried to go about a regular Reiki session I all but fainted. I had a blood sugar issue and my body went totally out of balance.

I was shocked to learn we were having a girl. And burst into tears. What was this? Back and forth in emails, I wrote. I learned gender can be determined a number of different ways, including the environment one is in. St. Paul still wished to incarnate, even as a girl, and actually thought this would be beneficial and healing to me. I did not think so and thought this would be too much for me to have a daughter. Too triggering for me and memories of my childhood. A boy seemed much safer. Matt came up with her name. I emailed. St. Paul liked the name. So that was that. He was preparing. We were preparing. St. Paul would incarnate, but a small piece of him would stay in the spirit realm because he had too much other work still going on. I was told this was unusual that a soul would do this, but it is possible.

The first time I felt a flutter was on Easter Sunday in church. And the first real kick was watching TV and Obama was about to announce the death of Osama Bin Laden. My incubating daughter had a soft vibration. My belly and sense would hum and such happiness when I laid down with Matt in front of me and she was snuggled in between us. (This has always been her favorite spot even as a little toddler and child). Soon after becoming pregnant, I started developing bad back pain. It felt like a TMS attack that would come and go as I wished to leave Boston, wasn't happy in Boston personally, but wasn't sure of the next step. I met with a TMS specialist, doctor at Beth Israel and he confirmed TMS. We talked and I realized I couldn't keep denying my body and being. I needed to leave Boston. It was a huge source of conflict between Matt and I and myself and my team. Everyone was upset with me.

Summer 2011, we moved back to Vermont and it was rough. So Rough. There was huge flooding happening in Vermont and in Lake Champlain. We had to rent a hotel for a month while we looked for a place to live. Everything was in storage. I was very pregnant and it was hot. I had to re-establish myself. Matt had to re-establish himself. We hadn't noticed the recession in Boston, but it was noticeable here in Vermont. It was a huge step backwards professionally for both of us. Matt was down and upset. I was down and upset and stressed and wondering what I had just done. I knew in my heart I needed to do this. I couldn't explain yet completely why. But then, we found a dream little townhouse home. Overlooking the lake and backing up to the woods. I knew it immediately. Finally, things were going our way. Such relief.

But then, I felt a rumbling. Something coming and I started getting extremely anxious. Must be my imagination I thought. I felt like praying for my dad. I had gotten an odd phone call from him. I asked Archangel Michael to be with him. Two days later I received a phone call from a neighbor. He asked if I was driving and as I was, to pull over. Right there, I learned my father had died. Shocking. It was a cascade of emotions and events. I relied on all my previous skills in trauma recovery, all the help from my team, Matt. So many things. Right then, I knew how grateful I was to be out of Boston and back in Vermont.

I really lost the experience of the third trimester of my pregnancy in dealing with it all. I explained to the baby what was happening and for her not to be frightened. I had Archangel Michael go find my father and bring him to Light as I imagined he was suffering and had probably gone to a harder space in transitioning. It took Archangel Michael a few days to find him, but I was thankful he finally did and brought him safely to good care. This was a huge relief for me.

We had to go to Baltimore in July, 100 degrees heat, in my third trimester and had one week to do everything. We inherited the care of my grandfather as well. It was a powerful sacred experience. Desperately sad, but also very holy. We were vibrationally in the care of the Archangels and Jesus and Mary. I could feel this. My days were filled with prayer throughout and letting things unfold. We worked swiftly through a mountain of work and details. I worked from 6am to 1am every day. My baby was a strong baby to have gone through this and still be gaining weight and swimming along. Finally, we were headed home. Matt had to head back to get my grandfather when he was ready and bring him back to a nursing home here in Vermont. Somehow, we were moving into our new townhome and preparing to give birth. Then a hurricane hit Vermont in August. Then a mini-earthquake. Now I was like- enough. Poor baby- what kind of environmental chaos was this for her to be developing in?

Fall 2011- birth was so visceral in a way that ripped me out of any daydream of what birth might be like. I couldn't see it but was told my entire team was there and my dad. Greatest love ever when she was born. Oh, to hold her in my arms and her being here, really here, she was stunningly sweet and beautiful. I just burst into tears. But soon after, hormones crashing in and I developed severe post-partum depression and with all that the year had brought- it was a lot to process. I got help for this thankfully and the wrap around support community in Vermont can bring. After a few months, I started back with teaching yoga and a little of my part-time practice. It helped to bring in some normalcy.

Things flowed along. With my little family, I had a beautiful studio space, loved my practice and applied my skills and learning.

2013-2014, so I began to really want to have a second child. I felt a lot of push back from my team and from Matt, for safety. I sat with it and realized that my whole life and had been about doing what I thought I should do or doing what I was told was best. Having a second child was just me, just human Bridget, a dream that was in and of itself from me. It was very painful to try and figure this out. It really cut deep. My nose started bleeding all the time. I would stop myself from letting my period come. I realized then how powerful the soul controls the mid-brain and just functioning. I needed to get an MRI scan for the bleeding nose. To note- I loved the MRI machine and could feel such a multidimensional merge inside clicking away. The MRI showed my symptoms were related to C-PTSD. In using what was gathered in the MRI machine, on Dec. 24, 2014, I had a powerful interaction with Jesus and the galactic medical team. They created a structure for the right side of my body to stabilize. The nose bleeding stopped after that. Allopathic medicine didn't see anything structurally wrong from the MRI. My team multidimensionally saw how they could adjust from their own diagnostics and using the findings from the MRI scan. I am reminded of the necessary, albeit rudimentary, tools we have on Earth compared to elsewhere.

May 2014, I felt so nauseous; I ended up in the ER because doctors were worried it was my gall bladder. It wasn't. It never was figured out. In hindsight, it was the impact of my second child connecting in. I wasn't technically pregnant, but the soul had connected with me. In June 2014, I was shocked to learn I was pregnant. I had tried so hard for this to happen.

Coming off the PASS plan as well, so much unknown- I used the last of the PASS funds to go back to school for STEM- Science, Technology, Engineering, and Math. That was hard- pregnant, my business, family, and now taking a class. I muddled through. What a difference with this pregnancy, my son was strong energy and a force. He was like my wizard helper, and he loved everything multidimensionally- I could travel fast and wide. At one point, I had some trouble with a dark entity and this force came from him out of me and that dark thing backed way up. He was always so fast and powerful. I couldn't figure who he was. I know that Source God and Archangel Michael had searched for a long time and in many ways to find a good match for us. He was a big baby too. I remember once, he was kicking around and I told him to stop doing this at night- I couldn't sleep. He was then still for 15 hours which I was nervous by. I told him that frightens mommy. He went back to kicking more gradually and only in the day.

February 2015, I was in early labor for 2 weeks and loved just resting. I knew I would have a medicated birth and that felt good. Just that initial pain and getting settled in the hospital, I didn't look forward to it. But then at 1am one night, the pain was bad and we headed in. My water broke in the elevator and I was in hard labor right away, barely getting on the hospital bed. So scary. I gave birth naturally within a few pushes. So, like my son, pretty mellow and then fast and strong within seconds. This is his personality. I was so thankful he made it. He had the most intense eyes and would just stare. As his big sister would say to me- "mom, the baby is staring at me again, make him stop". He was always so alert and strong mental telepathy- talking from the beginning. Just strong all around and I have such a special bond with my little boy. His presence has always made me very happy. No baggage, no nothing. Just pure unconditional love and not frightened of anything with him. It is just complete.

Just looking briefly from the star children/adult perspective. I am Indigo. Matt is Indigo with a bit more Rainbow in. My daughter is Crystal. My son is Rainbow. As I came to find out with my son, I believe this is his first time on Earth and he so enjoys his body. All of his past experiences are Reptilian, which maybe explains my great ease with him? It's not quite clear. He does have a unique blend of extreme strength with extreme speed. As a baby it was startling to witness. Like every Reptilian I have encountered, his sensitivity and empathy are high. He gets very nervous about startling people or hurting them. He is very intelligent, but is discreet. He has interesting wizard like abilities. I did see how he was killed in his last lifetime when the Regime entered his realm, being thrown up in the air before death. And as my human baby, he was terrified of being in the air- he would start panicking and screeching. My son reminds me of all my happiness and peace and love in the Reptilian Realms and life, family, and joy.

Spring 2015- with my son here and moving through maternity leave quickly, I needed a new studio space. Just nothing was showing up. I thought about what I wanted. Truly wanted and I had always loved a nearby medical center surrounded by trees, so peaceful and mature. I saw that an acupuncturist worked there and so sent him a note about myself. I learned later on my team had been working, checking on this scenario. I was surprised that the acupuncturist was interested- he was in the midst of some changes and was open to it. I went in for a meeting. Big energy in that office, altered, but maybe that was my imagination. He seemed nice enough and we thought alike in how we were seeing integrative medicine working with allopathic medicine. It felt a bit scary, but felt like something I wished to explore. I could feel the multidimensional pull. I wasn't sure what to make of it. But then there was structure. It almost felt too easy.

Archangel Michael assured me they would check on it and make sure I was safe.

Summer 2015- I had my private practice at the medical center. It was a little bumpy in the beginning. The merge was strong, but my team helped me manage it. They could also work with the acupuncturist, so I felt better. The merge was close enough into the third dimension I had felt in a long time. I loved that tiny space. It was awesome. I quickly could see myself and really gain a whole new layer and level to my skill set. The structure for me was great. I came into a session and the place multidimensionally opened up. It stayed confined to the tiny space. I could see how I had been like in the Amazon just wild and here I was like on a ship, a galactic ship and able to really work on my skills and fill in areas I had been missing- learning systematically case after case. The team on this ship could see where I was missing pieces and help me learn appropriately. I felt so home. And I finally stopped thinking about Greg. It really replaced him. I could pick up where I left off in in-depth multidimensional studies and was getting good help. I'm not sure how much the human acupuncturist understood, but whatever moved through him seemed to get me. I was glad to keep my distance from him. Our paths really never crossed. But just his presence, felt like a brother. This great holding container. Work felt good on many fronts. Three new opportunities had come my way and expanding and I felt the support. I began to think of the human acupuncturist and the soul acupuncturist as separate beings. Soul, or something moving through him, felt like the guiding captain on this ship. Human, I barely noticed, but captain of the ship was my steady help and companion. Beyond grateful. These new work opportunities raised the bar further in my work and this new support energetically helped.

In the studio, I experienced much and worked on, could catalog, organize what I had been experiencing since 1993 and see what I was missing. There was a place to work just in the space ship area and use different diagnostic tools and see how they interfaced with allopathic practices on Earth. I could bring the cases into furthering different dimensions using the space ship area as a starting point and the captain, his team, and my team could give me pointers- so many different places. I wasn't sure how this was possible. But there it was, day after day. Our technology on Earth is just not as advanced on what I was witnessing. I worked like this for the next year and a half and I was really truly happy. So brilliant to have such containment and power to move and explore my power and abilities. I felt extremely loyal to the fullness of the acupuncturist and just tried to stay out of his way. My private practice and work on a few projects felt so home. I had my dream- in the hospital researching, designing, and implementing a yoga program for the pediatric wing. Loved what I was able to do there and probably the best fit for me.

Around October 2015, I could feel the captain of the ship getting antsy. This really wasn't meant to be a long-term solution for me. Guardians of the galaxy, three of them with two attendants, came to visit and talk with myself and the captain. They evaluated me and the situation. They said to the captain- she is too weak to leave now, she needs to stay longer. He said he wasn't sure that he could. I didn't understand at the time, but he seemed concerned. He eventually gave in to the needs and requests of the Guardians. I was very happy. I realize now I should have questioned more. I got a note two days later from human acupuncturist saying how happy he was having me and my energy in the space. That made me feel good. Maybe captain of the ship was just frustrated about a change of plans?

I kept moving forward in my work- my private practice, my yoga classes, my oncology yoga classes and workshops, my two roles at the hospital- one for the pediatric patients and a different role for the Vermont Department of Health. It didn't feel like a lot. Everything was close by and naturally flowed into the other. And the stability and multidimensional home and union I felt in the studio space was very helpful.

I would make really interesting findings. I did stumble onto something and I believe this is when everything began to fall apart. I had two patients with cancerous brain tumors, one pediatric and one adult. I unraveled something. There are 100 universes stacked on top of each other. No new energy can come in and be created or destroyed. There was a dark force wishing to move into our universe and it was seeding. One way it could seed was in a brain tumor- it would kill the host but then expand into our universe. It was odd at best, but I saw it twice and I decided to go for it in unraveling the truth, and to see if I could save the child's life. I alerted my team what I was seeing and we could trace the one doing the seeding from the other universe on this particular tumor. Source God helped turn the seeder to light. But then, there was a hole in the hive it had been operating in. This seeder now in light could tell Source God and others what was actually happening. Which baffled those in the other universes.

This did not go over well with darkness trying to do something here. What I had done, discovered, and alerted light to- was a tactic darkness was using. Oh- it got bad- anything and everything connected to this darkness just came after me hard. This is what I observed. There were other things too, but I think this was the bulk of it. I'm more cautious now after that experience, but in the moment, I just couldn't sit back and not try to help a child save her life. Ultimately, the best I could do in the third dimension was help with the pain, help her sleep, and maybe buy a little time. I could also help in taking out the seeder and opening up the technique being used by darkness- for light to see what was happening. But this started a chain of events for me- layer upon layer, uncovered for the next two and a half years.

Initially Archangel Michael said he had this, all would be okay, but I truly felt I had a bull's eye on my chest by darkness. I began to see how darkness was preying on sick children and keeping them in the soul slave trade. There were human operators of this, ego-based self-serving humans, disguising themselves as healers. I alerted Archangel Michael who saw it too. It was just a nest. Well, I wasn't going to operate the way darkness wanted me too- the hospital project I worked so hard on fell through after 1 year. And it was my first real taste of the Regime in this lifetime and what they are capable of.

It's not personal, but if you are going up against them- they are technically brilliant in figuring out how to find your weakest most vulnerable areas to press to cause the most amount of pain. Brutal. It was shocking. Even with all the help I had multidimensionally, my team seemed shocked as well that they couldn't seem to help.

Summer 2016- just devastated, feeling captain of the ship comforting me in the studio space, I would just cry at times. I realized it was just a dimensional merge, but it felt good to cry. Soon after, I received an invitation to go to the National Institutes of Health inside of a biomedical Native American initiative- fully paid. It was a bright light. I went ahead there. It definitely felt like my elders pushing- especially Red Cloud. When I walked off that plane in DC, I felt like an entourage come with me of my native elders. In fact, when I had been traveling, the seat next to me was broken and I could see the faint outline of Red Cloud sitting next to me. What was this trip about? I had a great time. I loved the NIH. It reminded me strongly of what I had come to know later on as the medical center in the Archangel Realm- great vibrational rhythm there and many happy doctors and scientists- relatively speaking. I just felt so good. Meeting and spending time with those from other tribes- some from Rosebud and especially one from Standing Rock- felt impactful. So, when I learned from him later on what was happening at Standing Rock (the protest of a pipeline and trying to protect the Earth, water, and tribe)- I felt pulled to do something multidimensionally. That honestly felt like my purpose in going to the NIH- this hooking in.

That began the start of my session work at home. I would clear with Archangel Michael, center ground and open with Reiki help, and go where I needed to go. There was an urgency to the situation at Standing Rock that I didn't realize how, but for me had opened a new way of doing work. All my notes are documented in length in the emails. For after every session at home, I would document in detail to make sure I was accurate, send to my team, and if my team had seen the same thing. They could also see where maybe they needed to tweak my knowledge or skill set. I guess it is kind of like the "Matrix" movies.

Holy rituals and ceremonies happening in real time at Standing Rock- made it easier to hook into and work remotely. There were 12 snakes. Truly serpents. With my killing the first one- the next day there was an earthquake in Italy which upset me because people died. Each night I came into session, this was talked about, some Native shamans said it happens, there are these snakes in the Earth impacting the Earth. I said we can do this without killing anyone. I mentioned we needed help like that we'd find with Jesus or Archangel Michael which upset a fair amount- which rightfully so considering the holocaust in Jesus' name on Native soil. Many did not trust him. I said just for this particular matter. We need his muscle, plus what we bring to the table. The next snake killed- another earthquake in Italy after, but no people died. We kept at it. In one long session, I just went hard with Archangel Michael, very mentally tiring. Most of the snakes were of different natures from each other. There was the last one, the beginning of the snakes and it actually asked to die by my hand. Which made me sad, but honorable and when it died it turned back to light and went with Source God for a walk. They looked to be close that he had had a disagreement with God way back in time. Sigh. Later on- the pipeline with Standing Rock still went through- so I was confused by this whole experience. But it felt deeper than the pipeline. It felt like we helped move something out of the Earth that needed to be moved. I was tired. But good tired.

I tried to follow through with the NIH suggestions I had learned, but the Vermont hospital I worked in just didn't feel like a match for me. I was deeply saddened and disillusioned by the real darkness I witnessed in their integrative health unit, the out-of-control egos, and how this also spiraled within the hospital's administration and their egos and greed. But I continued with my other work and remaining hospital project, aligned with the State Department of Health. I wasn't sure where I was going. The only person in integrative health I felt safe with was the acupuncturist and the studio space we shared.

Fall 2016- things started to get tricky and deep, so many layers. I found an old television show, but new to me, called "Fire Fly". I really liked it, but a few episodes in- I started to come upon something. The captain of the spaceship- his wording, how he looked, how he talked with one of the people renting space on his ship to do her business- it struck a chord in me. The woman's business on his ship was helping people. Her relationship with the captain was an interesting dynamic. As I came upon this, I was flooded by a wave of sexual energy that felt like my studio mate, like captain of the ship. I was confused. It went on for about a week. My team solved it and said that it was some low-level darkness. The energy there was energy he had with his wife, but it was being crossed with me because the Regime was trying to find a way to hurt and confuse me. Hmmm. I guess- it was odd and made me uneasy. But it had stopped and so I let it go.

Then, there was the issue with the election. I became more and more fully aware of how the Regime was working through Hillary Clinton, that she had made a deal with them about when she was 14 years old. I became more frantic because while Trump was a jerk and buffoon- what would happen if she was elected? Humanity would be enslaved and we would have about 400 years left. I could see exactly what would happen if she as president put her hands on the desk- like an electric power snaking through. It was so bad. The whole thing with people dying around her- maybe she wasn't aware, but so much of it was the Regime. It's not political- it's who is hooked in with them and can best serve their Regime agenda. A lot was riding on her winning. The Regime was sure of it. Days before the election, I would do sessions with other twin flames and powerhouses on Earth and just uniting to keep our planet, to reclaim our planet, our species. It's mapped out better what we did as documented in the emails. It was intense. It was really standing up for those that could not stand up for themselves. I was deeply frightened. I was told by my team that Source God had a plan. I wasn't sure. There is no way she would not win. I thought how I could take care of myself, my mental and emotional health. My plan was to rent a cabin in the woods and while of course being with my family, I was going to spend my time in the cabin when they were away. I'd move all of my work into the woods and just sink into nature and completely ignore all media. I couldn't watch it unfold. I had also been following the Gabriel Method, helping with meditation, stress reduction, better relationship with body and food and health. I decided to do the Gabriel Method detox. So, I started that. I was sure Hillary was going to win.

But then, she didn't. I felt this huge gushing wave of relief- such a deep profound sense of relief that the Regime had not taken this planet. My soul knew first-hand what could have been. I emailed my team and they said Source God had intervened and was not going to allow it. He figured it out. How I felt, what I knew, what I had documented, what I had experienced at the hands of the Regime- I would not wish on anyone. They literally feed on pain.

It was hard though, so many people were deeply upset. Such a divide in our country. The pain of the people around me. I so wish they could see it from my perspective. I also felt like we were about to have a lot of flushing out and discussions we've been needing to have as a country for a very long time. We needed to figure things out. I kept on with the detox. First week was just a more whole based food approach. The real detox was the second week in. Things got weird. I so loved the way I could rest and breathe. I really loved this detox. I was so happy nearing completion by Saturday morning. On Thursday, I was in my sweet little studio space, resting on the table and had this amazing experience of my heart opening in a way that it exposed the entire galaxy, really the universe in there, like a gateway. So cool. I just breathed and rested in that space. Just really, really happy and peaceful.

Friday afternoon, I got an email out of the blue from the human aspect of my studio mate. He was concerned how I was doing with the election results. I explained my feelings, not quite the detail I give here. I thought it was odd he should email. That evening he wrote back, "You are uniquely important to me." Just the feel, the tone, felt deeply intimate. Wait, what? I got nervous and began trying to pull his cord out, the connection. It was in there deep and I couldn't get out of- what was this? What was going on between us? It would show up in my intimacy with Matt as well. What? Wait, what?

I told my team. They didn't see it. So, I opted to just ignore it for the time being. But then I got a long email from him that seemed to really know me. It was confusing. Why was he telling me this? Then himself, human aspect, third dimension- just started to treat me odd, like controlling. I pushed back which then led or was it just coincidence to him needing the space soon for another project and I was basically forced out. It was like whiplash. What was happening? I was so happy there, what was going on?

Dec 2016 was a whirlwind. I was cleared and clean and open from the detox and decided how good I felt eating along the Gabriel Method guidelines- I stuck with it. I felt so much light around me and could bring in a lot of light into the space. My skills now inside the space being able to flip with dimensions easily was like a home. It was a great portal and effortless after the past year and a half. But now, I was being forced out?

I saw what was happening with captain of the ship aspect of my studio mate/attached to my studio mate. I saw how I looked now. I had definitely matured and aged from my time where I looked like Indiana Jones in the desert and now had a more female presence and organized- a long teal/blue gown with wavy blonde hair and more calmness. I was in a sexual relationship with captain of the ship on a dimensional level, and not sure how this happened. This did not seem healthy and he didn't want me to leave, yet he knew it was wrong. I later came to find out that this loneliness was a weakness of his, this is what he was pointing to back in Oct. 2015- that he didn't think he could hold the line, he knew himself. He was used to giving and helping others and leading, but was deeply lonely. In the fall/early winter 2016, captain of the ship was offered a deal by darkness that he could have me if he followed their orders of what they wanted him to do. He agreed and made the deal. In reality, only later it was learned it was a set up. If the deal had been successful and I really had been led astray and taken from Matt, I would have been drained and killed. It was an Achilles' heel for the captain, his loneliness. Who only later I found out was not the soul of my studio mate/acupuncturist, but had been brought in and was supposed to be an ally to Light to help make the dynamics at the studio a safe place for me. In reality, the actual soul of my studio mate had left a long time ago.

2016- what a brutal year, one thing after another, and how was I to ever trust my team and Archangel Michael? At this point Source God talked to me through email directly and just pissed me off in his comments and I told him so. Jesus then took over the emails to help with better communication. I thought and hoped this would help. Things just felt and appeared more and more out of control.

Such speed. My human studio mate (no soul but cleaved with the captain of the ship soul) and I were going to meet for tea, to see if we could figure it out, but my team advised against it. I made the hard decision to just leave. Things were out of control and I felt in extreme danger. No one really understood at the time what was happening. At some point there had been an attack to try and get in at the opening of my heart to the universal experience I was having, and Archangel Michael covered it and blocked it.

Captain of the ship was in pain. I could see that. And the bare bones of my human studio mate weren't very nice. I kept getting away and cutting cords as I went. It was awful. On top of how awful and confusing the last 6 months prior to this had been.

January 2017- I started the year just in shock. The Regime was pissed, darkness was pissed, my life felt awful and I had lost so much. The loss of the safety I had felt with human aspect and captain of the ship aspect of my former studio mate was really devastating. Things needed to change. Dovetailing on session work I had been doing the year before, new nightly sessions opened up- to start really getting in to how to proceed. I have documented them. I think after around session 86, I went to every other day or just labeled them session. Some of the major changes and foundational work that needed to change happened in this time. What's hard is to know how hard I was working, not just for me, but for humans, for other souls and other beings, for the level of corruption I had stumbled on at the hospital and especially in integrative health. The levels of ego and pure bullshit was ridiculous. And how innocent people were being harmed. That made me work hard. To help and give a voice to those enslaved in something they didn't even have a clue about and for the Regime and darkness to be getting away with it. It felt like a labor of love and necessary and important, but it was hard on me. Even with all the protection in the world, I didn't feel safe, didn't feel like Light really knew what was going on. In fact, they did not, which was just startling and upsetting. Not to say it wasn't fascinating, but it was tiring work.

I'll document here what I can, but it's really in depth and full how full the year 2017 was. As mentioned, I document my session and send them to my team through email- so we can compare notes, we each see how much is translating for the other party, what adjustments to make, and also for my own growth and their growth.

The beginning sessions were about uncovering what the Regime was actually doing- showing this and presenting before galactic federations. Even with support from Archangel Michael and Jesus, I felt embarrassed to be on such a galactic stage. This was new for me. I could open up my entire being soul history and pull out pieces of the puzzle and put them together. The picture ultimately really showed that Source God and Light only had about 7% understanding of what the Regime was up to.

I'll start to explain with an email thread from February 5, 2017-

Jesus wrote to me- "Here are the facts. Darkness lined up a massive attack. The head of this attack was Hillary Clinton becoming President. The second wave focused on light workers. These light workers all had the same ship structure you had. It became obvious that we needed to focus on stopping the point of attack, Hillary. We succeeded with the help of many light workers, such as yourself. The attack was able to knock out nearly every ship structure that was in place leaving many light workers weak. The ship structure you had with your studio mate was safe until the days after the election. Now we are scrambling to restore order. The head of the attack has been cut off. The ship structures are weak. We are looking for the best way to not only take out your former studio mate, but all like him. We think we have to do this all at once. Do you have any question or need more detail?"

I wrote back "How many in number, light workers, do you speak of? I am aware now that the ship structures were not neutral, never safe, and were designed as entrapments for light workers. Do you agree or disagree? My former studio mate actively rearranged me and plugged me into the evil inside of (a grant funded project). My gathering awareness is that the attack started June 2015- as I was drawn to and brought on this ship. A ship that was already encapsulated and functioning in darkness. Do you see this differently? Why? How do you see that the ship structure was at any point safe? Why was this not stopped sooner? What is your plan to take them out all at once because- all I have intelligence on is that my former studio mate is part of others picking up speed and lacing the country in his plan, and our nation to have a global impact and universal impact? Your time is beyond extremely limited. You don't have a lot of time."

Jesus responded, "I will stick to facts as that seems best. Tens of thousands of light workers were impacted. The ships were safe at one point, but became contaminated when our defenses had to shift to Hillary Clinton. The plan here involved healthcare and keeping humans addicted to unhealthy practices. They were not designed as entrapments but became them. I will need more information to verify the (grant funded project) question. It seems more like those inside (the grant funded project) were weak and manipulated. The ship was not encapsulated in darkness when you were brought on but the time frame of the attack you have is accurate. The ship structure was safe because it was created in conjunction with light. Those tending the ships were greatly responsible for their care. We did try to stop this sooner in many ways but failed to different degrees. One example was Bernie losing the election. Bernie would have been an excellent resource in defending the ships. Instead, our resources had to be split up. It was better to not risk losing everything. Time is not on our side. Actions do have to come quickly. Does this answer your questions?"

I responded back, "A bit, but no. I strongly disagree that the ships were ever safe. I think even now you are being hid from the fullness of all information. The attacker behind Hillary Clinton- lives inside (the grant funded project). I firmly believe my former studio mate hooked me into (the grant funded project) on darkness's request.

I see with crystal clarity inside. Ask the galactic medical family of light team that just worked on me. They have dissected the 100's of chips extracted off the cord that was inside of me. You do not have all the information. I firmly disagree with you. You have maybe 20-30% of it, but you are missing a tremendous amount."

Jesus responded, "I will look at this as your information is generally accurate. We would not have sent you on a ship unless it was safe. If it was not safe, then this has to be examined and discussed. Light beings did have control of the ship. They could be incorrect that they had it well protected. I will work with the galactic family. They could be a good resource in how to proceed. I will use the information you share to move forward."

I replied, "You were fooled. I was fooled. Emotionally, I need to shelve this for now. Let's get down to the business of what happened. The galactic medical team family of light that worked on me this past week, please go to them now and look at the chips. They told me they were shocked. They said they had been looking for this information for a very long time. They are probably sucked right now into exploring the data on the chips. I wish they would have come to you. Why did they not get you? I'll have to find time to give you as much information as I have. Going back to the very beginning of March 2015. The cord that up until a week ago was inside of (the grant funded project) from me, still was beyond intricate and advanced. We've got an extremely bad situation on our hands. I know I'm right. I can't explain all the details without really going into the experience, but will do everything in my power to get what I can to you. You and Source God and Archangel Michael have been distracted and visually what I see is the maneuver in warfare where one side, dark, has unbeknownst to the other side, light, penned them in. Darkness is waiting for the kill shot and or letting by sheer mass suffocation to occur. Can you see the image?"

Jesus replied, "This is valuable information. I will do as you instruct and learn what I can from the galactic family. I will also await your words. They can come when you have time."

I responded, "I'm obviously anxious and will push myself. There is simply too much at stake. It's the large entire canvas. I can see it, but I can't describe it. I see pieces, but I can begin to see how they all connect. I feel like you all have been focusing on a select few pieces and not seeing the harmony of how they operate and the bigger canvas. Regarding pushing myself, if you were in my shoes, would you not do the same? At any point the galactic family of light needs a meeting with me to look at parts of my being scarred and marked- it could give clues. I know these chips. I have lived with them for a year. I felt like a carrier for darkness of these chips. But why? Who would I have been unconsciously smuggling them to, right under your nose? You now have dealt with the head of the attacker with Hillary Clinton, what I'm seeing is something that goes deeper inside- darker and deeper into a close connection with the heart of the universes Dark- like our Light Source God."

Jesus responded, "I understand that you will push yourself. I can relate. The information is important but your health is more so. I can meet with the galactic family. The information you provide can come a little later. Even if you push yourself, I still need to meet with the galactic family. In other words, you have a little time, maybe about 24-36 hours."

I replied, "I'm wondering if they are getting ready to call you anyway as they are thorough and the chips are taking time to understand. Maybe my urgent sense of you talking with them is converging with them about to reach out to you?"

Jesus replied, "It could be. Either way, you do have time."

I commented, "24-36 hours seems a lot of time. Why so long? I've been on edge for days now and now it's just over the top."

Jesus replied, "I am going to meet with the galactic family. Our discussions will be thorough and take a little time."

I wrote, "Okay. I just don't feel good. I feel how I felt before the election and that was knowing we were on the same page. Now, hearing you all don't have the same information as I do. And we're not on the same page. Is upsetting. I don't know what plan I can formulate to feel my sanity come back."

He wrote, "We are getting on the same page. Your information is proving to be very helpful."

I ended the email thread with, "I hope so. I feel vulnerable and uncomfortable when I fully can't explain why I'm so sure I'm right. But I've felt it pouring out of me to really shaking you and these emails- we need to wake up to the reality yesterday and now now now keeps screaming in my mind. I worry I project or it's my C-PTSD. I second-guess myself all the time with my scientific need to keep myself reigned in. I do hypothesize though it's way worse than I can explain. I'm afraid of opening too much information when myself is fragile. I'm afraid of not opening it and us and you being in the dark. So, I'm put in a hard position. But I know for a fact I got too close to the heart of what's going on in January 2016 in being inside of my patient's cancerous brain tumor and seeing things darkness did not want me to understand. Darkness underestimated me and my ability. They still underestimate me."

So. So, it can be seen how involved the communication process is. This is one thread of many email threads in one day. Plus, the actual sessions. Then add in my own processing and actual living reality in the third dimension. There is my business- private practice, teaching classes, and other projects. There is my own self-care. There is having a partner, family, children, and home. It is an incredible team effort and balancing act. Although another description in my brighter moments- it really is like a beautiful weaving tapestry and quilt with many layers, fabric, threads. They help and support each other. I've always been told as a child that I think too much or I go too deep. Well, now I'm glad to be who I am. I'm grateful for the strength of my mind and heart and soul and gut. It is different than others, but it is a way of living I'm designed for and have the skills I need to live it, as well as the support. Days are full though.

This next email thread I bring up goes into the uncovering process of learning more fully about the Regime.

February 5-6, 2017

I wrote- "So from 9:35-9:50pm I spent time moving my consciousness to connect in my pod and with the galactic family of light medical team. This is what I experienced- I was able to understand why you, Jesus, have not known this information. During my clearings last week in the pod, you were there, but remotely and as such, a screen up. You were able to help, but not witnessing the fullness of it. The galactic medical team apologized for not letting me or you Jesus know information, but wanted to be absolutely certain before alerting me and you. They have been guiding me in my speech and pushing to get me to talk better, communicate better. I mentioned I was extremely grateful for their help in navigating. (In reflection, I don't know why they didn't just get you). It was a very clear session even without opening Reiki, I asked if they wanted me to open Reiki. They said it was up to me, but it might expose me to an abundance of information quickly that could be triggering- so they would need to put buffers in place. I declined to open Reiki, but instead reflect back to them what I was hearing, and if I was off maybe I should open Reiki then. We all agreed. The lead being talking to me, to my left, showed me how you Jesus were taking in the information, going back and forth to your father, and that it may take 48-52 hours to fully begin to brief you. I was told the information on the 100's of cells that had been attached to me; the galactic family had been looking for this information for a very long time. That the actual knowledge Jesus, Source God, had of what was going on with dark plans was actually around less than 3% to 10%. That in securing and risking myself to secure this information I had done a great service and they would have expected nothing less from their queen. In this process, there had been damage done to my body that is currently irreparable, but they are working on technology now to be able to fix it. At this point I was glad I had decided not to open Reiki as I think it would have upset me too much. A question came up from me to them of why were all these chips placed on that cord. Was I a mule? Like running drugs for darkness unknowingly? They are leaning towards there is a very underground resistance and someone somewhere in time put those chips there, in hopes of them being discovered. At this point, I started to flood with overwhelming anxiety. Who is the resistance in there? I have so much confusion and such a limited ability to take it in. Is my former studio mate part of the resistance or is he dark? I feel overwhelmed and freaked out. They mentioned I would start to see movement in 48-52 hours on this information by Source. Does this seem accurate to you? Back to being very tense and upset in my body and nervous system, when I was doing better the last few hours. Please let my team know and help if you can."

Jesus replied, "These words seem accurate and I am doing work based on the words. Your team has great respect for you and will work to keep you safe and restore your health."

I replied, "Thanks. Good to know I'm accurate and method of seeing is accurate. Very disturbing and sad that this is the reality. I don't think my former studio mate is part of the resistance in any way, do you or my team? I imagine whomever, however the chips were placed is way deep in the dark matrix. I can't see it- it seems my cell memory has been blocked from remembering, no?"

Jesus responded, "I don't know that your former studio mate is part of the resistance. I also don't know that he is linked with darkness either. We do have to flush this out with some other details."

I replied, "I don't see him as being part of the resistance on any level, but I need the facts on this before I can be emphatic. I heartily disagree with your comment that he is not linked in to darkness as I'm thinking. I think he is way more linked in than even I realize and every single second that passes, under your very nose, he is replicating what on a larger scale Hillary was going to do. He is beyond able to hide it because he is extremely far up there in darkness. I will prove it. Please have my medical team show you the cuts on my body and the weaponry technology that was used to make them and who owns these kinds of tools and has access to this technology. There are not many in darkness that do. As they are having to find a way for me to heal, they are learning new technology and the ins and outs of its construct. My former studio mate is simply one of the darkest figures on our planet."

Jesus Responded, "I take your words as accurate and do not dispute your former studio mate's attachment to darkness. I was going off the fact that you proposed he might be part of the resistance, which would conflict with being attached to darkness. As I said, we are being briefed and these facts will help flush out details. Certainly, any work we do will be based on facts and I will be working with you here as well as with the galactic family."

I replied, "He is not simply attached to darkness. He is a walking dark lord, on Earth in our universe. I see this more clearly than ever. Of course, a musing thread of me would hope maybe he is part of the resistance, but that's my hope and it's not reality. Wanted to check in with you. No, he's a powerful dark lord. Yes, his power is ultimately less than mine, but in darkness, aligned, and a dark lord and master of dark arts- he's up there in the hierarchy. It is not a coincidence he can live in Santa Fe, New Mexico easily and that he went back there for a visit soon after I started in the office. It is not a coincidence I've been drawn to him because of how much I probably can spy and also, it fascinates me to be so close- not something I ever choose to do again, nor should have. It's complicated. But yes, he's not just attached to darkness- he is the walking embodiment of a dark lord and works extremely close with deep parts of dark."

Ugh. It's hard to read this and know- I was correct, but it was at an angle. It really would prove to be much, much more complicated than I could have imagined.

Part V. Anchoring- sessions

The sessions continued. Here is a snapshot of a few. It was a way to process information, contribute- I did wonder where this was leading.

Email thread February 7- February 8, 2017-

I asked- "So, we are at 52 hours, thoughts of how things are going regarding briefing?"

Jesus replied- "The galactic family exposed the screens and other technology darkness was using to shield us. We have started working with the galactic family on countermeasures. They have introduced some technology that will help us eliminate these screens. We will be working with them in the future because they are ahead of the curve from a technological standpoint. We are also now planning on how to handle the Sith Lords that stemmed from these ships. One theory had the light workers riding up and taking back the power from these Sith Lords. Once weakened to the degree they will be weakened, the Sith Lords can be conquered. We are going to continue to work with the galactic family on forming an uprising. At this time, you should be able to take part in discussions. Let me know if you cannot. I will give you more information as it is available. "

I wrote, "Hmmm. I began coughing hard this morning. A pinchy sensation at the heart and it felt like a cord tangled. My awareness of the following started filtering in at 12:10pm my time today- my former studio mate is the incarnation of the being that tortured me when I was stuffed away in darkness the time ago, I can't really remember. His heart cord is tangled around deep parts of my heart. With Source God, the galactic medical team has been looking at this technology and how to remove him. The solution was created and told it would begin to be applied around 2pm-5pm today. It was more complicated than anyone expected. It seems almost clear except for one very small spot to the right part of my heart. It seems stuck. With this completely freed, they will cauterize the cord. His heart will have no energy going to it. They are not sure what or how his body or being will respond. My truthful hope is he will die of a heart attack. And Source God can destroy him completely. I have zero tolerance and will not be subjected to this figure on any level in my life. The backlog of emotion on this is huge. How Archangel Michael can stomach having turned me over to the being that tortured me is almost beyond; surviving so long ago-to be tortured again. I'm at a loss of how to comprehend."

Jesus replied, "Michael cannot stomach it. Michael is undergoing the education the galactic family is providing. My father has been working on this cord for quite some time as referenced earlier today."

I wrote, "I imagine his pain is worse than mine. It is extremely important to my health and sanity on every level that I am no longer exposed to my former studio mate. It is not enough if you hide him from me or block him. If he exists on this planet, in this galaxy, in this universe in any form- I will feel it. I will know it. You made a promise to me that I would be safe from him, as Source as my witness- I was not. I was exposed to him again to be brutally tortured. I don't feel this comes from rage or hatred- it is the reality of me being able to heal and to work on living, instead of just surviving. And work on being able to trust you again. Do I need to explain why I will not live if he is allowed to?"

Jesus responded, "We are discussing the best way to do this with the galactic family. You should join this conversation to get a sense of what options are available."

I wrote, "I can't. I've got Matt mad at me. My daughter who won't go to bed. Bad TMS starting in my right hip and lower back."

Jesus replied, "Matthew is not mad at you. Our discussions will be ongoing. You can join when it is convenient."

I wrote, "I did from 9:40-10:07pm. That was a lot. You were to my left. I'm confused by this email.'

Jesus wrote, "The timing is off. I sent this before you arrived."

Email thread February 8-9 with session notes-

I wrote of the session, "I was skeptical of what I could bring to the table in discussing plans going forward, but upon your request went into a session at 9:40pm my time last night. Brought myself consciously there in the space reserved for me and this is what I experienced- huge stadium full of the galactic federation in front of us. On stage was Source God, Archangel Michael to his right, Jesus to his right, and me to his right. I felt really embarrassed and especially about having a pod around me. You leaned over and whispered that the family of light could make it invisible and that helped me feel less self-conscious. I felt supported in talking as I knew or felt familiar with everyone there. I basically said- "you all have the briefings and large documents that were found in the cells and you can see behind me on the screen above from my experience images of the levels and layers of torture." Everyone was in agreement. I said, "right now you are making plans, but I tell you now I have been on the inside and you know 3% of dark plans. That's it. What is here before us is only 3%." This seemed to startle beings. Lots of murmuring of what are we going to do. Somehow it began to dawn on me and I spoke again, "I apologize that I don't understand technology, time, and physics super well, but I believe it was me about a billion years ago that set the cells on the cord that I smuggled into this time frame. I must have somehow remembered and went in and got them." We then created a huge model, like for a large multidimensional puzzle, and plugged in the 3% knowledge secured, another 1% I collected this lifetime. I said, "if we can get at least 80%, no my mistake we need 100% it will click into place exactly what's going on and what we should do." It slowly dawned on me- yes if I've smuggled this piece in, maybe I have more and I'm really good at this point of talking to my energy and cells. I wanted to leave and work on it, but the family of light medical team said it would be more helpful to have those that care about me surrounding and supporting me. It felt better too. I agreed. I stilled myself and contacted the fullness of me- somewhere between 1.3-3 billion years old. I first thanked myself and told and could feel how much I loved me, the wonderful sweet beautiful me. I made the request to myself to show and highlight all the pieces that I had gathered to help light. And I could see it through time all these pieces and chips I had gathered through all I've been through. All these pieces were collected. And then I was told and shown we've got 100% and actually plus more information than we need. I was relieved and thankful. I cried and cried and cried. It felt very good, for the first time in my life, to be surrounded by family, friends, and loving ones even as I felt vulnerable and scared. I could feel the technique that tribes of old use, of surrounding their warrior after war and helping them heal, and come out of the war experience. I felt very grateful. 2/3 went off to start immediately going through the puzzle complete and a 1/3 stayed with me. Slowly coming back to look at the cord- a piece attached still to my former studio mate. I finally said enough. And even as the piece of the cord left, that part of me was like in shock- just repeating over and over like a broken record- no, all can turn to light with love, all can turn to light with love- like it wouldn't let up. Some family of light members just held this part of me. Next with family medical team and Source God removing the large plug that had been placed in my heart area so long ago I can't picture it- just a hole- Source filled with his substance and then the medical team put on another substance. My being started to calibrate with it. I noticed last remnants of my experience with my former studio mate would be absorbed and taken care of by Source substance. I again felt awkward and ashamed and the two family members used humor about how their oddly unique too and I felt more seen and normal. I was too tired to see the information and just wanted to come home. I did say that beings could come to me with questions, but I ask now that my medical team with Jesus filter out the requests and find a way so I'm not bombarded- i.e., triage it. Does this seem accurate to what you witnessed?"

Jesus replied, "These words are very accurate. Work will progress as you witnessed and I will find a way to triage questions. You have done well and it is nice that you can see how well respected. Please let me know how you are feeling and how you are feeling with Matthew and with your daughter and your son."

I responded, "Okay, thanks. My neck is really sore- more probably because my heart has 'bled' out of its dressing. It needs to be cleansed and redressed so it doesn't get infected, I think. Maybe my team and Source can address this?"

Jesus, "I will direct work here."

My response, "Thanks. Things feel good with my family. Is there something I should be aware of? I'd say my heart, I, just feels sad. I note that there is dark brown blood in my underwear. I think my period started, but this looks different. One thing I notice- I could be wrong- is some of those in the federation are commenting on things they find odd in the third dimensional realm- myself being treated badly, struggling with money, people disrespecting me and it makes them upset. Of course, it makes me upset too. I just don't need to be reminded of it; can you buffer me from hearing their talk- it's not helpful nor productive. Little longer day than I would like, some moms in the hospital to visit, 2:30 pm long distance session for client, 4:15 teaching yoga class, some grocery shopping and need a little exercise. Plus, any yoga or meditation on my own is helpful. Plus, I'm healing and there is a lot going on. Can you help me figure how to best use my time?"

Jesus, "I will honor these requests."

My response, "Thanks. Yes, I do have my period in full now. Just feeling a bit weak today and tired. I would like to know how things are going. My expectation is immediate change for my former studio mate and a plan really coming together regarding darkness. I can see all the puzzle pieces together in their formation- clicked into place has created a great multidimensional informational portal globe to really get the fullness. Is anything missing needed? Any questions?"

Jesus replied, "Things are going well. We are working very closely with the galactic family. At this time there are no additional questions and we are assessing what is needed. There is likely going to be another opportunity for you to join us this evening like you did last night."

I responded, "It is 9:45pm my time. It does not look like there is a space or need for me to be there. Things are moving quickly as you and others are traversing the galaxies and universe to talk with key leaders. In real time- you are just traveling and weaving in and out of time very fast. I don't feel I can keep up and it makes me sleepy and stretches my consciousness that I can't keep up and hurts my brain and spine."

Jesus, "We will convene another time."

I replied, "Is all okay? It looks like you are responding to the information the leader from the outskirts brought to you- regarding what was found in my former studio mate's left upper pectoralis area tissue. Is that correct?"

Jesus, "That is correct. We are working at a fast pace and covering as much ground as possible."

I wrote, "I don't wish to distract you from this. If it's possible to understand, how did the outlying wilderness leader have access to a biopsy of my former studio mate's human tissue? It seems to me the biopsy shows an operating in the cells you weren't expecting- can you explain? How, why do I know this leader- it's like I was a toddler soul when I saw him last."

Jesus, "I will pose these questions to the galactic family and funnel answers to you."

My response, "Okay. I really do know that I'm not going to be able to function nor progress in this life if he is allowed to live as a human being. It's extremely upsetting to not know what is going on. It's extremely upsetting thinking about what kind of bullshit excuse or convoluted answer I'm going to be given about why he's still alive. I've been able to talk with my deep powerful emotions, but I'm losing patience."

Jesus, "We are not sure he is a human being at this point. With the cords to his heart cut, he cannot survive. The galactic family is looking at a full walk-in situation or applying some other form of technology to overwrite his current existence. Discussions are continuing and options are flying around. I will mediate a form of discussion that you can safely join."

My response, "Are you saying that you're leaning towards- he may never have been a human being? That he's been a sophisticated hologram? I do not see the walk-in situation working for me. As long as his name is still in the community, in the papers, and his projects continue- doesn't matter if he's a shell walking around in that body and name- it will still be triggering."

Jesus, "We're not sure when he would have ceased being human, if that is even what occurred. A walk-in situation would not simply replace your former studio mate with another one. The plan would also entail discrediting the studies and work he stole from others or even having the light workers take it over in some capacity."

My response, "Can you more fully explain your statement here- We are not sure he is a human being at this point. With the cords to his heart cut, he cannot survive. The galactic family is looking at a full walk-in situation or applying some other form of technology to overwrite his current existence."

Jesus, "Simply killing him probably is not going to stop what has started. The galactic family is looking at options. One of them is having a walk-in inserted. If a walk-in is inserted it would come with other steps. The walk-in would not be just so that things could continue as they are. They are also looking at other technology which would erase the existence of what has happened. These concepts can be discussed with you when you next join us."

I wrote, "Unfortunately you have missed why I'm distressed. I'd like to understand how you understand me and my words I have expressed- why do you think I'm distressed?"

Jesus, "You are distressed that your former studio mate is still alive as a human being."

My response, "What have you gathered is my primary reason for my distress?"

Jesus, "You are distressed that you are unable to find valuable work in the third dimension which will allow you to help support your family as you outlined in a previous email."

I replied, "No- this is incorrect."

Jesus, "I will consult with the galactic family at this time."

My response, "Okay. I'm confused. I thought I was extremely clear through sessions, through email. I don't understand."

Jesus, "It is extremely clear."

I wrote, "No it's not. If you understood what is at the heart and soul of the matter for me- your response of why I'm distressed with my former studio mate still being alive would have been very different. This does not sit well with me. Not at all."

Jesus, "I apologize. I was looking in context of this email chain. I understand the greater picture and have been working feverishly with the galactic family to understand and use the technology they have. I have been working to open up the discussion to you which I think has been extremely helpful for everyone and am very happy that you joined. I see great value in having you in these discussions as does the galactic family."

I replied, "Okay, I'll ask again, why do you think it doesn't work for me to have my former studio mate walking around on Earth as I am walking around on Earth in the same time frame? Whether there is another soul in there or not. Why does it not work for me to his name continuing, his business continuing, etc.?"

Jesus, "I understand your point. So does the galactic family. We are working extremely hard to flush out options. This is why I am making you a part of the discussions being held. We are looking to address the fact that your former studio mate walking around is not good for you, or anyone for that matter, versus the fact that he may not be able to be simply removed without something else filling the void and continuing the work. We are looking for ways to simply remove him versus shifting the work he does back to the light workers from whom he stole it. It is not necessarily black or white, alive or dead. We have ruled nothing out as we look for the best solution. These discussions benefit from you and I will hold a space for you in them and help you to join them."

The end of this email thread. In summary, I believe this gives a decent snap shot of the email communications. These particular few days were about the Regime. The attacks on me would get increasingly more vicious over the coming months.

A good summary email comes from a session on February 10, 2017-

I wrote to Jesus of the session, "Thanks. Why did it feel differently this time? Hard to focus and not as crisp. I noticed we were in the stadium arena again, with the large swirling globe puzzle/pattern of darkness's plans. There were a few federation beings, but they looked like they were talking amongst themselves, writing, reading, or thinking. So basically, the few working with me and you- were just us. I was thrown a bit about how different I felt prior to last time. We went over the globe. You, others, us talking about it. It was shown to me how my former studio mate and his being have been spreading darkness throughout time- you can see it in the globe. If he were just wiped out, darkness would be alerted and it would call forth many more and much darker to fill the void. Kind of like with me, if darkness takes me out in such a direct way- it opens up a void that allows light to ramp up. So, this is the idea- his heart cord being cauterized and because of the dark he is- a normal human it would kill, not him- he can rely on a dark internal generator. It does essentially blind him. I see like an infection or dark mass covering his eyes. So currently, he's stumbling around, forgetting things, making simple mistakes, and confused what's wrong with him. In the meantime, the galactic family and federation with countless others have a whole series of things going on- to distract and confuse darkness administration. They can't figure out the pattern. It's too many things. For example, like dismantling what they are doing at the hospital's NICU to the babies energetically. I was told to let the family and federation to do this and not to try and do anything so I don't put myself in danger. Before darkness can put out or understand how one fire started, another starts up- creating deeper and more and more confusion for darkness. My former studio mate will continue to stumble and make mistakes- darkness will be so fed up- they won't really investigate, but will pull him and others back in to the mouth of darkness- really gather everything back in to regroup. Basically, you have set the stage for my former studio mate to be cannibalized by darkness in the next 24 weeks. We, on the other hand, are also regrouping, hence many lightworkers like myself going into different dimensions. Archangel Realm for me.

Pause.

In this pause, I will be working with you Jesus, Source God, etc. to work on a construct so darkness cannot proceed how they have been and other ideas. Currently, there are about 1,000 humans/beings as dark as my former studio mate on this planet. He is ranked at about 999. So, actually on the low end of this level of dark. But considering 7.1 billion people on the planet- that's pretty dark. It brings up a lot of emotions for me. Maybe I was hoping, he could just be destroyed- to save him this pain; if there was any thread of light it could've released, we could talk, and it would flow back into Source God. It's odd to me, how even after all he's done to me- I feel sad to see him suffer. I truly understand there isn't another way and this is who he is. I just hate seeing suffering. The image of a crocodile comes up and myself like a beautiful free bird flying around. I can honestly say I loved him. And he like the crocodile has nothing inside of him that knows how to truly relate to the freedom, beauty, and joy I have. Like there is nothing there- he is a manufactured entity of dark. His one try would be to eat me and see if he could experience what I have then. It makes me very sad. I still hold hope like in a few million years....but then I don't think he has a soul like human beings. As a manufactured entity, he's basically a robot- hence why the cauterizing his heart had virtually no impact. Darkness will think he's just malfunctioning and destroy him. The danger here for me is it stirs up my wanting to rescue him and feelings for him. I could be being attacked right now as I type this. Can you buffer me from his crying and pain? I think it's very important to get me involved in another project and to get my mind off of this. I wish another hospital in the area wanted me, my practice, and my expertise to work on projects for them. I need to focus on letting him go and just letting him be cannibalized.

Is this all correct? Do you have anything to add that I might have missed, especially regarding who and what my former studio mate is- his actual make up. Why am I being sexually pulled into him again?"

Jesus responded, "I'm not sure why it felt different. Maybe it was the way it was prepped. Your words are accurate and your understanding is getting clearer. We're not sure if darkness will even bother fully destroying him, though it is likely it will happen. He could become like a ship lost at sea. You may hear of the project but that project is not going anywhere and there is nothing behind it except the space it once occupied. I understand your compassion and it may come one day that he can return to light but that is not a concern right now. It is too unsafe to pursue right now. We will block you from sensing his suffering though I don't think he is suffering as much as you think. There are some voids in you as you bond more and more with Matthew. Your sexual desire stems from Matthew and until you feel good enough to allow yourself to connect with Matthew sexually then there will be an opening in you, more like an unattached cord because nothing will be able to enter the opening, that will be confused and pull on past parts. As you connect with Matthew sexually these parts will be flooded in light and healed. I can explain more on this. I will have the galactic family research this as well. We are working on getting you steered to a new project and focus will shift to here in the coming days and weeks, depending on some other things."

I replied, "I'm a little confused. It is shown to me that leaders in dark will create more of something akin to a black hole and absorb it in upon itself to regurgitate and come up with new plans- why would my former studio mate not be pulled into it. I'm confused in that if it's being shown to me, he is a manufactured entity of dark- never having an experience of light- how can he return to light? Why do you not think he is suffering? I need the galactic family to come up with something that helps this unattached cord in me to not pull on past sexual experiences- this will be triggering and have me push Matt away- and instead for this cord to be calm and at peace before it reunites with Matthew."

The end of this email thread.

In real time, once after working with a client and they had left, my uncle showed up from out in the wilderness (the wilderness being at the edge of our galaxy)- to say hello and deliver information. This kind of visitation would often knock out power in the third dimension wherever I was. He along with others were great trackers that could see stuff coming in to our galaxy.

As mentioned, attacks on me became increasingly more vicious. It became more and more apparent that I wasn't safe- especially as I became more aware and the Regime was starting to notice.

During 2017, I learned a lot of what I have already mentioned- like I was 3 billion years old. Pieces would be given in sessions and ways of understanding reality. I learned so much about myself and many things.

I learned about traveling more through the dimensions, relying on Jesus to help me. We visited many different places and planets. It was all relative to what I was going through. I began to piece more together about my former studio mate. He and his soul at one point used to be attached. While living in New Mexico moving into acupuncture, he was nervous about how good he would be or his business- he made deals, bad deals with darkness and the Regime. His soul tried to stop him and finally abandoned him- like jumping out of a fast-moving car. The Regime supplied fuel to keep my former studio mate going. My team knew this before I started working there. But then, them bringing in captain of the ship soul there, aligned with light- they thought it should be okay. My past twin Reptilian twin brother was brought in and used at one point. I had made a vow to find him and with the collapsing of human former studio mate- we could extract my twin and also could extract captain of the ship. It was good for me to visit both of them. There were too many debts that human former studio mate had accumulated that darkness wanted their return- so he was kept alive, fueled by darkness to get their debt repaid, or at least try to. Which frustrated me. It also wasn't as simple as ripping darkness out of the hospital or the integrative health community.

Part VI. Anchoring- transformation sessions

Spring 2017- in third dimension during this time, I was being harassed by darkness and the Regime left and right. It was awful. We tried so many things. For safety, transforming my whole being became the only option.

The first transformation was transitioning back into being an Archangel on Earth. It was originally slated for August by Source God, but with more and more safety concerns and darkness ramping up attacks- the decision was made for now. I technically already was, but this would give me added protection. It was unclear at first and I was very confused. I noted each session in this process numerically.

Session 1- April 24, 2017

"I'm not sure how that went, but here are my notes. Well, I was definitely nervous- deep anxiousness at a soul heart level making me feel cold, my back feeling like it would go into a TMS spasm, left shoulder blade hurting, my left sinus and left eye having a hard time. My daughter and I were snuggling before I put her to bed and she was asking all these questions. She must have been feeling the energy change- asking me about her grandfather and about who she was in a past lifetime. On and on. Well, I put her to bed and brought myself into session. I began by centering and focusing. I first opened to clapping sound from the Angels and then the scene changed. Oh, I've come to this space multiple times in the past year and a half. I didn't realize it was the Archangel Realm. My favorite spot is in one of the gardens by the big Akashic Library. I have my little bench I like with a fountain I like. I first noticed all the flowers. Very comforting. I looked up in the sky and saw different ships. The colors were all pastel dewy and light filled. I asked if this was heaven and was told no, but some similar colors. I felt myself sprout little rounded fairy wings with Jesus to my left, walking towards the great library. It was so big. I saw one of the Archangels walking into it and he was huge, gigantic which frightened me but then Jesus whispered about look at nature all the different sizes. I felt better. But still, felt like a little buttercup compared to a redwood tree. We walked in and could see the library in action. I've been here before too, just once or twice. We went to a smaller room and I sat down with Jesus to my left. I felt very shy, little, and afraid. I hid behind Jesus' cloak. 5 Archangels were there, but didn't seem quite so big. Jesus was introducing me and my history. At one point, one tried to take me to another place, very nice, and I got upset and didn't want to leave Jesus. At this point, I started crying- I don't know these beings, I have no experience with them, what if one turns to dark and squashes me. At this point, the one closest to the door seemed frustrated and said, she's not ready, this will be bad and as Jesus protested, the Angel walked out. That kind of woke me up a bit. I do wish to transition, but this place is completely foreign. Jesus went outside the room to talk to the Angel and I could hear the Angel's frustration- her body can't handle it- it will either harm her or possibly harm the realm, no. Him and Jesus were arguing. I looked around the room. The other Angel closest to the one who left is a good friend with the one who left and felt torn on what to support. The other three were all more female and very encouraging, oh he's always so glum, doom, and gloom. Come with us, this doesn't have to be so bad- sure it's an adjustment, but we can have fun with this. Sure, you'll have some educational lessons, but you can have fun too. This doesn't mean you can't visit other realms. Their chipperness and positivity helped ease me some. But I still worried- what if this is a mistake?

I worry my body simply can't handle the transition. But I also can't really stay where I'm at like a sitting duck and we really have tried everything to protect me from dark. I don't know. Thoughts?"

Jesus replied, "You did very well. This was a good first step. It will allow us to see how to help your body make the transition and it also allows us to see how to make you comfortable on all levels during the transition. The galactic family is happy with the way things went and see some techniques they can use to help you. We will continue with the transition which will include you visiting the Archangel Realm, probably a few more times, before the transition is final. It will not take long from this point. Are you feeling OK with Matthew and still feeling safe and protected by him?"

I responded, "I do feel better around Matt. Why did the Angel leave and who was that? How will things feel or look different once the transition is final?"

Jesus, "That Angel is a cranky old Angel and I would not let it bother you. I'm not sure I can answer your last question. It is a personal experience and I also don't want to make expectations for you that make you anxious."

I replied, "My father was mentioned (and my daughter was mentioning him a bunch last night)- how does he relate to the Archangel Realm? Are you concerned at all that when I've been in the Archangel Realm before- it's been when I was in my former studio mate's office- does that concern you? If not, why?"

Jesus, "Your father will have access to the Archangel Realm through you. I am not concerned. Your former studio mate has no access to the Archangel Realm."

I wrote, "Okay. I know my father was trying to be introduced to me and I started freaking out- like what is going on? It was confusing. Regarding my former studio mate- as I was on the ship moving through different dimensions in that office space- I've got to wonder what captain of the ship former studio mate thought was going on."

Jesus, "I don't think he paid too much attention but we can look into this."

I wrote, "Okay, this is a concern of mine- how much he understood when I worked in his office, translated to him, which could then be gleaned by dark."

Jesus, "We will look at this again but this has been studied and deemed safe. Dark cannot use anything here but again, we are always doing security here."

Some follow-up questions I had to Session 1 are found in an email thread the following day.

I asked, "Just some questions- So, can anyone related to me now have access to the Archangel Realm? I don't understand. If just my father, why? Are my kids in danger if Matt and I have transitioned into the Archangel Realm, but they have not done so? Which brings up- is Matt transitioning with me or is he already there and doesn't know it? How many others have gone through this experience?"

Jesus, "You will be able to bring beings to the Archangel Realm for different reasons, but the amount they will have access to will be limited according to the reason and the being. Your kids are not in danger and in fact will also be better protected. Matthew is part of the Archangel Realm but is focused on the human realm for this incarnation. I'm not sure I totally understand. It is hard to give numbers for how many others. The number is low at this time."

I replied, "Okay. I was surprised to see my dad. This could be a source of comfort, but not so if people connected to me just start popping up. Yes, I've brought a client there a few times and other clients, but it was always work related. I guess what I'm asking- will I appear different to Matt after the transition? Where does Matt fit in with all of this and his experience of reality? Yes, it was interesting that one of the three Angels that was happy and positive towards the end of the session- took a genuine interest in my other incarnations. She said she'd only been in the Archangel Realm. That made me feel included."

Jesus, "You will not appear different to Matthew. He will be with you during and after the transition just as he has been before. Your relationship with him will be an important part of the transition and be a big help."

Session 2- April 25, 2017

I wrote, "Thinking of joining again around 9:45pm this evening, but would you like me to wait?"

Jesus, "I can set it up. Spending time with Matthew would also help you. Physical closeness will help your body and mind. You can join us tonight. "

I wrote, "Hmmm, would it be better to skip it then?"

Jesus, "You can join us. I am pulling it together."

I wrote, "Okay. I did not consciously spend a long time. I hope that's okay. We ended up again in the garden, but there seemed to be some gathering and such a beautiful light filled young woman with so much gold around her- was on a dais of sorts but approachable. She was gaily talking with Angels listening to her adoringly. I kept staring, but who was this? You and little me to your right approached and she was happy and gave you a hug. Why it's Mother Mary- Queen of the Angels. That's right. I was so surprised- so much joy and aliveness and caring, but truly joyous. I felt very at ease with her and my so damaged 1–3-year-old self felt very seen and able to feel at ease (although I could see how much trauma was in my eyes). And with Mother Mary, I got on like a little cart ship to be shown around. Although she has a lot of energy, I feel I might be able to bring up anything and she would be still and lend me her wisdom. Just being in her presence is healing. And off we sped into the realm. You are so lucky to have such a great mother. That's about it. My heart feels very full and decided to close the session. Was that okay?"

Jesus, "Of course it is OK. We want to make sure you are undergoing this transition in a safe manner. This transition should go quickly. How are you feeling today? Are you feeling safe with Matthew and good with him?"

I wrote, "Yes, I think so. Are you trying to keep an eye on something that could go wrong with Matt and I? Or my experience of Matt I should say?"

Jesus, "No. We do not anticipate anything going wrong. I am just checking in."

I wrote, "It feels a bit better, but I know it will take some work. Matt is still struggling with being able to breathe, my son is home with an odd sickness. I know it feels like an eternity distant memory that I ever had feelings for my former studio mate or others. And in that, I feel more well suited with Matt and playful with him. The actual coming together physically feels a bit forced and odd like two positive magnets coming together- it pushes apart which I don't understand and find that odd, no?"

Jesus, "I will look at this for you. It does make sense that coming together physically would feel a little odd at this time. I am not pushing you to force it. I'm not totally sure why you experience it exactly this way but I will have the galactic family look here as well."

Session 3- April 27, 2017

"I'm always worried I'm not going to do this well. Opened up and with you to my left facing a very large building. In color and shape similar to the library, but more tiered and pointy and I think taller. As we got closer, I understood it was a medical facility. It reminded me a lot of the National Institutes of Health on Earth- it had a similar buzzy feel. We walked in and again reminded me of the NIH Clinic Center. Differences for sure, in ways I could not process. We buzzed up an elevator and to a room where a particular CEO kind of doctor/Angel was waiting. You talked briefly of my case. This doctor worked fast and thorough in a way I could barely keep up. He looked at my whole chart from the library, ran a patterning sequence. I laid down and went through diagnostics twice, a bit more emphasis on the heart. He felt he could definitely see where adjustments and help could be made in my overall state and in transitioning and that he could work with the galactic family-comparing his findings. Much agreement all around to not distort my evolution in the process. I asked him how many like me he had worked on, transitioning that is, and he said 5. I asked if it would be helpful for me to meet them. He thought no- that it might be overwhelming. Even with all his knowledge and stature, the doctor was so kind and respectful. I love how in this realm Angels are still with unique features and personalities. I asked why I wasn't brought here sooner; things seem to be going well. The doctor looked at you and said, "do you want me to tell her or do you?" It seemed it might upset me. I decided I'd rather Jesus told me.

Things seemed to be good. We walked out of the building. It so brought me back to the NIH. All these incredible Angels looking at all these wide and diverse medical issues. I did not feel though this was my calling. Which was odd. We went outside and sat on the lawn. I blew out a long breath and I just felt- finally a place/a realm I don't have to worry about darkness raiding. And then my whole being just started to do something different. That exhale and that sinking in- I began transforming before my very eyes. These full inhales and exhales- reconnecting into the matrix of the realm- I could feel it flow in and myself as an Angel flow out. Then all this light flowing out of my hands. I got huge and could see the entirety of what I'd been through the last 3 billion years with a different vantage point and could see how my essence could be in many locations at once. And then I settled back into myself seated on the grass with still that rhythm now of being altered- breathing in the Archangel Realm and breathing out as an Archangel back into it. There were chants and prayers I could hear floating around me and I felt your father Source God there too. It reminded me of a woman in labor, you never know when her water is going to break and the baby comes out and this full transformation takes place. But it seems like everyone was ready? Is that accurate?

Questions-

Why do Angels and Archangels keep fluctuating in height?

Why wasn't I brought here sooner?"

Jesus replied, "I'm not sure what you mean by your questions. Do you mean fluctuating in height from each other? By sooner, do you mean earlier in your life or in another life?"

I responded, "Thanks. Well, I know when I've visited, I've seen different sizes, why is that? And how can like such a huge Archangel fit inside the medical building or any building really in the Archangel Realm? I guess I should ask- what's the difference between an Angel and an Archangel? Do my notes of my experience last night make sense? What's your experience, meaning how did it appear to you? Well, I felt like I got really big and then I went back to a normal size, I guess I don't understand that. Also, the doctor seemed concerned about telling me why I hadn't come sooner. Like it might upset me. It seems like it's going well- why wouldn't I have been brought sooner to this transition and avoided suffering- I guess I speak of in this lifetime. You and the galactic team have spoken quite a bit if the time was safe and right, due to me, and I don't understand. Can you explain?"

Jesus, "An Archangel is a more powerful Angel, to put it simply. Your notes make sense. It looks like the transition is going well. Your ability to undergo the transition was not really an option until now. It is not because of you or anything you did or didn't do. It's just a matter of certain things lining up. One of these is your twin flame relationship."

I wrote, "Okay. At some point, I'd like to understand how these tall Archangels are fitting inside these buildings- or could it be I'm seeing their energy power and interpreting it as height? I don't really feel any differently today or in the world, same old same old. Regarding Matt, I don't know what to say. I felt closer to him at 10:30pm last night and then it just all fell apart. I don't believe I said I was coming up to snuggle with him. I said I'd be up early, but I believe that was it. I did want to rest and be close, but I wanted to write my notes or read an article. We've done that many times in the past. But last night, his behavior just has set something off in me. In my vulnerability of feeling closer and then his odd language and frustration and feeling abandoned and scolded- just has really upset me. My eye is a mess. I feel down in my heart and anxious. I don't feel good emotionally. Then on top of this- I called him to see if he wanted to go for a run during a lunch break- but it ended up just bad because he listened to me regarding scheduling but he didn't seem to remember, retain, process, write down scheduling information. And screwed it up. Now I'm just left mad at him and just feeling like I don't want him in my life."

Jesus, "The galactic family will drain this. It is certainly understandable and the work you have been doing transitioning to the Archangel Realm has left you with less room to handle things like this. We will work with Matthew in how to support you and you will see an immediate improvement."

Session 4- April 27, 2017

"Had a little more trouble getting focused this session- not sure if just overly tired. That being said opened up to a scene with Jesus next to me that couldn't understand. We went back to my little courtyard I like by the library and I rested on the bench. I focused on breathing with the Archangel Realm. Breathing in the realm I feel all the other Angels and Archangels and Source and breathing out I let go and connect with Source in me. Until we are just breathing together.

The realm is a very communal realm.

Jesus asked if I felt better and I did.

We walked back to the scene and it looked like all these Angels standing around looking down at a violent scene happening and an Angel standing their ground battling darkness. There was cheering and looking at it deeper- a bringing of energy from all the Angels and the realm present to the Angel fighting darkness. The realm is so connected to Source. It's an unlimited supply.

(This really being tapped into the Archangel Realm- I wonder if is throwing something about my human belly button area off. My core being overwhelmed and bulging seems related.)

Back to the scene. I was fascinated to also witness how Angels and Archangels through time have stepped into all manners of events- fully protected by the realm and Source. I understand I think better how Archangel Matthew has been able to protect me and if he started to get exhausted had help. I also think I grasp how Angel Zahid was created to be a communicator for Archangel Michael with me- part of the collective brought into form to help with a certain mission. And his words now make sense from 2010 that- he was created in the Archangel Realm.

I then was toying where I fit in with this work. I think I'm good and well crafted and enjoy being empathetic with those suffering. I'm fascinated by science and physics. And I am also of a warrior nature. But having spent so much of my soul feeling isolated, whether real or imagined- I feel a great kinship to those suffering and those not understanding what to do. I don't know, just toying with ideas.

My hands opened up with light and they were creating something between them. It seemed to take a while and couldn't figure what it was. Then it was an orb, shades of blue silver, very finely knit pattern that I came to understand- with my thoughts directing, I could go in on itself and I could flow through it to where I'd like to go. This would be helpful if stuck in a place I needed to get out of and felt caught. I could instantly leave. Which would seem a miracle, but actually follows laws of physics in our universe.

I was more curious, but growing tired and my belly hurting- like the muscles are all just so sore all the time now and can't keep form. Something is definitely odd.

I think that was about it. I laid down after for a few minutes. Does this seem similar to what you all saw? I'm trying to think if I missed anything. Some thoughts come to mind- whether I should take a night or two off because I'm getting tired? I wish my son would sleep longer. Also, does my lack of physics and how our universe works hamper the process?"

Jesus, "You can take a night off. We can work still. I'm not sure your lack of physics is hampering you. We will help you with what you need. Matthew as your twin flame is a good source of healing and strength for you as well."

Session 5- April 28, 2017

"Just coming into the realm, I appear to be fully surrounded by flowers. I believe I was shown- how if I look at myself as gridwork- Angels were figuring which flower (with its particular educational and healing properties) to place and allow to flow through each individual line of me. The idea being to prepare my whole being to make my permanent transition to the Archangel Realm as smooth and less jarring as possible. I was fascinated by this. How Angels appear to be a mosaic of pastel rainbow of colors. How flowers are an expression of different traits found in the Angels and breathing through the realm. Like if the ocean produced flowers- the waves (Angels) and the flowers (if the ocean created flowers) and the ocean itself can never really be considered separate from each other. Just expressions. Does that make sense?

I was concerned that in my treating of the wart, on my foot in the third dimension- I could throw things off. They didn't think so and thought as the virus is gone and a hole created- they can bring a flower to heal that particular line.

I stayed a little longer following my breath, but then as this work would continue- decided to come back."

Jesus wrote back, "You are doing well in your time in the Archangel Realm."

I replied, "Thanks. It is a little challenging to have some of these deep experiences of anxiety, reminds me of how I felt when I was 0-7 years old. Any suggestions or requests as I continue on here?"

Jesus wrote, "I will see what the galactic family thinks."

Session 6- April 30, 2017

"A longer session, but I felt awake and alert. I opened up and immediately was hit by a lot of feelings- really describing what I was experiencing, my perception, how it correlates to other times in my life. I notice as I was having a lot of these feelings and thoughts- my left wrist had like an IV in the wrist there, something with the left ring finger closest to the heart too. That felt like Jesus directing that. It was a lot of information I went through which all really boiled down to my fear of hurting others, that I'm causing harm, or worry that I'm not doing enough to make a situation better. How this shows up- worried with my neighbor's recent weight loss (my mind goes to she has cancer and all my work I've been doing has impacted her cell tissue negatively); a nuclear war breaking out (worried that by transitioning to the Archangel Realm, in that real moment- a nuclear bomb will be dropped). Well, we went through a lot of information. Another big one was my exhaustion on trying to navigate through anything and always having darkness rear its head and try to suck my soul dry. Like here in the Archangel Realm at times I argue with Archangel Michael or Jesus, but there is a huge difference of disagreeing and conflict that's healthy to open up dialogue and being honest vs. then adding in darkness and all the crazy that brings. The biggest thing the Archangel Realm is to me is safe. Safe to just be my authentic self without fear of repercussion and anger of rattling wasps of darkness and their wrath. I'm aware of how much I self-doubt myself, all the time- which does lend me to check constantly my accuracy in my work and in helping others, but is exhausting in just living.

And then Jesus said finished with the left wrist and put a patch on it. Then, I had no more images or emotions flowing. Next, we were in an amphitheater space. In the center was a suit like contraption. I entered into it and lots of monitoring and movement around. My experience was it and myself dissolving together- first my head, and then down through my heart, and then my arms and torso, into my pelvis, and flowing through legs and feet. I asked what this was. Something about calibrating my soul/lifetime experiences to be a match when I fully transition into the Archangel Realm. Once that was completed, I stepped out and someone was checking a chip or something through my left eye and into my brain area left side with like a light. And that's when I grew tired and asked if it was good time for me to come back to third dimensional realm. That seemed well all around."

Jesus responded, "How do you feel overall? I apologize for the communication error with Matthew. This should be better as well."

I replied, "I don't know. I want to feel okay about it but something snapped inside. Last night I dreamt about all these men with Matt right next to me. I don't think this was a communication error. This was more of the same."

Jesus, "It was a communication error between Matthew and his team, not between the two of you. One of the adjustments did not get made correctly. It has been corrected now. Your energies now line up appropriate for your pace into the Archangel Realm. "

I replied, "I can hear you, but my subconscious and unconscious and deep parts of my soul have just shut down- hence the dreams last night. I'm not sure what to do. This was a bad error for me to have experienced/ happened at a very critical time."

Jesus, "I agree. The galactic family will intervene here."

Session 7- May 1, 2017

"Feeling a bit confused by the session. I opened up to standing on the deck of a ship- the Angels around me and the galactic family and reality in front. I was told that I was ready and this was a hand off of my care from them to the Angels and that realm.
(But what does that mean? Does that mean no more pod? I'm so confused. They said to ask Jesus and he would explain).

They said we'd see each other again. I felt sad. I thanked them gratefully for all that they have done and do. The Angels were gently tugging me. Finally, I finished and then was ushered inside where I was on a stage and part of a ceremony and there were many Angels in front. Like graduation day. I was brought forth, had a thin gold crown on me and my golden hair. Went to sit down. Next to me on my left was Matt, although he too looked different with golden hair. And on down the line there were 30 beings presented. I asked Matt and it looked like we were the only two humans. We were all given red envelopes. And presented as those that would be helping with Earth at this critical time. Lots of cheering among the Angels. I felt a bit tired.

(I found it odd I was observing this, but not actually in it like I have been in all the other sessions. What does this mean?)

Matt and I retired to a little spaceship pod. We intertwined and went to sleep. The pod, along with the 30 others and their pods- were dispatched moving through space and into the Sun like a giant sphere of Source energy and when we landed in the Archangel Realm- we landed in a large pond at the bottom of the hill to some buildings.

(I'm wondering if that's what I noticed on my first visit to the Archangel Realm- I'd see little ships coming and going).

We got out and were greeted warmly by a few. The Angels we saw were surprised and very happy to see Matt, who they knew well it seems.

(It still was/is unclear to me- why was I experiencing this as watching it? I was in it when talking with the galactic family, still in it when I moved into the theater space and then became this witness to the experience soon after. I don't understand what happened. I'm also confused where Jesus was).

At this point, I decided it was a natural pause place for me and this session."

Jesus responded, "I will still be working with you as will the galactic family. I am thinking you experienced this session as a look ahead to what might occur. Once you are fully immersed in the Archangel Realm, however, there is no specific plan to have you do anything. You were brought together with your twin flame because of the great love you have for one another and not so that the power you have between the two of you could be used for an agenda. We will review this session as well."

I wrote back, "I feel extremely confused and this doesn't settle well with me. Please consult with anyone that might be able to clear this up."

Jesus, "It seems these Angels were giving you a tour of some of the work being done and possibly a little recruitment. The galactic family will still be working with you but did hand you off for this tour as they worked on you from behind the scenes. What I mean here is they continued to work on you as you took this tour with Matthew."

I wrote, "Did I miss the tour? I don't understand. This simply doesn't settle well with me. I'm upset, confused, and angry and obviously rattled as I made a very stupid mistake this morning and harmed my eye."

Jesus, "I guess I am confused by your experience. Your care was not handed off on a permanent basis. I will be working with you and so will the galactic family. I will also serve as a mentor of sorts for you when the transition is complete. We will still have a very close relationship. This will also be true of the galactic family. I am guessing that you are talking about the time you spent with the Angels. Your care for this part of the session was handed off to these Angels who showed you a few things and allowed you to rest and get acclimated to the realm. While this occurred, me and the galactic family watched over you and continued making adjustments to help you transition. You were introduced to some more Angels as they will be working for you as messengers and such. They were excited to meet you."

I wrote, "The words I wrote in my initial note felt crystal clear in accuracy. I don't understand what the graduation ceremony was about. I don't understand what was in the red envelopes. There is a lot I don't understand and feel unsettled. Your experience and mine seem to differ quite a bit. Just not feeling good and stuck in limbo like this is not healthy."

Jesus, "We both went through the same ceremony. The Angels were welcoming you to the Archangel Realm, giving their seal of approval in a sense. It is an important step in that it will open up your transition and make it that much easier. The Angels will work with and for you. They will serve as your messengers among many other things. They have completed their portion of the transition."

I wrote, "Ugh. I just don't understand. Hopefully this will clear up in time. I prefer feeling part of it and not just witnessing it. I don't understand why that happened in this past session. So, when you've said you have lots of experience helping others transition into the Archangel Realm- you were talking about beings in other forms, not those in human form? As Matt and I witnessed, the other

28 at the ceremony were in other life forms. Is this accurate?"

Jesus, "I will bring your confusion to the galactic family. Under no circumstances are you to not be a part of the transition. Your words about other beings are correct."

I wrote, "Right? I agree, maybe that's why I feel grumpy, on edge and weird today. Why did this split happen in the last session? You mentioned in history- there are some humans that have transitioned to the Archangel Realm. Do you think it would be helpful to know their names or meet them or simply not helpful?"

Jesus, "It might be helpful in time but probably not at this exact time. Let's make sure the transition continues to go well."

I wrote, "Okay. So tired today."

Session 8- May 2, 2017

"Hard to shake how unpleasant and ugly Matt was after I came down from tonight's session. I'm tired of it being blamed on him being tired or sleepy. That's not right. I'll try to focus here. Feeling a little more natural to flow into a session and then out. Not too bumpy tonight. I opened to a lecture happening. I felt a little silly, but I did speak up and tried to explain to the leader of the tour that I was doing this merge, feeling nervous and if he could take this into consideration when speaking to me would be much appreciated. I'd like an explanation of what was happening. He paused and had someone else take over the tour and pulled me aside. He looked like some leader from out in the wilderness, kind of like my uncle, but he was taller, more statuesque, sterner, but fair. He removed this and could see he was an Angel. I was surprised. He explained- he wore the "clothing" that made him feel most at ease. I questioned why don't other Angels/Archangels have this- I just see them as light figures- he said because they haven't had an incarnation out of the realm. That felt accurate to me. It made me happy to meet someone that I could relate to in this way. I asked if he knew my uncle. Oh yes, they are good friends. This leader/Angel is from the North Wilderness of the galaxy. It seems that my uncle is of the West Wilderness. I called him Archangel and he said "No. I'm an Angel. You're an Archangel, well, Archangel in training, but we are different in that." I like how I feel there is equal value and weight- maybe we have different properties, but we are equally valuable- if that makes sense. I like this and is calming. (Most current cultures on Earth do not do this). I asked him what he does here- in what looked to be a display teaching venue inside of a larger school system. He said he was a teacher and educator for those to understand. He felt a great need to educate about what was happening in our galaxy to those Angels running messages and just basically to help. We looked at a figure preserved. The story behind it is a woman (or female being) was being turned into darkness and she cried out for an Angel to save her. An Angel was able to whisk her away in this exact moment of transition into dark, halt it, freeze it- she was unable to be saved- but this metamorphosis was able to be captured in time and was displayed here in this display center. She had large bumps on her back, but I was too scared to look at her face. I questioned why this wasn't brought to the galactic family of light. They could have figured it out. I was told this was a long time ago. Which brings me to the point- how long have you Jesus, Archangel Michael, Source been working with the galactic family of light working with me? Why was it not brought to light's awareness sooner than this past January 2017 what technology was being used by darkness? Can these questions be answered? I'm feeling confused. The leader brought me to where the tour was at now. A large case showcasing in great beauty and detail about creation, galaxy, etc. I paused to think about how I would like to look in the Archangel Realm. I like being human and me, Bridget. I like having very long, maybe more wavy hair- maybe some softer blonde woven in. I like the idea of wearing long feminine simple and flattering dresses. I like feeling more feminine than I currently feel and honoring this. I'd like to feel much better in my physical body than I do now and really figure out how to feel much better in my belly and core and to be more fluid and at ease. This seemed a good space for me to pause and completed the session."

Jesus responded, "These words are very accurate and reassuring for us. We are thinking that we will open a cord or link to keep you connected to the Archangel Realm during the day and in between these sessions. Do you feel like this is a good idea at this time? As far as why I did not work with the galactic family in helping you sooner is difficult to explain in full. I will say that it was my father working with you and I pulled in the galactic family soon after I took over for my father. I called them in as soon as I saw that they would be of great benefit. I have been working with the galactic family of light for a long time as has Michael. My father has been working with them even longer. I'm not sure why my father did not call them in. I think he did not see the need for their technology as brightly as I saw it. I also don't think my father planned to transition you to the Archangel Realm as soon as I am. The galactic family of light is very helpful in these transitions. As far as Matthew, we have a very solid plan in place to do work on him in a way that does not interfere with the work you are doing. Matthew does not always go to bed when he is tired and instead falls asleep when he thinks he is only going to rest. We will look for some markers that are now in place to tell us when he is truly asleep and when he is just resting. "

I wrote, "I think this is a good plan. Can you explain how I might feel different or how it might change things? Is it part of the usual transition process?"

Jesus, "It is part of the usual transition process. You will feel more of a connection to the Archangel Realm. We will monitor how much energy flows to you from it so that you are not overwhelmed. Because your reaction and experience will determine how connected you will be, it is difficult to tell you exactly how you will feel. You should feel like you do when you are in the Archangel Realm and be able to apply it to the third dimension. However, this is a skill and you should not be hard on yourself if it is not like a switch being flipped. Also, you should inform me if you want to shut off the connection even if just to get a break. I will discuss this with the galactic family as to when this should occur. Do you have a time or window of time where you would feel more comfortable with it? We can even go with it for window of a few hours at first if you would like."

I wrote, "Hmmm. These are all good points. From 9am-noon I am at home getting stuff done. Then I am working from 12:30-6pm and then with family."

Jesus, "Maybe it is not good to rush it for today. I think it makes sense to establish the link since you will have that as part of being in the Archangel Realm anyway and then we can turn it off and on at times to help you make the final parts of the transition. The goal would be to turn it on on a permanent basis and allow you to control the energy flow. You would reside in the Archangel Realm at this point."

I wrote, "Every day ahead of me is going to be like this. I'm happy to start right now or wait. It's really your call. I can see problems if I'm alone. I can see problems if I'm around others. Like being pregnant and having a baby, a huge transition- I don't know that there is ever an ideal time. Does that make sense?"

Jesus, "I am not looking for an ideal time. I just want to make sure things get set up properly. We will work with you in all of these scenarios."

I wrote, "Any information on how this is shaping up?"

Jesus, "We plan to have you ready by morning. We will assess things after your session and then plan to have you within the Archangel Realm during the night and as you wake."

*Update to session 8, May 3, 2017

I wrote, "Just wondering how things seem to you all."

Jesus, "They seem ok. Do you agree?"

I wrote, "I think. Little more prone to a headache. Tired and a bit down today. Nothing unusual. What comes next?"

Jesus, "We will increase this link until you are fully able to handle it and then we will pull you into the Archangel Realm. There are smaller details as well."

I wrote, "Okay. Well, I just don't notice any difference at this point."

Jesus, "That is good. You are transitioning well."

Session 9- May 3, 2017

"I opened up, but had a harder time "landing" so to speak. Was in front of the little fountain I like, but felt like I was waiting and waiting. That split thing started to happen where I observed myself, but not in it- so I paused and waited some more- being very clear with my words I wished to stay engaged.

Felt the scene shift to being like in a castle top, looking out over the beauty of the realm. Most of the focus was put on my presentation, what seemed to feel good to me. I liked this activity.

After going back and forth fine tuning- I look to have two "outfits". I have my Archangel self and when I'm at rest/play I like to have wavy golden long hair, white/light gold long dress with a band around the waist, simple shoes, simple jewelry if any at all. When I'm at work, I like incorporating what is meaningful to me for the last 3 billion years of my life. I find this very comforting and complete. My hair is brown, maybe swept back with a piece of jewelry in place. My robe or outer covering is like that of the blues in the galaxy with billowy blue see through sleeves, and sparkles like stars throughout- paying homage to my Pleiadian lifetime, Reptilian, science, creation, time with Merlin and Avalon- weaved in is the ritual, essence of strength, working as a tribe and values I find in traditional native cultures. Instead of a crown, I like the ornamental band around my head with a jewel near my third eye area. I like simplicity and graceful old grounded power. In a moment's notice the bottom part robe can be moved away to more action wear. I don't want any shoes with any kind of heel, so I can feel my pelvis and chakras well aligned. I like the simple scepter I have in my left hand with a blue small globe on top that in moving to my right can immediately turn into a shield. And my left hand can reach behind into my left back pocket area for a sword or dagger. I'm reminded of those James Bond movies where simple clothing and objects actually has great functionality and can serve multiple purposes.

I was pressed on jewelry, like a ruby, but I don't know. Nothing came to mind at this time. Everyone including myself seemed pleased with these outfits. I felt good to come back and end the session. "

Jesus, "These words are very accurate."

I wrote back, "Great. I really don't feel any different this morning. Is the cord there?"

Jesus, "It is and this is probably a good sign. It means you have been adapting well to the Archangel Realm during your visits. We will keep allowing the energy to flow and monitor it. Report anything that seems off."

I responded, "This isn't really any report, but a request for help that I'm struggling with my rage regarding Hillary Clinton's current denial and behavior. I don't often feel like I want to strangle someone to death, but her I do. It's upsetting to me. Pours rubbing alcohol into a deep wound and causes me terror. I wrote on Facebook to vent- Are you f***ing kidding me? Quit trying to blame others for your failure Ms. Clinton. Accept that you lost and move on. Besides, if you wouldn't have cheated on Sanders in the primary, you wouldn't have even been running. Because you forced your way to be the candidate, the worst possible candidate to go up against Trump, the only one shown statistically that would lose to Trump- that divided our country further. Your ego is the reason we are in the mess we are currently in. Just. Go. Away. "

Jesus, "I will see what the galactic family can do to help you here."

I wrote, "Maybe what they view. What is going to be done? I know that dark entities are still attached to her and kill people in her wake, creating destruction and chaos. The Democratic Party is afraid of her, there are many afraid people scared to speak up. This is an ongoing situation- what is going to be done? These dark entities may not have won the election, but they still control the Democratic Party. They are operational and plotting. My hope would be these dark entities get absorbed with others flowing out, like my former studio mate in August/September of 2017 and Clinton goes with them or is incredibly weakened to the point that she stops wreaking havoc on this country and world. She may not be President but nothing has changed. She's still operational and in her mind plotting her return come 2020."

Jesus, "We are aware that we may have won the battle with her but the war is not over. We are also plotting to stop these forces as well. We are making progress and will continue to organize our forces."

I wrote, "I'm not sure how or if it's a good idea for me to help here because I feel so violent and am in this time of transition, but I do feel passionate on this topic and if I can help- let me know."

Jesus, "We will likely call on your help when it is time."

I responded, "Sounds good. I also see the need for a few different colored outfits."

I wrote again, "I'm struggling immediately after I sent this message. Pressure at heart center, coughing, overwhelmedness feeling, heart center is spinning, disorientated, hard to breathe, anxiety. I'm not sure what happened. Is it imagining the ruby outfit? I can't handle my fiery nature yet. I feel I'm too impetuous and too young. I don't trust myself yet. It frightens me."

Jesus, "I will inform the galactic family who will make the adjustments accordingly."

I wrote, "I mean- it could be something else? I was doing just fine until I sent that email and I'm not sure what happened."

Jesus, "It is good to report. The galactic family will look to see what is happening."

I wrote, "Thanks, please let me know their thoughts. I'll let you know if I feel any differently."

Session 10- May 4, 2017

"Felt like a very brief session, but it actually was 20 minutes. Opened up to find myself high up- like on a walking path- where one could look down at the clouds. I was aware I was so close to the sigh and breathing and thinking of Source God (explains my fascination with studying weather). Mesmerizing to watch the ebb and flow and how He interacts and flows into the Archangel Realm. I see how each soul out of Source God eventually comes home to itself. It made me ponder- in seeing all the different personalities and interests of the Angels and Archangels- well who am I, what do I wish to focus on? I really don't know. I'm keenly aware that I don't really know what my interests are."

Jesus, "We will help you find and follow your interests. Are you feeling OK being in the Archangel Realm upon waking and feeling good and connected with Matthew?"

I wrote, "I believe so. As I said, I feel exactly the same- I don't notice any difference. I wish I had more time to rest and play with just Matt. I feel somewhat bored and frustrated by the structure of my life."

Jesus, "I will note this and ask the galactic family to help me arrange this."

I wrote, "To note- thoughts from my past have been swirling around, especially New Mexico and my former studio mate at times. Not sure why. I guess I just feel down and sad I'm not here nor there. In my breathing pattern, I notice I really love the exhale and just to stay empty in emptiness and I begrudgingly inhale. Odd."

Jesus, "I will inform the galactic family so we can make adjustments."

I wrote, "Thanks. I'm not sure why I feel so blah lately."

Session 11- May 5, 2017

"A bit on the later side than my usual time- in dealing with my poor daughter upset. She reminds me a lot of me in dealing with anxiety and stress. I hope we can help her to not go through what I have been through. I know her strong emotions scare her, confuse her and she lashes out. I can see she is overwhelmed and feels ashamed and confused. I feel so sad. My son keeps touching my face and heart and face tonight. I wonder if my kids feel a change coming.

That being said. I did go ahead.

Session seemed to open up smoothly. I felt lots of Angels around me and lots of puffiness ethereal white clouds and felt like I was being helped to walk up a small few steps onto a little platform and there was this like cocoon like structure- going inside I was aware it would be about 1-3 days of transformation into just pure Archangel self, joining the realm and I would wear my "outfits" as best fits situations- human sheath in third dimension, my relaxing human sheath at rest in Archangel Realm, and my galactic human sheath when I am working amongst multidimensional components. There are other human outfits, but I just haven't felt up to exploring them at this time.

Not super important, but I was really craving to understand how this transformation happens from a physics point of view. That information couldn't be provided. Can you explain it?

The 1–3-day marker would bring us to Sunday evening my time. The reason for the variance was it is not clear how my body and being will respond. I personally feel like my brain says slow and my body and all systems say fast. So not sure what that means. It could mean I indeed transition fast in one day, but my brain doesn't catch up to awareness for 3 days.

I was told last night in a dream, but also here in this session- there would be a surge of people coming at me initially, but this would be buffered as best as could be and then managed. If this is accurate, I will definitely follow my comfort zone and take care of myself and talk to you all and Matt. It reminds me of a plane landing- there is that initial rush and push and intensity as it lands. And then it levels off and settles in. That seemed about it. I do wish I could understand the science of how this transformation/transition looks like from a science perspective. I will Google how caterpillars to butterflies go about it."

Jesus, "These words are accurate. I will consult the galactic family about helping you understand the physics."

I wrote, "Thanks. I don't know that the caterpillar to butterfly description is a good analogy. They digest themselves and from stem cells create a new form. If that's the case, I'm going to be exhausted. To note- I did run into the once Pleiadian Regime General's son at my daughter's school this morning. My knees are hurting and lower back."

Jesus, "I will look at these symptoms for you."

I wrote, "Thanks"

Session 12- May 6, 2017

"Glad that I could start a little earlier. Opened up the session and found myself in the cocoon. I believe the galactic family of light team showed me the following; this is what I gathered. So, when a soul comes out of Source God- it is of a certain nature, vibrating. When the soul begins incarnating, the fabric of the structure it incarnates as imprints on the structure. As the soul goes through lifetimes, it continues to imprint layer on layer. So, for me now, in this cocoon is like a vibration- like the feeling I have when I walk into the butterfly exhibit at our local science center. It is there with the butterflies slightly I can sense it. Well, here in this cocoon I'm in now, its amplitude is very much turned up and with the ability to restructure the soul. Kind of like the caterpillar into a butterfly. So, I can observe how the vibration moves through layer upon layer of imprinting gently teasing it apart and restructuring it into the pattern that is the Archangel Realm. I had some concern if I would lose all my memories of different lifetimes and experiences. It looks that those "cells" or "molecules" that make up the soul remember but form a new formation- i.e. I can access those memories if I want to, there is a recording, but it's not front and center as I am no longer residing in that imprinting. That is comforting. I've done a lot of work these past 3 billion years and I find the experiences will be valuable, but no, I don't need to keep re-living them. Hence, once the transition is complete (I'm told I was about 1/3 through)- others will see the Archangel Realm as the only imprint. Now I understand why darkness will see no point in fooling with me- because in the Archangel Realm we are all unified- separate, but unified and endlessly supplied with energy from Source Himself. I did try out the power flowing from my hands. I had some concerns on my heart and mind- for example, the heroin addicted mother at the hospital today, who gave birth to her twins at 24 weeks, the boy will most likely make it, but the baby girl may not. I pray for the whole family. It makes me very sad- all of them. I pray for those making decisions in our government. I pray for the Earth. I can feel my heart and soul and mind feel very fragile right now. I get impacted by things and feel a crushing sensation of pain in my heart- like I'm having a mini-anxiety attack. So- I need help in buffering and editing because what I used to be able to handle- images, information, story lines, etc. I feel the suffering deep right now. Please help to buffer me or balance me out. For example, now more than ever- I have never at the heart of it relished anyone suffering- even those- like my former studio mate- who would kill me if they could get their hands on me. I still ask for him to be removed fully, but there is no joy in it. I always think I can help a situation. It's just like an engine inside of me that wants to dial back to first ripples of when things went dark and mediate a different outcome. My empathy for those suffering is deep to the point I know it's been used against me, but I'd rather have that because I have helped in ways that others have not been able to. Then coupled with this is still my great anger at key local figures in the integrative health community who are so steeped in their own ego, it's shocking. It's a confusing jumble of emotions.

Some questions for me that I couldn't understand- what is the point of all this imprinting and layering? Why have only so few humans through history been brought into their original Archangel selves? Why did Source God not see this as the original plan for me this lifetime, especially if I'm happier?"

Jesus, "I'm still gathering information on the layering. Not many people make this transition because it is very difficult. As you gain power in your twin flame relationship you can make the transition. My father wanted to make sure of your connection in your twin flame relationship so that he did not put you in danger.

My response, "Thank you and okay. Yes, the imprinting and layering serves a purpose, but I'm not sure what. Does this session seem accurate?"

Jesus, "Yes, it seems accurate."

<u>Session 13</u>- May 7, 2017

"Just an aside- still having tightness and pain at high heart area if close with Matt. High heart having anxiety all around. Opened up to still in the cocoon. Interfacing with galactic team. Looking like transition at matrix of soul level will complete around 6am on Sunday my time. Still breathing out charge on soul left from my former studio mate and from Greg- breathing the charge back over to them and letting those emotions and charge wash over them. On my end, with charge released, more ability for that fabric piece of the soul to work with the vibration in the cocoon and shift. I'm standing before like an ethereal white ocean. Once the process complete, I will wade into this ocean and like dunking a sword that has been forged in heat, this ocean of Archangel Realm will help seal in the process and seal in the work. Will take about 12 hours. And then the careful process of completion- coming out of the ocean, drying off, preparing to leave cocoon, leaving cocoon- etc. I'm to sleep more which I'm not doing a great job at."

Jesus, "This is all accurate. We will help with the closeness and Matthew."

I wrote, “Feels a bit better. Don’t feel that stingy pain sensation in high heart. Very tired today. I did sleep 8 hours though, not sure why I’m so tired. “

Jesus, “Extra rest is a good idea.”

Session 14- May 8, 2017

“I'll keep this short as I'm tired and upset by this all. I asked my question in an earlier e-mail. Why wasn't this discovered sooner? You can look at my conversation with Matt at 9:55pm on Sunday night of why I am upset. In opening the session, I thought it would be great- rising up out of the forging process and leaving the cocoon. But, just like what has been happening in the brief hours after the forging complete, there is something wrong.

I had to lie down in the session on a bench by the ‘forging’ ocean. I came out and I looked down and there was a hole- a hole from my pubic bone to my xyphoid process. I had completed the vibratory change, but my human sheath didn't work. There was this hole. We were staring at it wondering what to do- implant, Source grafting, helping it move along? The decision seemed to be made to remove the whole thing and just be in my Archangel self and go see the doctor.

I was led in and lied down in a hospital bed to rest while the doctor went to examine the sheath with the hole in it.

As mentioned, the damage is profound. Came about from time I was captured and has never healed. No wonder I have been thinking about my former studio mate these past few days. I thought that was odd. I don't even know what to say at this point. I'm angry, sad, and disheartened. I'm so done with this drone existing."

Jesus responded, "These words are accurate. The damage is not as great as you imagine and it is being repaired. It looks like your twin flame relationship will help to reproduce the damaged area and this will be weaved in for the repair."

I wrote, "Can you explain what you mean by reproduce the damage? Have I made it through the transition process?"

Jesus, "Reproduce the damaged area. I'm not sure I phrased this well. This means that the damaged area will be replaced by a reproduction of the healthy cells from your twin flame. It's like cloning or stem cell work. This healthy cell structure will replace the damaged area and graft with you being seamlessly because it is in essence your cells. Your twin flame relationship looks strong right now so this will help with the process. Does this make sense?"

I wrote, "Yes, that makes sense. I was just staring at it last night, looking at this hole- it just looks seared on the edges- so I don't see how the human sheath could repair- not by implant or Source grafting or time and healing. I did see that being in the Archangel Realm- the vibration is intact- because that always has a healthy supply of life force no matter what comes at it. Hence, the shedding of the human sheath and handing it to the doctor and myself as just pure Archangel resting in the medical center. Have I made it through the transition at this point?"

Jesus, "You are considered through the transition but there is still work to do in getting you acclimated and helping you understand the realm and various other things. The procedure to repair you is one such item."

I responded, "Okay. Is there anything I can do on my own to help myself? I still am aware of the hole. It gives me a headache, makes my heart fluttery, and a weird airiness in my belly. I don't notice any crush of people or real change in my life. I do wish I didn't have to work today. My work feels a drain on me right now, but maybe I'm just tired."

Jesus, "Rest is good. Also, feeling the flow of energy that is between you and Matthew would be helpful. What do you mean crush of people? You will notice the changes slowly. We did not want to send you into shock with instantaneous change."

I wrote, "In session past and in a dream, and your confirmation, that people would be drawn to me like a wave of people- but that you all would help buffer it."

Jesus, "I understand. Yes. This is being buffered so it is not overwhelming and also for safety."

I wrote, "I feel like I'm missing something I need to feel at ease, joy."

Jesus, "The galactic family does see a few items yet to be cleared that will help once cleared."

Session 15- May 8, 2017

"A bit thrown by Matt, but know it has nothing to do with me or my daughter or my son. Decided to still open a session. Looks like I am in my hospital room. It has been buffered in a way that makes me feel like I'm back in the cocoon. I have my human sheath on- but simply me now. Big healing happening where hole was. Told it would be another 24 hours of healing and 48 hours before operational. Different beings in the room. I was eating red Jell-O to my right. Not sure why. (Could be why I'm very uninspired by food right now in third dimensional form- hate eating, although my body can digest it- I just don't like eating right now). There was a messenger over in the far-left corner. Reading a letter from my uncle in the wilderness- "Greetings and Congratulations. Very proud of you. To note- there is a grave concern headed our way." Then an image flashed in my mind with the message- like my uncle at the edge of our galaxy watching lightening. He seemed to express more concern for the unpredictably of how it will land. He felt he and his tribe can protect themselves, but not sure how it will land in the galaxy. I wasn't sure where to go with this message. Or why it was sent now? It seems like 10-20 years off, but then I don't understand how physics work in this arena. What do you make of it? I can see as I'm healing there is limited amount I can see, process, or do at this very moment."

Jesus responded, "Your words are accurate. I will investigate the message."

I wrote, "Thank you. Yes, please let me know what this message is and why it came now?"

Jesus, "I am still exploring this. It seems this message was not sent to upset you. The galactic family has asked for support to be sent out to monitor this concern and to supply help as needed."

I wrote, "No, I understand. I didn't send you notes to session 16 last night because I was too upset by Matt's behavior, your response, and how I felt."

Jesus, "I understand. Your notes will be helpful whenever you can send them. I apologize for last night. I will work with the galactic family here to make sure the work I am doing in helping you and Matthew matches the work they are doing in the transition. I may need to emphasize my communication with the galactic family now that it seems it is more necessary to communicate more often."

I wrote, "I don't understand. Can you explain what you mean? This is absolutely not about me spending more time with Matt. This is about quality and Matt is very aware of this if only unconsciously. As I have been repeating for a few days now- I'm completely checked out and it's getting worse."

Jesus, "I understand. Matthew is aware of quality. We have been trying to provide more opportunity for time. I see that this is where the confusion lies. I will resolve this confusion. We have been trying to understand why you are checked out as you have indicated you feel on a good path with Matthew. We have been recently exploring your professional and personal life in connection. Does this seem like we are now headed in the correct direction?"

I wrote, “We can have quality time just making dinner together. There have been multiple opportunities. I just have not been available emotionally or mentally. I'm basically a zombie.”

Jesus, “I will look into this and work with the galactic family.”

Session 16 part 1- May 10, 2017

“These are my notes from last night. Feeling bad and out of it still, but decided to go forward. To add to my symptoms- I keep bleeding when I have a bowel movement, looks to be a hemorrhoid activated; so tired all the time, I can't keep my eyes open; I can't tell when I'm hungry or full- like I just don't have awareness regarding this cue. I opened up to a beautiful figure at the top of a short staircase- all glowing and pastel colors and went up to this- and it opened up to like a spa, pampering facility at the Angel Medical Center. That was nice. The emphasis seemed to be on me pampering myself and relaxation. Coming down from this. I noticed my belly is mostly healed- still not quite operational, but filling in. At the bottom of the staircase and off to the right was a lounge area with some comfy chairs, low lighting, tea, etc. I noticed you, Thor, Michael, galactic members, and a few others and of course, I sat too. A screen dropped down in front of us and it was crackly as it came to life with a direct transmission from my uncle out in the wilderness. It was crackly, it sounded very windy there too. After this message he said he was taking down the antenna and him and tribe were retreating underground until this passed. They would be fine. He is concerned how this will impact the galaxy. He had the video direct to the image of like lightening in the sky. I asked for this image to be stilled, captured, and saved- so I could look at it in depth later. The video than went back to him. I questioned him about why now, I heard your messenger say 10-20 years. He tried to explain, but I couldn't follow. Basically, yes, but because of physics- the storm would hit where I could see the impact around June 9 and 10, 2017- maybe sooner- he wasn't sure. And then the image broke up. I had the still picture opened up so I could study it. I thought, when he was talking, it would just be about lightening hitting certain targets and destroying. But that is not what it looks like when I study it. It reminds me of a powerful lizard, pounding through the sky and striking with its tongue- destroying for sure, but more importantly collecting data to transmit back to darkness. The idea here was, at least with Earth, to secure all potential areas where it would be best that no data could be gained. A shielding placed in front, as soon as possible- until this sent "storm" passed. Does this make sense?"

Jesus wrote, "This does make sense. This is also accurate. I did say in an earlier message that help was sent out. We will secure all potential areas where it would be best that no data could be gained."

I wrote, "I thought you meant help was sent out to my uncle, which doesn't seem to be what he requests. I'm fine with him reporting to me, but wonder.....why? Is there something I'm to do with this information in particular or is it to just be aware of it?"

Jesus, "For now you can be aware of it. At some point you will be able to help make counter plans and execute actions using the information."

I wrote, "Hmmm. But I thought that's what you all do already, no?"

Jesus, "I don't understand."

I wrote, "I was responding to your statement- at some point you will be able to help make counter plans and execute actions using the information. And, I'm not sure what I can bring to the table to help that isn't already there- that doesn't already have help, i.e., you, Source, Galactic Team, etc. Does that make sense? I feel like my greatest asset has been being who I am, with my connections, but being in the Earthly Realm- so could get inside the belly of the beast. Although....I would not recommend this, it has traumatized me, and don't wish to do again. But I'm good at being a spy. I've really, really enjoyed being a spy (although I know it's bad for me, which is odd). My cover is blown as I'm fully in the Archangel Realm. Although now protected."

Jesus, "I understand"

Session 16 part 2- May 10, 2017

"After the session, a few things happened later in the evening- I learned that Trump fired the FBI Director which I found startling and unnerving. Matt responded as he did when I came downstairs and then I think your response- all making my heart feel on edge, beat fast, and pushed me more deeply into feeling isolated, shutting down, overwhelmed. I tried to finish the evening, felt more tiredness come on, exhaustion, then I hurt my hip. Did a relaxation audio clip which helped me go to sleep.

Dream or visitation- not sure. I was somewhere in the woods with cabins and a bunch of people. Trump and Melania were in a cabin and I was talking with them.

What sticks with me is a childhood friend driving up and feeling like him rescuing me. He was talking with me and it felt comforting. I remember the feel and look of his hand. And I remember his eyes looking deep into me. I felt this energetic barrier between us, but he didn't seem bothered by it. He seemed to indicate he would wait.

It was a very bizarre dream in how vivid it was. Today, I definitely have felt worse than yesterday. Very floaty and not here- like a zombie."

Jesus, "The galactic family is studying your words and will help you."

Session 17- May 11, 2017

"Opened with me staring at the beautiful Earth through the large picture window on a huge ship. I was dressed in my galactic outfit- which fits nicely and my belly feels operational and good. Walking over towards me was a galactic figure. He said your education and training begins now. I asked where was I- he said on a subship from a galactic family of light elder I've talked with in the past. That made sense. He also said that they had been told about my sadness with my mission being over as a spy and had something new for me to do. I was interested. He handed me a folder. I wanted to read it then, but when I opened the folder- it was in a language I didn't understand- with symbols and different than two-dimensional writing I'm used to seeing. I appreciated the ability to make the decision myself to bring it to you and others back home in the realm. He said to think about it with Jesus and that you would help me understand it. I went to bow and say thank you so much for considering me for this mission and he stopped me with no no, the elder said you might say this, no no let's practice here- this is how it goes. You say to me "Thank you. I will consider this request" and stand tall. I say to you, while deeply bowing, thank you sincerely. We practiced this.

And then, it took a little effort, but I dematerialized and set my focus on the Archangel Realm. I materialized in my home, the bedroom of my beautiful home in the Archangel Realm- looks more Earthy and reminds me of New Zealand. Which confuses me- this looks like a part of the realm where those that have been human like to have their homes. I feel there are about 35 homes. 29 from those that transitioned closest to being human and the other 5 were human at some point.

I was tired so closed the session with going to find you and bring the folder to you."

Jesus, "These words are accurate. You only have to consider what you want and I will help you with this."

Session 18- May 12, 2017

"Just will be brief here as I need to sleep. Opened up to an underground place, still in the Archangel Realm, but very Earthy feel and ancient underground. Jesus was with me walking through this cavern. The very ancient beings were exceedingly happy surprised to see Jesus in their home. Two of them- a twin flame couple-this is the form they are most comfortable wearing. Reminded me of like Yoda in the 'Star Wars' movies. We handed over the folder and they examined it. They took the letters and dropped them into prepared cauldrons and bubbled up and out images and language I could understand. I'm thinking now- it must have been coded in a certain way to keep the message safe? I'm not sure. The basic idea is some ancient seedlings that turned into dark, talking with them back in time, before they take a dark path. The folder contained 5 case studies. If I was interested. This very much interests me and I like this kind of work. Once that was resolved. I stayed with the beautiful ancient couple and they began to educate me about Earth. I don't remember what they said, but I trusted the process and returned fully back into my Earthly life and closed the session.

Seems good, but unclear how this relates to my being human on Earth. Thoughts?"

Jesus responded, "I will get clarification for you."

I wrote, "Thanks. I mean how does my journey here in the Archangel Realm and in conjunction with the realm translate into the physical Earthly Realm I live in as well?"

Jesus, "I'm not sure I understand."

I wrote, “Well....right now I feel like I lead two separate lives. It's a bit odd.”

Jesus, “They will blend naturally.”

I responded, “Okay, but I just don't see how. I can't dematerialize here at the hospital where I'm working and then materialize at home. I don't live in a home like the one I have in the Archangel Realm. I could go on with examples like this.”

Jesus, “That's true. You are looking at third dimension limitations. The two realms can blend together in many ways. The peace you feel in the home in the Archangel Realm can be felt in your Earth home, for example.”

I wrote, “Okay. I just feel so tired and out of it; hard to focus or be positive.”

Jesus, “The galactic family is working on this.”

I wrote, “It's hard for me to see- Is it the medication? What I'm eating? Severe anxiety that has me disassociating?”

Jesus, “It could be a combination.”

I wrote, “Hmmm. I'm not sure how to help myself then. Just down.”

Jesus, “We are trying to clear a few things.”

Session 19- May 13, 2017

“Last night- I opened up and saw that I was sitting at that retreat spot in the Archangel Realm- way up high- looking down into the engine/mind of Source God (sort of how I would feel when I would sit on a cliff and look out over the Mediterranean Sea). Jesus was sitting to my right being comforting.

So much raw power that my human mind feels perplexed why I'm so comfortable here and this is my retreat spot and where I go to think or when I feel down.

I talked with Source and dropped my prayers thoughts right down into Source. Along the lines of, ‘I really do love the soul that is now known as my old Pleiadian friend’s current name. That will never change. His soul is very special to me. I'm not mad at him for myself being captured back then in time. I think I can see how darkness played the situation and he had almost no part. But now is not a good lifetime for us to meet each other. There is no part in this lifetime. I have too much C-PTSD going on. He has too many issues and is being played by dark again as a pawn. It's frightening me too much and keeping me from connecting and grounding into my life, Matt, and the Archangel Realm. Even when all is clear, good, and healthy around me- I am still going to be dealing with fear. It's that intense for me. I choose for my old Pleiadian friend to have as much support, love, and help- he can allow, but it won't be from me and he needs to leave the area completely.’

I heard in response from Source very quietly, ‘your wish is granted’ And that felt settling, but I don't know. I don't see how this is going to play out.

Last night then I had some weird dreams. I dreamt of seeing old boyfriends from my past. And then I had a very weird dream that I was getting ready to marry the neighbor from next door. It was just very odd and vivid.

I need for Matt to stop highlighting how much he can't stand my old Pleiadian friend. It's upsetting and awkward. We are caught in a very uncomfortable and odd position."

Jesus wrote, "This is accurate. We will help facilitate this."

Session 20- May 14, 2017

"I had a hard time concentrating on opening up. I breathed with the realm to help. And then stumbled my way over to like a holding dock of messenger warrior Angels- like they hold shifts to always have Angels ready- like firemen here on Earth. I stumbled in and sat down and must have told them a little that was going on. They started flying down into the Earth Realm and collecting information. They seemed gravely concern as they began coming back, one had a specimen jar. I was told to just lie down and felt myself softening. I was on like a stretcher and they wrapped me in this bubble cloak and as they raced me to the medical center my whole being just started coughing out dark black bugs. The bubble contained them and killed them instantly. I was so sick. In the diagnostic operating room, there was a lot of chaos and I was upset and crying too. How had things gotten this bad? A shield was put up with a white cloth neck down- on my request as I didn't want to be traumatized by what they were finding. Mother Mary was by my side to help me and she was fierce. I did hear her say to the room- what happened here? Why has this happened? I took comfort in her speaking what was in my heart and her sticking up for me. As the medical team worked, she had me look her in the face and repeat over and over- I am beautiful, I am courageous, I am strong. And also- I have got this. The main culprit seems to be a large bug wrapped around the left side medial to my heart. Will need to be killed with medication so it doesn't damage my heart if pulled off out right. I was told to sit up. I was back in a hospital gown- lots of wires and IVs off of me. I was told to revisit the realm before I went to bed and three times tomorrow. I was also advised to stay off the computer as much as possible on Sunday."

Jesus, "Yes. It is being discussed. It is accurate."

Session 21- May 15, 2017

I wrote, "TMS in my lower back starting."

Jesus, "I will inform Michael. "

I wrote, "Still very bad TMS and has gotten worse."

Jesus, "Michael will address it himself."

I wrote, "I can barely walk the pain is so bad on the left side of my sacrum."

I wrote again, as deeper truth had begun to dawn on me regarding my old Pleiadian friend, "Where does this leave me? My whole first lifetime was a lie and set up.

How did such a dark figure end up in the Pleiadian Realm? How did you all miss seeing this?"

Jesus, "It's not exactly the case. This being did not make your first lifetime a lie. We are certain that you were not responsible for this being entering the Pleiadian Realm."

I wrote, "True he didn't make that whole lifetime a lie, no I don't feel responsible for him coming in, but there are very upsetting facts that remain-

- I thought he was a friend. When in reality he was scouting out whom to recruit to darkness, that had abilities well suited and wanted by darkness.

- I never thought he was responsible for myself being captured, when in reality he was.

- All the ensuing hell that happened to me came from this being. He started it all, he marked me, and he allowed for a dark raid to overtake me and my fellow Pleiadians that were on the project."

Jesus, "He was under orders which means you were already marked. What I mean is this being alone is not responsible for everything, however, we will act as if it was."

I wrote, "This was my first frickin lifetime! How could I have been marked? He didn't have to cozy up to me and be friendly and act as if we were friends. What was that about? It still hasn't been told to me- how could the likes of him have infiltrated and incarnated in the Pleiadian Realm? Is this new information to you? Because you have not brought this up before."

Jesus, "It is difficult to explain. He used various others. You were friended because everyone was friended. He came into the Pleiadian Realm because he was turned. It is not new information but we must examine this to stay ahead."

I wrote, "Do you mean he came into the Pleiadian Realm before he was turned?"

Jesus, "I believe so."

I wrote, "I disagree and strongly so. Again- he's doing exactly what I have done but myself for light. He's a spy."

Jesus, "We agree. He was likely converted through pressure. We are looking at when this happened."

I wrote, "My heart and somatic feeling in my body really point to that he was born from figures of dark. I don't know how that's possible- i.e., everything comes from Source or is manufactured like drone former studio mate. I just feel in my body there is something very different going on here that you all are not seeing. I can't shake this strong awareness."

Jesus, "We are looking at it from your view. It is easier with you in the Archangel Realm."

I wrote, "Okay. TMS is still in my back, whole lumbar spine and my pelvis just feels really impacted and full of energy. I wish I could be more present in my life, but I can't shake this thing with my old Pleiadian friend/dark entity. Do you all see what I'm saying? I feel like I'm struggling with how to speak up to describe what I see- for some reason it's very triggering."

Jesus, "You are speaking very well. We see what you are saying. Your presence in the Archangel Realm has helped here and it is keeping you safe. We will work with you so you feel comfortable trusting what you are speaking. We will also help you with your symptoms."

I wrote, "I'm confused what happened with Session 21. I opened up and was speaking- like where I've spoken before in the amphitheater- galactic warriors, team captains. I had on my working galactic human outfit- so I don't think I was in the Archangel Realm. But I was speaking. On the stage with me were Jesus, Archangel Michael, and Source (outlined figure of his energy that is). I was speaking, but then as I merged into this- I grew very upset and fled the area and went back to the Archangel Realm, in my home, on a sofa in front of my balcony. I was just so upset and Mother Mary was helpful. And I just feel awful in my body. My back, TMS, the medication making me feel weird. Just awful. I know I'm right regarding my old Pleiadian dark entity/thought was friend. But for some fear and rage, I can't let my consciousness see it, so then my back is in pain."

Jesus, "The galactic family will work with you and call in help as needed."

<u>Session 22</u>- May 16, 2017

"Just my notes here from last night. I opened to being on a galactic ship. The size reminded me of the last time- when I was looking at Earth through a huge window and was given the case notes for 5 individuals. So, the ship looks like the same or similar. I was in my work outfit.

And placed, standing in front of me, was a gigantic globe like thing. I was told it could change the pattern, (of what had been programmed in to me for unhealthy sexuality to keep me away from being able to connect with my twin flame).

I walked in and felt fine and could listen to instructions coming from like a speaker. So, I was to relax and expand fully to the fullness of my 3 billion years (the globe could contain it) and then was to go ahead and go with the fullness of the energy my old Pleiadian dark entity was offering. Did that. And they were tracking it and making adjustments and then, still with him sexually, things began to shift- real power of light and it terrified him. He started running away, as did other parts of the pattern- that amount of light, pure and strong. It reminded me of the movie the 'Matrix' when Neo climbs inside the body of one of the dark figures and breaks the pattern by light flowing through it and then dark starts running away from him. I tested this out, but my old Pleiadian dark entity had no interest in me and was frightened of me. And through the pattern in time, regarding sexuality and sensuality and beauty, dark intentions had no interest.

I could see the pattern- how it's been and truly threatening when I've been flowing in myself, beauty, calmness because the program had been set to then have darkness come in and attach- like a beacon for them. Now, they just wish to run in the opposite direction.

I came out of the globe and that was the end of the session.

I spent some time with Matt downstairs, but he's obviously been jarred by this whole thing. I just need to feel where I'm at, independent of Matt. I just want to feel good in myself regardless of where he is."

Jesus wrote, "What you write here is accurate and reflects the work being done. The pattern has been exposed and it has turned to allow you freedom from it. The galactic family will need to help cement this new pattern and allow you to grow strong in it. Matthew has been frozen, temporarily, so that no damage could be done to him while the work you performed could be started. We did not want darkness running to him and hiding in a pattern there. With the work you did having a good start, we will unfreeze Matthew and he will match you where you are. It will be good for you to allow his pure energy to combine with yours. You are correct that you will need to feel where you are independent of Matthew and the galactic family will help you here. This can be done in connection with Matthew and in connection with allow healthy sexual energy to flow. In seeing darkness run from you, you are grasping the power that flows within the Archangel Realm. We will continue to work here as well. You will find it helpful to spend some time with Matthew. Do you have questions?"

I wrote, "I'm here with my therapist at the moment. Telling a rape survivor, a 3-billion-year rape survivor, to heal by having sex or intimacy with Matt is damaging. I ask you to meet with women, your mother, female entities to understand this. Your words cause me great anger, distress, and my back to hurt with TMS pain. This doesn't feel like my choice anymore. There has been

100's of times I've gotten close to Matt and something has gone wrong- internally or externally. I'm exhausted and depleted and burnt out. I will be restored and consistently restored before I consider Matt. My therapist wrote this- In order to say an authentic 'yes', we need to know that we have the power to say 'no' authentically. The more I'm told I must consent, the more I want to resist. I need the space to explore my no before I can consider yes."

Jesus, "I agree with you 100 percent. I am not trying to force you toward intimacy. I apologize my words come out sounding this way when we discuss this topic and I do think your advice of meeting with women is a good idea. I am simply saying that we are working to get you to the point where healthy intimacy is a possibility. Intimacy is not healthy if you are forcing yourself to do it. There are many, many things that have to be cleared and healed so that you can get to this point on your own and naturally. Our focus is on helping you heal in this way and not the end goal of simply having intimacy. We see your twin flame connection is strong and know that speeding this up beyond your comfort zone is counterproductive. We are looking to restore you and help you trust that you will not be depleted before taking a leap like the one you suggest. I apologize this keeps getting blurred in our communication. I will learn to communicate these points with more care and understanding of how my words fall on you."

I wrote, "Thanks. Just really tired and depressed today."

Jesus, "I will report this."

I wrote, "Thanks. I'm just barely functioning and I can't figure out why."

Session 23- May 17, 2017

"So, I was a little confused when I opened where I was. I double-checked myself. I was outside Jesus' tomb and I was hesitant to go in because I didn't want to see a dead corpse. With some prodding, I went in. I think Jesus was there alive and a man, I think St. Francis. I was shown this portal of light was open- from Source God to where Jesus was resurrected. I was asked to sit up here in the portal. So, I understood and did that. I felt fine inside that level of light. It seemed to me the galactic family of light team was checking something and then the serum shot in my right upper arm. I spent a little time there and then coming out of the tomb said goodbye to Francis and Jesus was to my right. I felt too weak to make it back to the Archangel Realm on my own so I touched Jesus sleeve with my right hand and we both traveled back.

On entering the Archangel Realm, there was a big commotion and while I wanted to investigate, I really wanted to understand what was going on with my health. We went to a galactic family of light facility in the greater medical facility here. Diagnostics showed me and explained- it looks that the meninges in my body are getting confused. They adjust to the Archangel Realm, then they have to try to adjust to the third dimensional realm, but they are staying stuck in the Archangel Realm and then with things changing- they are confused- causing an imbalance. They showed me with the shot, adaptogenic helpful to adjusting, but more importantly the serum can stay in talking with the meninges from the galactic family medical team- monitoring the situation and talking with this living tissue as there are more changes coming. This seemed good.

The commotion felt louder and Jesus and I went to see. It was my brother and uncle from the wilderness. The Angels were happy to see them. They always have a robust jovial rough around the edges nature about them. They spotted us. And my brother and uncle addressed me as Queen and bowed. I felt concern if all was all right.

My brother, uncle, myself, Jesus and later in came Michael, Thor, galactic team- we went to a private conference room. They explained that the time had sped up. Because of my ability to rebuke my old Pleiadian dark entity soul, things were picking up. The darkness they saw would be coming my way May 20 and most likely sooner. They didn't feel I was safe in the human realm. Which made me nervous. They showed pictures of what they had seen this darkness could do. I opted not to look at it, but you all did. While concerned, Jesus assured them that I would be safe. Measures would be taken. It left me a bit nervous. Can you explain? Thoughts?"

Jesus, "I would not worry as we receive intel very frequently and we take countermeasures. We are actively planning for this advance of darkness you speak about. Darkness has lost some key pieces and is not really aware of their weaknesses right now. You will be safe. We are working still to return your health and to help you with the adjustments you are making. Do these feel better?"

I wrote, "Why would I have been involved this time though? I'll go over some dreams I had last night. Although scattered sleep- very tired- feel a lot better, less drugged- did you find anything wrong with the medication?"

Jesus, "I'm not sure I understand your first question. We helped your body to understand what was happening and helped it to read the medication a little better."

I wrote, "I meant- I was surprised to see my uncle and brother come visit me. And if it just was a regular alert of darkness- this seems an unusual thing. Do you think Greenstone changed the chemical binders in their 25mg or 50 mg tablets? I have so many questions and concerns about the medication. Did Greenstone 25 mg tablets change from 2013 (the one I took last night) to their present-day copy? Is being on Wellbutrin during the day and sertraline at night okay?"

Jesus, "I will consult with the galactic family on the medication questions. I think you might see your uncle a bit more now that you are in the Archangel Realm."

I wrote, "Okay. Well, last night, I took the Greenstone 25mg of sertraline from a 2013 year batch. Felt okay. I did not have Wellbutrin XL- would have been 30 hours since last dosage. Was told by my psychiatrist to wait until morning. Very sleepy, but then started having some interesting dreams. I dreamt of my childhood friend, at her family home in Baltimore with her mother, but now she was an adult with two kids and her husband. She let me know she and her husband had separated- he was abusive. He looked to be dark haired and Muslim. She is a doctor, but said she was taking time off to be with her children. Volunteering. Seemed happy enough. Then there was another scene where I was having an altercation with a dark figure and we had guns to go outside and fight and once outside he said I don't want to fight you. And we kissed, but it was yucky feeling. Then there was another scene of being back in my 11-year-old bedroom at my mother's. And there was Matt and we were being intimate and it felt great and good. And I was so happy. I was an adult, but my little girl self was very happy too. And then I woke up at 4am very happy to finally have had an intimate dream about Matt. And then I wanted to be intimate with real Matt in this time frame. Then our son interrupted us. Matt put our son back in his crib and we were intimate and that feeling I had in my dream has lasted through the morning and now. And now I'm terrified of taking some medication that is going to ruin it all. I took the Wellbutrin at 9:30am and feel okay. Should I take more sertraline? What am I going to do if Greenstone changed their bindings in their sertraline?"

Jesus, "I will share this with the galactic family. They are looking at how the medication is working with their work and they are making adjustments to each so they can coexist."

I wrote, "Ugh. I just don't wish to take any more medication. I don't see the point."

Jesus, "The goal would be to get off medication but it must be done safely and at a pace that can be handled."

I wrote, "Okay. Took Wellbutrin XL at 9:30am and here I am lethargic, drugged feeling 2 hours later. If Matt walked in the door, I would not have the same reaction I had to him this morning at 8am. At 8 am I was tired and hungry, but I had connection with myself. I could then connect with Matt. Now I don't have connection with myself and would not be able to connect with Matt. What do you want me to do?"

Jesus, "I will have the galactic family drain as much of this as they can. Is there an option for not taking Wellbutrin in the future?"

I wrote, "Sure, I've been off it before. It has helped tremendously in time of great fear, chaos, change and then when that time is over- it has stopped working. This has happened twice before I think, but I'm not sure. Like pregnant with my son worked well and then once he was born and here, stopped working as well. It's very confusing. I left a message for my psychiatrist. What does the galactic family think is happening regarding Wellbutrin XL?"

Jesus, "They are looking at it and will now study the cases you just outlined here. They seem to think that the Wellbutrin might be flooding you and are looking for ways to help control this."

I wrote, "I'm not sure what's going on. I know that for people who have ADHD- Wellbutrin can make them incredibly sleepy. I don't technically have ADHD but I am dialed to other dimensions. As Doreen Virtue says- ADHD should be known as attention dialed to a higher dimension. Now maybe more than I have been, I'm dialed in. Unlike people with ADHD- I have help and mastery with this skill."

Jesus, "This makes sense. I will have the galactic family explore this."

I wrote, "Okay, just in talking with Matt now over the phone - felt nothing for him. All the feelings from last night and this morning are gone. So sad."

Jesus, "I will report this and the galactic family will make adjustments to what is happening with the medication."

I wrote, "I have no interest in taking Wellbutrin anymore. It's awful."

Jesus, "Can you safely come off it or should I have the galactic family assist with this process?"

I wrote, "I'm going to need help for sure. I know my psychiatrist will want me to taper, but I just can't. You can't cut the pills and it just makes me feel so desperately unhappy and disconnected- I can't imagine taking it anymore."

Jesus, "We will form a plan and help you execute it."

I wrote, "Please help to get my psychiatrist on board. I can't tell her I've moved to the Archangel Realm and my brain is operating differently."

Jesus, "Agreed. I will help here."

I wrote, "Thanks. Have had no change in how checked out I am since taking the Wellbutrin at 9:30am. Teaching yoga was absolutely brutal. As well as giving a massage-just suicidally awful. I don't get what's so wrong with me."

Jesus, "We'll try to clear the medication."

I wrote, "I wonder if that's even it. I mean- if it created a cascade affect in my brain and it's layered- I don't know really what can be done. Does the galactic family see something I'm missing? I mean, I'm so baffled by how badly my brain feels."

Jesus, "It's important to strip away some of the elements so we can assess it."

I wrote, "Okay. I have talked with my psychiatrist who is fine with me stopping Wellbutrin. So as of now will be taking small amount of lorazepam at night and 25 mg of sertraline morning. Still feeling bad, but at least feel some connection to kids and Matt."

Jesus, "We will build on this."

I wrote, "I'm thinking, as I've started feeling better and especially since being in the Archangel Realm. When I've woken up and taken Wellbutrin now, my soul feels cast aside. Like Wellbutrin is doing the work I can now naturally do- so I then sadly check out and feel lost and down. Just a thought."

Jesus, "This makes a lot of sense."

<u>Session 24</u>- May 18, 2017

"Not too much to report. I felt out of it, but opened up to be in front of the Archangel Medical Facility. And fell asleep in a field of poppies in front of the building. Taken up to the galactic team where diagnostics were run on my brain and being. And then came up out of it. Did they find anything of note?"

Jesus wrote, "They were looking at the best way to wean you from Wellbutrin."

I wrote, "Great. I feel okay today. Tired, but connected to myself and can feel my soul and life force chatting away. Sertraline makes me feel a little odd, but more help with stress about all these changes. I guess eventually I'd like to be off everything, but I think a bit of sertraline and lorazepam is okay? no?"

Session 25- May 19, 2017

"I just couldn't focus or stay awake. I think my uncle was talking to me, but couldn't understand. Can you explain what happened?"

Jesus, "We can revisit this session when you are able."

Me, "What happened?"

Jesus, "You were tired and that is okay."

Me, "I just feel so odd lately. I'm not sure how to help myself anymore. Any word on my right jaw area and that tension in my tooth area? I feel bad being on medication. I feel bad being off it. I don't know what to do. I don't even wish to take the sertraline anymore because it makes me feel weird."

Jesus, "I am having Michael look at your jaw. The area seems structurally sound. We are working with your body to help with this medication change."

Me, "Do you wish for me to keep taking the 25 mg of sertraline? I don't see that I can stop taking the lorazepam, do you? At least not for a while because the threat of a seizure is too high."

Jesus, "Let's not stop the lorazepam. Sertraline can be stopped. Can you cut way back on it to see the changes and to help calibrate?"

Me, "You wrote- Let's not stop the lorazepam. Sertraline can be stopped. Can you cut way back on it to see the changes and to help calibrate? Cut way back on which one?"

Jesus, "The sertraline,"

Me, "I'm already at 25mg. I don't know."

Jesus, "Would a decrease in times taken work?"

Me, "Can you explain what you mean? I'm just not able to follow."

Jesus, "Could you take it every other day for example?"

Me, "That's what I was thinking. Today I'm not taking it, but tomorrow I could. I might take some Tylenol or Advil to help with head pain. What should I focus on with feeling this poorly? When should I expect to feel better?

I can't do what I normally can. I don't see life the way I normally do. And it makes my fear worse that I'm spiraling into a deep depression and not just going through withdrawal. It's extremely hard to not catastrophize the situation."

Jesus, "Our goal is to get you to feel better as quickly as possible. We will need to see what happens with sertraline and help your body accordingly. We do not want you to slip back to where you were prior to starting medication a short while ago. It does seem you were feeling pretty good a few nights ago and you did gain some strength in drawing in with Matthew. We are looking at this and trying to use light and healing energy to build from here."

Me, "Gosh- I don't know. This all feels way too slippery and not well thought out. This is simply not good. Not good at all. That night, a few nights ago, I forgot to take the lorazepam and took the sertraline at 25 mg instead. "

Jesus, "The galactic family has thought this out. They are looking at their work vs. the medication at that time and will mimic it in future work. They are wondering if lorazepam is having more of an impact than it should."

Me, "Could be. None of the medication is working as it originally did prior to being in the Archangel Realm and there is no one I can truly get solid advice on what to do. I feel like I live on Mars and now have a broken leg and I'm being asked how do I think I should fix it and what PT I will need with a broken leg on Mars. Can you understand my distress?"

Jesus, "Yes. The galactic family is the lead for this. They feel the medication does not interfere with your awareness and can see how it is challenging for you to slide back into the third dimension. Some of this is an adjustment that helping you acclimate to this will help and some of it needs to be addressed by working with the medication. They realize to you it feels like two different worlds and you move between them. They are looking to make technology that will keep you in the Archangel Realm while you are in the third dimension until you can better acclimate to doing this on your own. Does this make sense?"

Me, "No, this does not help."

Jesus, "I will mediate this during a session."

Me, "There is nothing tangible here. There is no understanding of how I should take care of myself or medication regime. It's not good. It's extremely unhealthy for me in fact."

Jesus, "I understand. We were planning to move forward with you taking your medication minus the Wellbutrin. The galactic family is helping your body clear that so the focus can be turned on the sertraline. If you are unable to take the sertraline then the galactic family will help you wean from this. Taking it every other day will suffice. While we are adjusting your medication it is important to rest and to have comfort within your family. We understand your personal and professional life factor into this so we are settling your environment by honing your medication so that this area can expand. It is not a good idea to change all of these variables at once. Since you have been feeling good with Matthew and your family the galactic family will use this as a grounding force. Is this more specific?"

Me, "Not really."

Jesus, "Where can I be more specific?"

Me, "You can't- yours and the galactic family of light have just smashed and broken my heart. I'm done for now."

Jesus, "I don't understand. We can definitely help you. I need to know how to communicate better so you can understand what is happening and how it is happening. I apologize I have been struggling with this. "

Me, "I really don't know what to say anymore. I feel this was all just a huge and colossal mistake and am very upset.

- I can't guide you how to deal with medication; you all are obviously unprepared in how to help me or lack understanding; my psychiatrist can't help me because she doesn't understand- so I'm essentially left on my own to flounder. I'm pretty furious about this.

- Prior to this transition, I was doing okay on medication.

- I keep repeating myself over and over again, but you all don't get it

- I cannot take any solace or feel my family if I am not connected to myself. The fact that you brought this up again- to connect with them- shows me how you are not able to hear me.

- Right now, I wish I had never transitioned, huge colossal mistake. I'd rather be in the hands of darkness than be mistreated and harmed by those working in light that clearly do not know what they are doing."

Jesus, "I understand. Continue to take the sertraline and lorazepam as you are. The galactic family sees that the Wellbutrin was causing an imbalance. They are going to help clear the Wellbutrin from you so that there is a balance. Once there is a balance, they will assess the best way to move forward with the other medication. In the meantime, please report anything that you feel so the galactic family can address it.

Does this make sense?"

Me, "I just feel after I take the sertraline high, weird, and sedated. I don't know if that's the sertraline or the lorazepam."

Jesus, "I think it is the lorazepam. I will have the galactic family tweak this."

Me, "I think so. But if the lorazepam is causing issues- why do I still take it?"

Jesus, "We will look at eliminating it. For now, the galactic family will work with it and then assess going off of it. Do you think it will be hard on you to stop taking it?"

Me, "I can't say. I just don't know."

Jesus, "I mean physically. Have you experienced withdrawal from this medication before?"

Me, "This is a class of medication called 'benzos'. I was on a higher dosage of Klonopin starting Dec 2008. Before I became pregnant, I tapered to a lower dose at .75mg I think. By fall of 2016 I found this just too sedating. My doctor switched me to lorazepam at a low dose. That is what I'm on now. My system has been on some kind of benzo since 2008. I probably don't react well to this level of sedation. What would you like me to do?"

Jesus, "Can you take less? Is it possible to take half?"

Me, "Yes, I can do that .25 mg for now. I might take the sertraline and lorazepam at night. I don't think the sertraline is the issue, but I don't know."

Jesus, "Sertraline does not appear to be the issue. Try the half dose tonight. The galactic family will monitor it."

Me, "What works better for you all to monitor- sertraline and lorazepam tonight or just lorazepam?"

Jesus, "Do what you normally do, but take just a half dose of lorazepam."

Me, "Oh dear- things have been all over the place. I don't have a normal. As of this morning, I thought I might be stopping sertraline so I didn't take it. I'll take lorazepam before bed, but I don't know what to do about sertraline. Thoughts?"

Jesus, "Take it when you are comfortable and we will get on a pattern from there."

Me, "This is not helpful."

Jesus, "Go back to the pattern you were doing before, but cut the amount of lorazepam."

<u>Session 26</u>- May 20, 2017

"Seemed to go better yesterday. I came into the session wearing my casual human outfit and other markers made me aware I was in the Archangel Realm. I wandered into a smaller meeting with my uncle, some galactic figures, and an Angel you work with discussing tactics in dealing with darkness. Small conference room. I felt bad about interrupting, but they paused in their briefings and I was feeling upset that I couldn't figure what I was doing regarding my work on Earth. Your Angel aide took me over to where you were discussing this very matter- we sped along down into the cavern area I've been before with the ancient elder Earth twin flame couple. You were there discussing this matter with them. No one seemed surprised when I showed up. Those cauldrons they have seem to be able to decode anything. Like even one of my tears on this matter. The elder woman said she could be frank with me because I could handle it. Basically, it boils down to my role on the Earth in human form is as a yoga teacher. That's who I am. And she asked me to think about it. Yes, there are tools inside of helping people unite with themselves- whether massage, yoga poses, changing the structure of thinking, etc. She pointed to how effortless it used to be to move along on this path. Now I've kind of separated from it, and it seems like I have no one coming to my classes. She talked on other points and even after I no longer was consciously there, I knew she was still discussing this with you. While I can see her point, I also don't see it- where do I fit in the yoga world as it currently stands? I can't even wrap my head around how I don't fit, have no direction, no understanding of what kind of yogi I am, no teacher, and no idea how to make a living inside of it. It's also so ridiculously competitive. I don't understand her words, do you?"

Jesus, "I will get some clarification for you."

Me, "Yes, that would be helpful. I mean- I understand you spent time in India when you were human and in regards to yoga. Which lineage is a match for me? Not sure how I apply this personally or professionally."

Session 27- May 21, 2017

"That was a bit of traveling. It will take me some time to write my notes, but there just doesn't seem a path for my job professionally or even how to find my way personally."

Jesus, "There are paths and options. I will wait for your notes."

Me, "Okay, so I opened up in my casual outfit in the Archangel Realm, but opened up to walking towards like a speedboat in the waters with Jesus beckoning me forward. We got in the boat and traveled quickly, some physics blending and entered a different realm. It looked like a beautiful bazaar in ancient Egypt or Turkey or Morocco- but it wasn't scary feeling or dark- just lots of orange and gold hues and laughter and ringing of bells. Those that are Buddhists might come here after death?

We headed down some back streets and ended up in a little room with Sri Krishnamacharya- who was very jovial and seemed to know you or have a comfort with you.

We discussed and going over my case. It is true that even with the depth that Sr K has brought forth into yoga as we see it on Earth- he scoffs it off and talks about just translating for Source. He saw the dynamics I was wrestling with. He said he was in a bad mood when he worked with Iyengar because of the very similar dynamics I am dealing with in the yoga field. He continued talking with you and going over my case, but there wasn't an easy answer or decision of good direction for me on any level.

We decided to leave and he said he would keep thinking on it and exploring and send word to Jesus when he had more something to share.

I felt a bit sad leaving. I'm not Buddhist. The 'To be or not to be' soliloquy came up again. Seemed more focused on my career.

Next, we got back in the little speedboat and I was told to buckle up as it was a more dense and bumpy transition where we were going and yes, we went into a realm that looked like it opened up to a forest and very Earthy, where Native People that would feel most comfortable might go. Here we met Chief Joseph and his tribe around him. He was very happy to see you and seemed to know you well. It looks that when he was alive and younger-had a visitation with you and became a follower of yours after that. I'm not sure what the history books say, but he had an easy jovial relationship with you.

He seemed happy and concerned on seeing me and we talked, had a meeting. I mentioned how sad I was that all the work I had done for Red Cloud and Standing Rock didn't seem to have made much of a difference as the pipeline is still going through; how much devastation is happening around the Earth; how this white culture dynamics is just so cruel to each other. I feel very foreign in it. I also feel foreign in the native culture and there is darkness there now as well.

We talked about my case with yoga and personal and professional career direction. Jesus mentioned, as did I, about gathering the elders that have worked with me-Crazy Horse, Red Cloud, Black Elk, Sitting Bull, Joseph, and trying to see what they come up with. Again, I believe Chief Joseph would send word to Jesus when they had anything to share.

We got back in the little boat and headed back to the Archangel Realm where I just felt sort of sad with all the inconclusiveness. I headed to my little home there, with an Angel aide helping me, took off my human outfit and just sat on my balcony resting and playing with a little bird that came by.

And that was it."

Jesus, "I am reviewing these words."

Me, "Okay. Please let me know your thoughts."

Session 28- May 22, 2017

"Well, this session felt good and I think integrated nicely into how I feel on Earth.

Opened up to being in my room in the Archangel Realm- opted not to wear my human outfit- just vibration as me. No real focus put on those helping me. Laid down on a bed of pink lights with pink flowers around, very shallow hint of roses, but not nearly as aggressive. Then turned over with a pillow under me and the lights turned to green- such a nice shade- and it made my heart feel very good. I liked this very much. Moved into child pose and felt massaging into muscles on either side of my spine. Then cat cow with focus on beam of light through golden third chakra. Moving wrists and stretching out. Then seated. Felt a bit nervous with this one so we didn't stay long, an Angel or figure held my right hand- a cylinder like cone coming down over 5th and 6th chakra emphasis in blues and just saw like the worse fighting and blood shed (hence my angst and pain today regarding cobalt blue netting).

Then white crown chakra connecting with deep root red- just a line of energy.

A swift sweep of orange over my 2nd chakra- again a tender place of suffering, didn't stay long. Back to line between white crown and root red.

And then that was it. That felt nice. I was reminded of John of God in Brazil who talks about using these crystal beds. But that's neither here nor there. Feeling better about starting a college course and a bit more focused on healing feels a lot better.

Still frustrated on finding a bare bones minimalist routine in how to care for my face skin. It's very out of balance- I probably just need water, honey, and an oil moisturizer or well, something this simple. But I'm not sure what."

Jesus, "This sounds good. We will continue to move in this direction and help you heal."

Me, "Okay. My facial skin is just a disaster, stinging, hurting red scaly patches- I don't know how to care for it. So, upsetting"

Jesus, "We will try to calm it."

Me, "Thanks. It could be any number of things. I so wish-I didn't have a reaction to Cetaphil. I've been using that for 20 years and after the detox- my face stopped being able to use it. Or I'm not sure what's happened. I just don't know how to care for it going forward."

Session 29- May 23, 2017

"So, I opened to my room in the Archangel Realm again-with my human outfit to the side. And the focus was with a machine with my heart. Lots of green and different shades of green. I think that my work in physical therapy is dovetailing with the work you all are doing. It looks that it was seen the bug I picked up on in my top right upper rib, there's an implant there. Not sure how it relates to my former studio mate but there is some connection. With beings around helping to repair my heart and any damage he may have implanted. Then I fell asleep. When I woke up, there was like a surgical suture thing at my heart and has been there today.

Was very cold and hot after I woke up and had a hard time regulating my body temperature. Had weird dreams last night, but can't really remember. Something about my old Pleiadian dark figure trying to find a way back in. But just can't remember.

Have had more bowel movements today and bleeding from rectum which has been going on for a few days now."

Jesus, "We will continue this work in the next session."

Session 30- May 24, 2017

"Just notes. To note, I haven't had any correspondence with my old Pleiadian dark figure since May 13. Last night, he did post a 'like' on one of my pictures. Thoughts?

So, I opened up once Matt had gone to bed and worked downstairs. It opened up to this amazingly colored indoor therapy pool. It was intense and I was a little worried. I was told we were in the Archangel Medical Facility. (Then I remembered at the NIH, they would use water tubs to help in diagnostics and healing). So, I entered the pool. It felt so good to move around in. I took a break and laid out of the pool on a chair. The walls seemed to be of white salt. Then, like in my daughter's 'Tinkerbell' movie, the galactic family wanted me to pick out things and see what gravitated towards me. First was a pyramid of objects. The orange cylinder like object upper left hand pulled and highlighted to me. Back in the pool swimming, see what felt comfortable swimming with me- a dolphin on my left side and a baby shark on my right. They felt this gave them the information they needed and that was the end of the session. What did it mean? No weird dreams last night."

Jesus, "I will have to examine what is happening with the old Pleiadian dark being. What did he like? The galactic family is working on healing and part of this is aligning you with appropriate work. This diagnostic work helped them with this."

Me, "I'll send you the pictures."

Session 31- May 25, 2017

"I'll talk more about it- But why Jain yoga and then a push to bring in Sikhism. I'm confused. I'm never going to be a vegetarian. "

Jesus, "I will explore this."

Me, "I'm confused- you were with me."

Jesus, "I want to look at it more and see the rest of your notes."

Me, "Session 31- I was surprised to open up to being like at the NIH grad/career fair in the Archangel Realm. Lots of Angels and beings displaying their information booths. I waited to see what I was attracted to (again just like in the 'Tinkerbell' movie) and what glowed for me was this little old lady with a booth. She was working on a sewing project and to the left of her was a boy, who was working on some calligraphy work. I stopped there. It was the only thing that drew my attention and had a soft glow around it. She said she was here about Jain yoga. And she looked like my uncle to an extent. We talked a bit. She said to tell my uncle that Marilyn and Robert (Bobbie) say Hi and that he would explain the rest. You and I kept walking out of the venue and into a huge glowing white room. It was huge. There was the galactic elder I've spoken with. He in the past was the one who encouraged me not to bow down- as that wasn't right, and did not do well for the energy exchange- but to place my hand on my heart and say, 'Greetings'. Also, at the table- looking to my right in an oval shape- were the galactic family of light, my uncle, medical team, Source God, Archangel Michael, you, me, and Angels.

I really couldn't gather what the discussion was about. I mentioned my need to have some direction. An elder advocated patience. I grew frustrated and asked you to step in. You explained it well to them. It wasn't that I needed all the answers. I needed things to make sense in my heart and mind. I needed that I could feel I was moving forward in the right direction especially with all I've been through recently and C-PTSD- it erodes my mental health otherwise. That made sense to them.

I mentioned my experience with Jain yoga.

They all seemed to nod in agreement with Jain yoga (they did not say Jainism). Part of the medical team mentioned and advocated for Sikhism and kept emphasizing

Sikhism. I said- but I'm not Buddhist and while I respect Buddha, I'm happy with Jesus and the Angels. I'm Native American too, but to open up all into Asian culture- well, I just don't know. I mean true with me- Johrei, Reiki, Japanese influences.

That was pretty much all I gathered.

My uncle did not have much to say regarding Marilyn or Bobbie- so I didn't understand that.

There was round table agreement that my old Pleiadian dark being is looking for a way in. For some reason, I didn't hear more than that. I grew tired.

With your help and touching your sleeve, I had help getting back to my home in the realm. There we worked with the green heart machine. Energy up through my spine, flowing out through my heart and that cord which hooked into my high school."

Jesus, "You have demonstrated your power over the old Pleiadian dark being. You may need to demonstrate this again but we will try to remind him. As you connect into yourself and with Matthew, he should stay far away. Jain yoga is not necessarily the path for you, but there might be elements in it that would be helpful to you. I will continue to look at this and help you. It might be more of an earlier version of yourself that is being shown to you."

Me, "I don't understand. It seems to me that this session was a waste of time. I don't see any value coming from it except confusing me. I still feel exhausted and tired, barely able to keep my eyes open, spacey and out of it, not connected or grounded in my body at all. My face is still a mess."

Jesus, "I wouldn't say it was a waste of time. I will share your thoughts here so this will be reflected in the next session."

Me, "If I had more energy, I'd probably be furious, but now I'm just angry and disheartened. This session was inappropriate. I do not know how to emphasize any more sharply, clearly, or powerfully that I am barely holding on to being alive.

Do you understand this? Do you think I'm wrong? Do you understand the level of the high stakes I'm up against? I am using every ounce of my strength and mental reserve and power to keep myself alive. Do you not want me to stay alive? Does it not matter? I mean I don't mean to sound flippant, but currently I am so weak the deck is not stacked in my favor."

Jesus, "I will make sure we stay focused on healing."

Me, "I feel, now you all may disagree, but that part of my healing is getting grounded in my physical body and life-work is part of my life- a decent part- having some focus here I think would help my soul pain. Like with choosing my son as my son. Whoever chose him nailed it spot on. Why is my work so hard to figure on?"

Jesus, "I do agree. It is hard to hit on because you are evolving and so is your work and the space in which it happens. "

Me, "With my son- it truly was/is a miracle all around. Now I understand Matt and my daughter are too. But I just can't feel it yet and it always brings me a bit down. But with my son- this desperate need, in this one request I- the most vulnerable youngest part of me wished for- and my son just met this part of me, so damaged by my upbringing. And shed a light, so powerful that- he is the first and only thing I've ever been able to love unconditionally as Bridget. Feeling this is so round, full, and complete- it's always complete. I would be heartbroken if something happened to my son, but I would also be at ease because I never have regrets. I always feel unconditional love for him. Always. I feel me in a new way. I have hope for me. I feel proud of me because I feel how good I truly am when I experience my son. By having the opportunity to experience love in this way- I love myself. I'm not sure the equation or the model how Source God and Michael figured on my son's soul as my son, but I am floored by their accuracy."

Jesus, "It took time and hard work. It is the same formula we are using to help you now. We are building on this as well to help you to continue to heal."

Me, "I understand. I do know that I reached a final breaking point. That my soul and lungs were just unable to handle it. I mean I literally stopped being able to control what the cellular tissue in my lungs would do. I started to go mad. I got pregnant a month later, but it felt too close for comfort in it ripping my soul apart. Darkness- and those that work for dark- may be waiting on this. I have no doubt they can sense my weakness. I honestly just don't feel like time is our friend right now."

Jesus, "It is why we moved you to the Archangel Realm early."

<u>Session 32</u>- May 25, 2017

"My notes are a little late here. I'm feeling a bit better. Okay a lot better at times. Matt also seems to be doing better- we both are less spacey. I'm feeling a bit more here. Matt says I was very hot last night- like burning up. I don't remember any odd dreams, but just that I was dreaming.

So, I opened to walking into my Archangel Realm home, the bedroom area like usual when I'm there, and I noticed all these beautiful bouquet of flowers from different Angels- as they knew I wasn't feeling well and that touched my heart. I lied down on my side, left side on the bed.

There seemed to be something about a port.

So, this was the sequence in and the sequence out of healing session-

- I noticed the flowers

- I lied on my side

- I felt massage techniques being used down my posterior self, releasing energy

- I lied on my back

- Acupuncture needles used, especially around the wrists and ankles

- Then looking at creating and having a port in upper right lymph duct area

- coming into Goddess pose- use of energy going up along spine and meeting behind the heart, but this time in helping the heart heal- from the inside, the energy not going anywhere, not going out any cord that is

- port being opened and a way to manually help the lymph system drain and restore properly

(the thinking seems to be that part of the issue is my lymph system is not working properly for the work being done and is causing a back log of symptoms I've been experiencing)

- then back to focusing on the heart

- then back to looking at needles and not just pulling them out, but taking out the needles and placing magnets, so those points can be stimulated

- massage techniques

- back to lying on my side

- back to noticing the flowers in the room

- sitting up

Session done."

Jesus, "Yes, I will share this."

Session 33- May 26, 2017

"Opened to just being in my Archangel Realm home, bedroom. Emotional heart centered talk and session. I can't remember all that I said or felt right now. Some basic themes-

- my fear of feeling good and then having it taken away. again. of something happening

- of how much I love my son and fear of something happening to him

- my sadness for those murdered recently in Manchester and for their grieving parents

- my fear for my children that if I couldn't care for myself as a child, how can I possibly help them

- my fear for my daughter in starting elementary school and what if herself, and my son, go through what I went through as a child

- just my abyss of loneliness and deep sadness, confusion, and relentless pain from the age of conception to 20 years old.

- why did I incarnate into such absolute hellish/misery? I would not wish how I felt from the age of conception to 20 years old on anyone, not even someone that is dark- there just aren't any words how awful I felt- day in and day out with no relief. I can't adequately describe how awful this time was. I don't see how I can truly trust myself or anyone or anything that let me incarnate into such misery and such a nightmare.

Now, before bed, I hate taking the medication. I just feel this wave of feeling like a zombie wash over me. I'd say it makes me sad, but I can't feel anything. It like sticks me in a prison. I hate having to take the lorazepam for at least 7 more weeks. It's triggering."

Jesus, "Your notes will be studied and used in sessions going forward."

Me, "But my question?"

Jesus, "You did not incarnate into hellish misery. The experiences that made it hellish misery were produced after your incarnation by choices and actions of others."

Me, "But my earliest memories started this way. I don't understand. Choices and actions of who?"

Jesus, "Your parents, those around you, beings that were connected to you and beings indirectly connected to you. A lot of these actions fell on you and without strong support around you they carried bigger consequences. Does this make sense?"

Me, "It does, but I don't understand how this wasn't observed before I incarnated, why I still incarnated, and why I wasn't pulled out? If I had it to do all over again- I would not have incarnated."

Jesus, "There was some support in place before you incarnated. A lot of what happened went contrary to the support. In other words, many beings ignored the support and followed a different path other than the one outlined for them."

Me, "I think I need to stop looking at reasons or how well I did, considering the situation. It was a devastatingly awful brutal soul ripping experience that I would not wish on anyone or anything. It is hard for me to remember, try to process how truly awful I felt."

Jesus, "I agree."

<u>Session 34</u>- May 27, 2017

"Again, I'm not sure what happened. I don't seem to be able to really access the Archangel Realm awareness very easily. I tried though. I seemed to be somewhere very foreign to me. You were with me, but I could hardly feel you. Why?

I was wearing like a gold silver armor- so I wasn't in the Archangel Realm. Sand. All about sand. Amongst sand people/beings. In like these incredible caves with sunlight flowing through. People meditating. And I worked my way back to a guide amongst these people. And he heard my request in trying to understand my grandmother. And then this huge force entered the room- like if the Sun could talk, but it wasn't the Sun- and I felt much easier talking to him and things became clearer. So, this force helped me to see- he ruled over about 5 planets and they all help each other. He rules, but is in service to those that rely on him. A mutual benefitting construction. Than to the left of him he showed me how my maternal grandmother is- she treats those under her as slaves, through fear and torture. Her coming to Earth was an experiment and gathering of data for her own agenda.

That was about it. The Sun force called me 'my queen' which I didn't understand. And I don't know where we were."

Jesus, "I will get clarification for you."

Me, "Alright. I'd like that information."

<u>Session 35</u>- May 28, 2017

"Opened with-

- something has definitely altered my ability to join in on the Archangel Realm. Third session struggling to connect.

- I found last time when I connected with that large force that watched over and has a symbiotic relationship with its inhabitants and 5 planets, I was able to relax.

- tonight, still couldn't connect and then found myself at the top, lookout place over the 'brain' of Source God, the engine, reminds me of the ocean, rolling clouds, a still sea, and thunder and lightning, peaceful and brooding at the same time. I found myself there and then wandering out onto like a rock, whale like structure that was breathing, and laying down, felt I could just sigh with Source God. I felt it echo into me- 'you know it's all been trial and error for me too. It's been devastating when certain things reflect back to me and I don't understand what's happening'. Sort of chatting along.

- and then I noticed Jesus at the railing calling me back. That I need to come back.

- I reluctantly gathered myself and climbed up out of where I was and onto the railing area.

- Jesus said, 'You can't be going out like that' he was brushing stuff off of me. 'Maybe in the future, but not now. Your system can't handle it'

- which confused me.

- I felt like I didn't want to go down into the Archangel Realm (I noticed I felt at ease with the large forces, but resistant to the Archangel Realm)

- we were back in my Archangel Realm home and I was extremely uncomfortable. I kept saying I'm more comfortable with the brooding depth of sadness, not this- the vibration is jacked up too high here- this isn't me.

- then there was some diagnostics looking at my left arm and I started getting a headache.

- so, I brought myself back

I don't understand. Do you?"

Jesus, "This event with your family has knocked you way out of balance. We will have to restore balance so you can continue to reap the benefits of the Archangel Realm."

Me, "I just don't see it happening. Every day I feel worse."

Jesus, "This connection to your family will be cut so you are not impacted by their unhealthy behavior."

Me, "I have been trying my whole life and I feel like if I cut it then my mom and step-father get to say- see I told you about her bratty crazy behavior. She has mental health issues. I've tried to have distance for the last 17 years and that has gotten me nowhere. I don't understand what you will do differently than I already have. Can you explain?"

Jesus, "Since we can trace it back to your grandmother, we can cut all of the cords. Your family knows your mother is not well. They are under a spell in a sense to appease her. We can cut the entire web and free up everyone."

Me, "I don't understand how this changes anything do you?"

Jesus, "Releasing your entire family will not allow your mother to blame you."

Me, "So are you saying my mother was invited to my cousin's wedding and they didn't invite me to appease her?"

Jesus, "I was speaking in general."

Me, "I'm not saying there isn't a way. I just don't see it. I grew up in this family. It's all I know. They've rejected me. It really doesn't matter why or how- it still hurts and carries a weight and pain that makes my life non-functional. I can rationalize with my brain, but it impacts my heart and soul in a way that is hard to describe. Even if you cut all the cords and do lots of clean-up work. These people's patterns are old. They aren't going to suddenly change. Even if they did, I could never trust them. They all know my mother is unwell. They've known this for years. But for some reason, they felt it makes sense to ostracize me, Matt, and our children. I guess I'm just really confused by what you think you can do and how it will realistically play out in real time and realistically make an impact in my life internally and externally. It just does not make sense what you're saying."

Jesus, "Their patterns are unlikely to change in this life time. You would be right not to trust it. You will be free from their patterns. That is the idea here. To break the web that perpetuates these patterns so you can continue to grow and be healthy. In time maybe one or two of them will use their freedom to seek health. The idea is so that their power is cut off and no more damage can be done."

Me, "But.....what difference will I feel?"

Jesus, "It will help you both heal and not feel the weight of their actions like with this recent event. It will also help clean up past trauma."

Me, "When do you expect this change to occur?"

Jesus, "We would look for you to feel changed quickly but spread out over time."

Me, "Okay. But when should I expect this change - tomorrow, a week from now, 6 months from now or you just don't know? I'm also concerned when my mother finally dies or my stepfather and being roped into the drama this way. And then there are my brothers."

Jesus, "We will begin the process right away. We will protect you from future drama. The relief you feel should begin right away and gain in power."

Session 36- May 29, 2017

“I felt a touch more present and grounded in the Archangel Realm. I did notice the thin sheath around me- it feels very much like a thin cocoon you see around the butterfly- I can go through a metamorphosis safely- yet practice as I go. It's an active sheath, can sink down into micro areas and help as well as relay information back to the galactic team. As usual, it is extremely advanced technology we simply do not have on Earth. That being said- I was like on a pastel colored hilltop inside the Archangel Realm- like at the edge looking out into the galaxy. Could feel the buffer of the realm. And as I stood there, I felt this rumbling and then creatures flying- and then my maternal grandmother soul warlord like a beacon towards me. As she approached- like a thin wire in front of the realm- she ran into and severed her head and she went down screaming. I felt more annoyance and disgust. Ugly disgusting thing. Screw you is how I felt. There were some other minions to it that came flying along and they met the same fate. It seems my grandmother’s whole point with Earth was experimenting and riding the coat tails of darkness fooling light with technology.

I feel bad for the section/planet she was ruling in terror and looks like plans are in place to help these beings. I don't know what will happen with my Earth birth family. I really have loved them. Truly. I hope someday in some life form they see and feel this. My mom- well that is just so, so sad. All I can say- is it's real clear to me why I am passionate about trying to help those in dark.

I do not understand why I incarnated inside such an evil line- can this be explained to me?"

Jesus, "Your entire family is not evil. You did not incarnate into pure evil. I'm not sure this is the answer you seek but you were not intentionally placed into evil and nor were you placed into danger."

Me, "I said an evil line. One of the lines. My maternal grandmother was evil. You said you did not know who she is when I incarnated. You disagree with this now?"

Jesus, "I understand what you mean. I will seek an answer to your question."

Me, "Thanks. I do not understand how you see that I wasn't in incredible danger."

Jesus, "Your father's line was the line rooted in light, or at least they had access to the path of light. This line could resist any darkness rooted in your mother's line. "

Me, "I guess, but honestly coming off a lot as a soul- I mean my recent past lifetime had been where I watched my son murdered, my tribe murdered, myself killed- I do not see how this was a wise choice to incarnate with one of the lines being a warlord's line. That makes no sense. The risk for my committing suicide/internal implosion was huge. This was a bad risk. I don't understand."

Jesus, "I will seek answers for you."

Me, "Thanks. I feel very confused."

Me, "Any thoughts coming in? I was hoping my deep sadness would have lifted some today, but no."

Jesus, "I am still tracing this back. It seems that your grandmother was not supposed to include her own family in the experimenting she was doing and somehow other family members did get pulled in. I am looking at how and why this happened."

Me, "That was never her intention. We were lab mice for her. She lied to you."

Jesus, "That was the agreement her creator had. She left the tutelage of her creator to carry out her actions as they unfolded. Yes. She lied. She lied to her creator. It is here where we have opened up the possibility to seek repayment for her actions. We will carry out steps to do this. You have asked to be a part of this."

Me, "I thought her head was severed in session 36. Is that wrong what I saw?"

Jesus, "No. I am speaking of that and the events of returning power to victims in the aftermath."

Me, "Hmmm. I don't understand who her creator was. Do you? All I know, is she decided to get in on the technological action that's been happening for quite some time and seeing if she could fool light. In the same way darkness has been doing for a long time. That finally got exposed January 2017."

Session 37 & 38- June 1, 2017

“Session 37 opened with me in the tower in the Archangel Realm and working with the fashion/clothing expert and his team. We seemed pressed for time and he worked quickly. I've been drawn to this beautiful pristine sacred spring with lush greenery and a deep blue green waterfall and pool of water. He worked with these colors to create an exquisite dress- green silk like on top and cascading into the deep blue green bottom dress. A crown of gold with my golden brown wavy hair. Then it was time to go. I came out of the tower and I was aware how large I was- really tall and big- with my right hand I took hold of a scepter from Source given to me and entered onto a plane. It took us a long time to get to where we were going and I was briefed by an aide as we traveled. At one point I grew tired, so I just relaxed and meditated. And then we landed.

Doors opened up to the planet of where my grandmother had ruled. And I walked out to a very large crowd. I felt at ease in this role. The aide was to my left, giving me information as I spoke. I talked on about how light had come to this planet. The scepter I placed in space in front of me and took off the top and the vibration was of pure Source and allowed the planet to change its vibration back to Source and to begin to heal at an energetic level.

I worked inside of three roles- one with Source, one with the beings/people before me, one with the support I had. I opened up to the Angels that had accompanied me who had taken on the role of helping this planet in all the small and large ways- economic changes, social and political changes, etc. Angels were placed so that beings/people who did not wish to be part of this vibration change could leave of their own free will. This is to be a socialist community where we work together in harmony and fairness, etc. It felt very nice to have power flowing through me to them. I asked the aid as an aside about the ruling here- it was one planet with about 100 million people. So- small, don't see it as a huge undertaking or taxing.

I felt sad to bring my consciousness back to Earth and my third dimensional reality. It seemed extremely odd to walk back downstairs with the TV going and my life resuming. It just felt very off and odd.

The next day, today, was unpleasant- dealing with a former supervisor was awful, dealing with confusion about work awful, fighting with Matt awful, thinking about my old Pleiadian dark being and missing him confusing- missing more his ability to get the level of sensuality in how I experience life; that we are very similar as artists in that way and appreciation of sensory experience and beauty.

Just down today and extremely worried about sinking back into a dark depression and snapping at people and being out of control.

Session 38- I had a hard time opening. Just felt down. I was thinking I'd be in the Archangel Realm, but that is not where I was. I was still in my green outfit- although a casual version of it and I was talking with the ruler of the 5 planet system that was next to my grandmother's old one. The Sun ruler I had met before with the people very dedicated to him and him to them- prayerful sacred communities.

Well, we were chatting about things. I felt comfortable talking to him and good. Although confused where Jesus was and confused about not being in the Archangel Realm. The planet I've been helping with and this Sun ruler nearby- all seem incredibly far from the Archangel Realm. So that made me sad and a bit homesick and panicking at my heart.

In talking with the Sun ruler- we went through some information. Well, first I was tired and rested a bit and was brought back to a medical place where the galactic team did have access to me and worked on me. And then I felt better and sat up and was ready to have tea with the Sun ruler and chat.

He is powerful, humble, and peaceful all at the same time. So, it turns out he was the creator of my grandmother's soul- it was a piece off of him. He's not sure what happened to cause her to go awry. She was moving along in her caring for a planet and then she wanted to be a human on Earth and try it. I think then when she came back- she then enslaved everyone and it turned into a hellish nightmare of power and greed. But I could be wrong.

This saddened the Sun ruler. I asked him why didn't he do something. Well, that seems to be like asking a rock or tree to sprout legs and go walking. He said he prayed to Source God and then I showed up- and he smiled. And was very happy. He has a strong love for Source. That made me happy.

We went through some information. He said I reminded him of my grandmother- which was a little confusing because she was so, so mean. But I let that go. He noticed that I don't receive. Like that I give and give, but don't receive. Like look at when I was talking to my people- I gave so much, but I didn't take in or receive their thankfulness or love or adoration. That is wise and true. As an aside, I know there are deep painful reasons for this and it brings me too much suffering. But I did see his point.

I felt like I could learn a lot from him. He mentioned how on Earth- I don't receive the gratitude from my students or patients. That is also true.

I said how I was struggling with work. He mentioned it would be good if I had a leadership position to work through these issues.

I noticed how lonely it must feel though. Isn't he lonely? He said he didn't feel that way. He gives to his people and they give to him. He feels complete in following how Source God created him.

That made sense, but it seems awfully lonely to me.

Then I got to thinking how far away the Archangel Realm was and I felt sad. I wondered- is this helpful to me, shouldn't I be healing in the realm; is this too much to be doing what I'm doing.

He tried to emphasize how I could go back and forth from here to the Archangel Realm, but I felt confused because it felt very far away.

Then we talked about my old Pleiadian dark being- the Sun ruler said that we were alike in our affinity for sensuality and Pleiadians experience sensuality differently than humans. He felt that there was no harm left in my current old Pleiadian dark being. He could help bring me back to my sensuality and then I would by-pass him, outgrow his presence so to speak. He didn't see how he could be a threat with all the protection I have around me.

I didn't know what to make of that.

The Sun ruler didn't think much of the PharmD program. He really seemed to emphasize my work was in learning how to rule and lead right now as there are some real issues I have with this.

That was about it.

I imagine we talked more, but felt best I should come back to Earth awareness. I felt a pang in my heart of not being in the Archangel Realm though."

Jesus, "We have been looking at this information. I will speak of the last session. The galactic family thought it best to get some answers to you. They saw these answers as helping you heal. They were most interested in you learning of your grandmother. While you were speaking with the Sun ruler you were deeply connected to the Archangel Realm and some work was being done to help you heal. Sensuality is important and it is ultimately Matthew that matches your sensuality. The old Pleiadian dark being is able to pick up on this frequency for some of the reasons the Sun ruler mentioned. The old Pleiadian dark being is far less powerful than you, but we are not going to underestimate him as it is possible he can do damage if he is simply ignored. You have far too much protection around you if he is not ignored and the protection is utilized.

I do understand the duality you mention in being on Earth and then in the Archangel Realm and then back. These do blend together and this is why the galactic family thought acclimating you to the Archangel Realm would help you see how. The focus is on healing you now so the disjointedness might seem a little more pronounced. I will have the galactic family address this without diverting from your healing."

Me, "Thank you for these words. What does my old Pleiadian dark being want from me? I feel confused. Again, I thought he was frightened. And can you clarify this more. You wrote-

I do understand the duality you mention in being on Earth and then in the Archangel Realm and then back. These do blend together and this is why the galactic family thought acclimating you to the Archangel Realm would help you see how. The focus is on healing you now so the disjointedness might seem a little more pronounced. I will have the galactic family address this without diverting from your healing."

Jesus, "He might be drawn to the connection you have with Matthew and in not having that in his family. I mean that the difference between the two realms can feel sharp until you are acclimated to them. The galactic family was working on acclimating you but then saw the focus was better spent in helping you heal. For this reason, the two realms might still seem as if they don't line up. I will see what the galactic family can do to help you without pulling the focus off healing you."

Me, "I feel like there are 3 places right now. The Archangel Realm, the Sun planets, Earth. They all feel very separate from each other. I just don't know what I'm doing on Earth anymore."

Jesus, "Your connection to the Archangel Realm will make Earth feel better. I will consult with the galactic family."

Me, "How do you figure?"

Jesus, "There are many ways. You will be protected from darkness. You will heal from past trauma so things that come up on Earth will not impact you as they have been. You will be able to use the skills and power you have in the Archangel Realm on Earth. There are many other ways. I know this will take a little time to feel and realize but it will happen."

Me, "I do not see how I can use the skills and power I have in the Archangel Realm on Earth. There are no opportunities. Just feeling depressed today."

Jesus, "I understand. I will report to the galactic family."

Me, "No offense and no disrespect. But I've been told what you are saying in some form or another since 1995. I really don't know what to say anymore. I'm somewhere between depressed, grief stricken, hopeless, suicidal ideation, lost, beating myself up for not being more patient, angry and enraged."

Jesus, "I understand what you are saying and I know you have been told these things in one form or another. I will invite some beings to session that will help you understand better why this is not the same as what you have been told before."

Me, "I cannot over emphasize and really stress the importance of having a solid career track on Earth at this time. I feel I have all this help and guidance in other realms, but none on Earth. Why? How is this healthy? You all are setting up this split to be worse."

Jesus, "I will report and reflect these words back to the galactic family. I agree with what you are saying and I will make sure the galactic family understands and sees this."

Me, "I want these words to make me feel better but they so sadly don't."

Jesus, "I understand and so does the galactic family."

Me, "Can I ask, what's the plan?"

Jesus, "We have to help you heal. To maintain the healing, we are planning to use a buffer so that any healing you do is not being torn apart internally. The buffer will help keep Earthly interactions from undoing your healing. The galactic family is developing an antidote to help undo the damage you have received from your profession. They are also healing this area with light and energy. This will help you understand the value people do see in you even if their own behavior doesn't always reflect that. The galactic family will also develop a path for you in your profession. Before they can do this, they have to make sure you can take the path by making sure you are healthy enough to take it."

Me, "I don't know. There are too many levels and variables. I don't see time in our favor. I'm sorry, but I just don't see your plans working."

Jesus, "The plan addresses these levels and variables. There are ways to merge them and to bend time to achieve what is needed. What do you see working?"

Me, "I honestly don't know anymore. I feel like we've tried so much, so many things. And this life has just been beyond brutal. Yesterday just punched me in the heart. I just don't feel I can recover anymore. Like some parts of me definitely do, but more and more I just feel I've given up. There's never any consistency and there is always another level of pain. I just don't have any interest in being alive anymore. I have a bad headache right now and it plays on my heart, mind, and soul how my cousin has not invited me to his wedding, I've been ostracized from this family line, and no one seems to think it's cruel or odd or is shocked. Even if one or more comes around. The damage is done."

Jesus, "We can see how your cousin's actions have impacted you. There are many in your family that do feel he is terrible for not inviting you. As we cut the web that keeps these people tangled in unhealthy behavior, they will be able to act. I will seek special council to help you with this pain. I know a few elders and beings who have special abilities in this area. I will employ them to bring help."

Me, "Why am I feeling the pain so badly right in this moment? Like so bad it takes my soul's breath away and is creating a terrible headache. Like if I had access to, I literally would end my life right now- that level of torture pain."

Jesus, "This has hit a very raw part of your human essence. It has served as a lead domino that has knocked over some of the healing you were able to do. It reaches back into your soul's history. The galactic family and I are very sad by what your cousin has done. We have contained the domino effect and are working to grieve with you and to heal you."

Me, "You understand why then this gives me no hope for my future. It's always something you weren't expecting, playing catch up or reacting. I'm still on the front lines being brutalized."

Jesus, "I understand. This is not something we weren't expecting. It is difficult to explain. I will consult the galactic family for words."

Me, "This doesn't help me."

Session 39 & 40- June 2, 2017

"I'll start with tonight- session 40. I opened, but saw nothing, had no experience so just stopped and left. Just sinking into my comfort with letting my body and being shut down. I'm not interested in being alive anymore. I have a feeling you all will block this, keeping me in suffering, pain, and torture to work through it. Which puts me squarely at odds with you all. I'm crystal clear that I've lost the will to live and my soul has been broken in a way I don't wish to discuss.

Session 39, the other night, I was facing the Black Hills in South Dakota. Native elder upon elder was in front of me wishing to help that they had all been through such misery and had found peace. I sort of just fell over. And was taken to like a shaman's lodge where they worked on my heart and created a structure. I remember the shaman saying that my soul is very weak and sick right now. Once the structure in place, I sat up, and the elders were there talking about how they would lend me their strength and awareness."

Jesus, "I am not sure why you did not see it tonight. I will reset this for you."

Me, "Hmmm. Well, as you pointed out, the text from my aunt a week or so ago has made it hard and sometimes impossible for me to be aware of the Archangel Realm anymore. As I predicted- the decline is consistent and steady. I'm not sure that it really matters anymore."

Jesus, "I have made some adjustments to make it easier. We can work on healing without you coming but your presence in the Archangel Realm does matter and is beneficial. "

Me, "I'm not sure how it's beneficial. I have felt awful ever since I arrived and steadily gotten worse each day."

Jesus, "The Archangel Realm is not doing this. We do need to make repairs."

Me, "I'll let you know as things pop up. Like this morning dealt with a past supervisor again basically attempting to prove to a colleague how she was right and I was wrong. She is a lying, manipulative, and ugly person and I said as much to my colleague. That the past supervisor is lying to you, has not set a good tone for the morning again. Just does not let up."

Jesus, "I am personally angry at the situation your past supervisor has created. She has lied and attempted to manipulate the aftermath of her lie to make herself look better. This is disgusting and insulting to me and extremely hurtful to you and your team. Michael is looking at how to take strong action against her and that which she is connected to. Fortunately, her lies and manipulation is observed by beings on Earth and throughout the universe."

Me, "Okay. I'm just sick of it. I need a break from people like this, but it doesn't happen. The fact that I was accosted by this information again before teaching my class and already in a hard space is....well I don't have any words left. Then I have to use every ounce of my strength to be professional and care for the students who've come to work with me. I just feel exhausted and beat up and it's only 10am. I simply can't go to Church now because of dealing with her directly accosting me."

Jesus, "She is not a good person."

Me, "I appreciate you seeing the true picture. I doubt that anyone will here. I mean beside myself and my student. She's in a position of power in the community and a cancer survivor- hence untouchable."

Jesus, "Many, many others see the true picture as well. She may be all of those things but she is also a bad person and that means she is not untouchable."

Me, "Well I must be in a different reality than the one you observe. This is my awareness and what has been presented to me-

1) My past supervisor gets to tell anyone and everyone who will listen how right she is and potentially trash my reputation like she has done with my colleague. I'm sure done with her husband, anyone at Church, etc. People may not like her, see her deceit, but she's a bully- they won't want to create waves or risk themselves being attacked by her, they'll make allowances for her. She will and does continue on in her positions unscathed and unchecked.

2) My former studio mate has a nice space, holds his positions in his profession at the hospital and continues his work.

3) Colleague same thing

4) Colleague same thing

5) Colleague same thing

6) Colleague same thing

7) Colleague same thing

8) My birth family some may feel a bit like oh that's harsh or sad, but oh well, and leave it at that. They will continue on in their lives as if nothing happened, a small blip at my

cousin's wedding, but ultimately life goes on. My cousin just used me and tossed me aside like most people do with me. Your reality Jesus sounds great and interesting, but these are not the objective observable facts placed before me. The world and life and community before me is not one that sees nor values me, but one that ostracizes and attacks me. Is cruel, abusive to me, and pain inducing towards me. Why you subject me and force me to stay here is beyond my comprehension at this point."

Jesus, "I understand your points. They are all not facts. Your past supervisor will not trash your reputation. She is not unscathed or unchecked. This holds true for the others you mention. People value you very much. You are correct that your family lacks the skills to stand up to the oppressor. This is being cleared by starting at your grandmother as we have done and going down through."

Me, "Thanks. It's nice to daydream, but reality before me is the only shown reality I've been given. And the facts presented before me do not line up with your words. Your words are null and void."

Jesus, "My words are not null and void. I do understand why you feel that way. It does seem that your suffering has led nowhere and those that caused it carry on. I see why you say this and can understand why this is what reality is. I will work with you from here and help you see otherwise."

Me, "Sorry, no disrespect intended, but I can only look at third dimensional facts brought before me. At this time, they are different than your wording here. This morning with my colleague reinforced my position. This is after emails sent to me from you- we are helping you, etc. How were my colleague's words to me this morning helpful? How were you protecting my fragile soul during this exchange?"

Jesus, "I will illustrate this to the galactic family."

Me, "This is achingly sad that this has to be illustrated to them. I think at this time I'm no longer interested in communicating on any level- not through email or my nightly sessions or any level. I just ask to be left alone by everyone- you, Source, Archangel Michael, the galactic team, anyone that has been on my team."

Jesus, "I understand what you are saying. They are aware of what you are saying. I will reinforce it for you. Our communication is important. I understand that it is frustrating, especially now that you are not seeing results. Your team will always work with you. My communication with you greatly aids with this."

Me, "I don't want to anymore. I will do everything in my power to help myself die a respectful death in the coming weeks and months. You deny me this or block me- you are my enemy and disrespecting my free will."

Jesus, "This is not helping. I am not your enemy and I am not disrespecting your free will. I know that you are in a very bad place. The galactic family knows this as well. They see the parts of you that have been triggered and know how to stop it. Until they can, my words will feel hollow. I understand this. I can assure you that the galactic family knows how to stop the dominoes from falling. Simply dying as you state will not stop it. Our work will take hold quickly. Your sessions in the Archangel Realm are integral."

Session 41- June 5, 2017

"I opened up and was wearing my active green outfit with the gold crown and a very long blade sword to my left (which looks more like it's capabilities are to shield harmful energy beams being thrown my way). I was in the conference hall with the galactic federation and others in front. There was a panel in the front on the stage area. I walked in and people were a little surprised. I talked, but unsure exactly on what- about the history and damage done by clans working together on my human Bridget body that has been uncovered. After speaking I went off to a little room to examine how I was doing. This is probably the reason I've always been saying I'm a permanent two-year-old. There is a growth like a tumor that has stunted my heart development and infiltrated, like a poison infection through all areas of my being- the heart, heart chakra, all parts of the brain, all organs, energy bodies, etc. It seems shielding my soul, cutting out the tumor, letting attachment sites bleed out their poison, and then sending in healing and cameras through the open channels is where we are at."

Jesus, "These words are accurate. The galactic family saw benefit in having you speak of your past experiences in order to accomplish several goals. Of these goals is to spread and reinforce the word throughout the universe, to get help and protection for you, and to aid in healing. You are correct with the healing process. The galactic family is also using technology to help with the healing and to make sure the poison does not flow into other areas of your being. Are you feeling OK following this session?"

Me, "Yes, I think so. Currently, upset by again here in my college class having it rubbed in my face about the awesomeness of the integrative health community happening at the hospital- and acupuncture. I have no doubt that my former studio mate and colleague know and work with my teacher here at the college. It's very upsetting. How am I to believe you that those I have mentioned are in any way held accountable for their past horrific actions with me, with others- when it's rubbed in my face here? I'm really baffled? Why?"

Jesus, "Those working inside of it are not aware of how bad they are."

Me, "But what does that matter? Honestly. They are supported by the hospital and the community, keep growing, no real checks and balances, and can harm others. Where does this leave me with my awareness and skills?"

Jesus, "I understand your points here. Your skills represent the direction integrative health needs to go, where it would do the most good. Those inside of the hospital represent integrative health as an ego boosting mechanism. Light needs to align with what would do the most good. I can arrange to show you the matrix of what is happening inside of what you are seeing so you can see the direction things are headed."

Me, "Here we go again. Can you explain my point?"

Jesus, "We are looking at options for you. It makes sense now for you to grow the work you are doing now as an independent practitioner. At such time when we can find an appropriate and safe team, or assemble one, it would be an option for you to work on it. Now, you are still easily triggered and working for the wrong organization would be bad for you. We are also looking at a parent organization that you could work inside of independently. In the immediate now, we are working to preserve your client base and to help it grow. Does this help?"

Me, "No."

Jesus, "What do you think is a good path?"

Me, "I'll guess I'll try to see it how you see it. Currently, I work out of my home and had three strong months in a row with plenty of clients. How does that look on your end? Have I been happy? Expressing happiness and contentment?"

Jesus, "I do not think the home office plan is optimal and not a permanent situation. I understand it has not been making you happy and content and we do not feel that it has. I'm sorry I was not more specific. We are working to create a space for you in which to work. Forcing you into the wrong space would be disastrous. We also feel it would not be healthy for you to just shut down and have no clients so the home office is a stopgap situation. Once we can establish a strong place for you, we will open it. This is a priority. The process might include flushing out a few incorrect spaces. What we have achieved is protecting you from darkness. Darkness will not be able to penetrate your working space. I also understand that we need to move as quickly as possible in finding/creating this space. We are doing just that. Getting you to the Archangel Realm created the need to shift around a few things but not reprioritize them."

Me, "I think I understand. I am not willing to scope out a few wrong spaces to find the right one. The right one will either appear or it won't. I also don't know that I want to do this line of work anymore. It just doesn't feel worth it, feels humiliating, shame and pain producing to me."

Jesus, "We are vetting spaces. Your final approval will be needed. We are also considering a lot of different lines of work. You are not locked in to anything at this point."

Me, "Gosh, I don't know. Like I went to an integrative health building and whatever is going on over there and it just upset me and freaked me out that I can't even follow up on it. It's extremely hard and painful to deal with a community of integrative health professionals that at this point just scare me."

Jesus, "I know. We are cleaning this up."

Me, "Can you explain what you mean?"

Jesus, "We are driving out the bad practitioners and helping to make it what it needs to be."

Me, "Okay. I feel like they are just snakes that keep breeding and replacing each other. This area where I live is so full of them. So full that my former studio mate seemed a good one in that I didn't detect much ego from him, because it turned out he was a drone, but still....you get the picture."

Jesus, "There is a way to stop the process as you describe it. I do get the picture and know it will take a little time to cleanse the field entirely. We do want to allow light to get back into it."

Me, "Sigh. I really feel lost and now I can't even get in the Archangel Realm awareness."

Jesus, "I will continue to work here. This might be an internal blockage but I am looking at every possibility."

Me, "No-it's a complex attack as I described in my other email."

<u>Session 42</u>- June 7, 2017

"I must say that my life there multidimensionally is so much more me and happier than my life on Earth. My life on Earth sucks- is hard, painful, isolating, and confusing. I pretty much hate it. Earthly life sucks. Anyway, that being said- odd session. Please let me know your thoughts. I felt more focused which was good. I'll just write here what I experienced.

I was in some parade, in the Archangel Realm, going somewhere and beings were happy and cheering. Then I was at a podium in my green outfit- dress with active part of it underneath. I felt like I was to give a speech and I had notes but I decided I didn't want to use my notes and put them away. I talked for a while- my gratitude for all that have helped me get this far, Source for entrusting me with the scepter of his vibration I wear on my right side, and I thanked for the broad sword I have on my left to deflect energy attacks and send an offensive strike if need be. There was you, Michael, my wilderness uncle, galactic members, and lots and lots of Angels. I felt a crown or something golden placed on my head- Queen (but queen of what I was thinking). I ended with my pledge to do my best and then I left in a unique way. I went up in the sky and moved quickly over to the planet I'm helping rule and also am learning how to be a healthy leader (in the tutelage of the Sun ruler).

Physics part of the session was learning that now I had the ability to 'arc' between places. It wouldn't take as long to travel from the Archangel Realm to my planet. Eventually I would be able to walk from one to the next without much effort."

Jesus, "What would you like my thoughts on? I see this as accurate. You will feel better on Earth once we can fully connect Earth and the Archangel Realm for you. I understand they feel like separate places at this time. You are getting situated in the Archangel Realm and it is good that you are focused and happy with it. This happiness is you and it does move with you to Earth. I do know the trauma and the blocks that keep you from experiencing it this way and that is to be expected at this time. The galactic family has been healing you as well during your time in the Archangel Realm. I do sense there is more you need from me. Please let me know how I can help."

Me, "I'm not sure what you sense. I feel like I'm stuck in varying degrees of hell and am miserable all the time. But you know that all ready."

Jesus, "You asked for me to comment. I know this part of the transition has been very hard. I am sorry. The plan is to have consistency between the two realms for you and we are working to achieve this quickly. It sounds like you are good in the Archangel Realm. We are building on this."

Me, "Thanks. I was looking forward to helping at a health department class. Again, not my field, but good to have a position of authority and I love babies. But in walks a woman and I thought just fine who discusses how she's a massage therapist and works up at the hospital- why have me exposed to this? TMS in my back now."

Jesus, "Michael will help with the TMS. I will vet this person."

Me, "I was so bummed. It's constantly getting rubbed in my face. It felt weird. Can you see where this is coming from?"

Jesus, "It might be a pattern from within. Something from within is reproducing this pattern. The galactic family will run diagnostics."

Me, "Thanks."

Me, "Has anything turned up?"

Jesus, "The galactic family is working at breaking the pattern."

Me, "It has kept turning up throughout the day today. Most days now. Like everyone's in this big club and I'm left outside. It's constant, consistent, and hurtful. I don't get it. It doesn't make me want to be around people- in any capacity."

Jesus, "It is a strange loop inside of you. The galactic family is going to break it."

Session 43- June 9, 2017

"Just my notes from tonight.

I wasn't sure if it was going to work tonight or my emotions would be too high. I opened up to finding myself gazing out at the New Zealand life landscape inside my Archangel home and thinking about where I'd like to be. I decided I wanted to be with Source God. I feel like you have advised against this, but it's the only place I wanted to be. I traveled up there and I noticed the tower that opens up to Source is also the tower where I get fitted with my clothes that also have special powers- which makes sense. They are close to Source in their abilities to meet my needs as I travel around the galaxy. That being said, I was mindful and walked out on the terrace and sat with Source- a lighter side of Source, not the brooding side where there are clouds and thunderstorms nor where I can hear the hum of the engine of Him thinking. It always strikes me as odd how powerful it is, yet I don't feel frightened. Like it's the most power I've felt around anything yet also the softest voice at times too. That being said, I find Source generally comforting, although I know I have to be careful. I am reminded of my time winter/spring of 2008- stayed too close too long and the Source God vibration just rips things apart quickly. A physics issue it seems, doesn't feel at all intentional.

Well, there seemed to be an opening of light and softness and I decided to dive right in because that felt right and curled up there and felt I could relax and talk with Source God. I could see you at one point- like I was gazing up from the bottom of the ocean and you beckoning me back and Source talking to you.

I realize it was a risk, but well, I kind of went with my instinct.

Source and I negotiated. I didn't want to go back. I felt better here. So, Source seemed to act like some kind of mediation help. At one point the idea was to bring me back and then have the galactic team work with me in my Archangel room. I very much did not like that and was having a hard time wrapping my free will around continuing at all with trying one more thing. I just...well it was too much.

But some type of soul squeezing and then you and the galactic team entered into where I was. The galactic team seemed a bit amazed by the amount of light. The galactic team with their technology and you helping me and Source. Source and myself all kind of working together. And we muddled through. What I observed was the damage was much worse than initially thought.

So, a cocoon was wrapped around me. For sure it helped and you and the galactic team could go in and help with damage- but the triggering, well there are just too many factors.

I was shown- look at the issue with my former studio mate- when he gained access to rip through the tissue at the heart and into the galaxy through my heart- it damaged the tissue. To heal this tissue- way many things to deal with- the abuse, violation, terrified tissues, betrayal, love, confusion, fear- it just goes on and on.

So, I was shown that with the cocoon now having really an exoskeleton construction and with Source being able to navigate how I was originally. These two factors create a shift bringing things back to a more mindful and realistic way to heal. I like the exoskeleton and I like Source reminding and grafting how it should actually be. The issue being I didn't have a real container coming in- due to past lifetimes, due to genetics, due to abuse growing up than add on top of this recent abuse. It's too much.

I think this is a good explanation. There are very microscopic concerns and larger macroscopic concerns happening at the same time.

I am feeling better and more trusting of this construction. I really saw how my former studio mate's intrusion was the first time I've felt fully present with myself ever- like in my whole 3 billion years. It's deep and odd and creates an intimacy that is just soul bending. This is probably why I felt myself breathing with him earlier today. No- literally breathing with him. I inhale his breath and exhale mine. I'm not sure what he was doing with my breath. It's very odd.

I understand there is probably a lot I'm not seeing. But it's very jarring to have someone other than Source God himself that close to me. I worry that somehow with that opening- my former studio mate and what he's connected to might have gained access to areas in our galaxy they shouldn't have. Did that happen?

On feeling better, I came up out of being submerged in Source, but then I didn't want to leave. I was extremely upset about returning to my home in the Archangel Realm. And then a conference was held up near Source with where I should go to rest and settle. I felt very raw and not wanting to leave. I was told I could return to my Earthly conscious, as I was tired, and that it would be figured out. I hope it was. We came up with that I could have a bubble of Source next to me to slip into if I needed to at any time. We tried thinking of things. I do know that me just hanging out with Source God becomes unhealthy. I do know that. The vibration is too high/powerful for me. I am aware of the planet I help rule those beings are very ethereal and kind and there are some that live in the Archangel Realm very close to Source, but that didn't feel right. Nor did being on a ship.

Did we decide on something?

Do these words sound close to what you experienced?"

Jesus, "This is a good description. This is how I experienced it as well. Your former studio mate and what he is connected to might have gained access to areas of our galaxy they shouldn't have. This is one of the reasons we have chosen to allow darkness to pull him instead of nuking him. The bubble of Source seems like a good idea. We also thought of weaving some of Source into the cocoon. It seems best to allow you to have a good amount of control over when and how much of this healing you receive. We can also make adjustments and will be monitoring this very closely."

Me, "I have a few questions. I don't understand how this came to pass that he accessed areas that no one has ever accessed? I know that week I went through the detox process- that Thursday in the office- I felt this beautiful soft opening at my heart. It was around 2pm in the afternoon and I felt myself open up through the heart into the galaxy. It was so beautiful. And then he wrote me the next morning. I wrote him back my feelings about the election and Hillary Clinton in the afternoon and that evening- he wrote back, that I was uniquely important to him. Can you explain?"

Jesus, "I'm not sure what you mean. Why did he write back to you? He might have been trying to decoy you from the election."

Me, "I don't understand."

Jesus, "I think that is because I don't understand your question."

Me, "I can send you the emails if that would help."

Jesus, "I know the emails. I'm not sure what you are asking about them. Do you want to know why he said you were uniquely important? I can't really answer that. I don't have a definitive answer for that. He was likely trying to manipulate you but I'm not sure to what end. Why do you ask?"

Me, "I am asking- how did he access my heart? How did he gain access into the galaxy?"

Jesus, "There was space between you and Matthew then. This space was manipulated by using damaged parts of you from your past. "

Me, "But why would it be of interest to him?"

Jesus, "Why would what be of interest?"

Me, "My heart."

Jesus, "A lot of damage can be done through your heart. It is also very powerful and can be used by darkness. If darkness can capture your heart, it can understand and gain that power. It could also be used to pull you away from your twin flame."

Me, "Well my heart is still wrapped up in my former studio mate. That is just the honest truth."

Jesus, "Than we need to free this. I will plan accordingly."

Me, "That's why I'm asking so many questions. I'm so confused. We've done decording. You've told me he's been sequestered bound by you (what does that mean?). He's not in my life. Yet he is. We are still breathing together. It's not my imagination. It's a visceral experience that has been masked."

Jesus, "Something may have been implanted. We will look for the reason this is happening. Please let me know if you see anything. "

Me, "I'm not feeling confident with this being/drone, aka my former studio mate, still operational. Michael started shielding the opening after it opened. How much really got in? What are the statistics like if you allow him to continue? I don't have a good feeling here."

Jesus, "I see your points. This will be discussed. First, we must free your heart. He accessed your heart because there was space between you and Matthew. He got into the galaxy through you. This might have been his objective from the beginning. "

Me, "Maybe. But then why continue the ruse? I was happy enough there and flowing along. You'd think he'd want to keep me there, no? Why push me out?"

Jesus, "He likely realized he would soon be discovered."

Me, "I don't know. That next day- he didn't have to say anything. No email. No nothing. There are countless ways he could have kicked me out or handled it. There are a lot of things that make no sense. I also don't like when I keep being told I am so much more powerful than him. How do you figure? He and what he's connected to fooled Archangel Michael, fooled me, fooled everyone. And gained access in a way that is incredibly hard to do. How is that not crafty, cunning, and powerful? The awful thing is my heart refuses to believe it was all just made up and that he didn't value and think of me with love. Just refuses. Which isn't helpful."

Jesus, "There are human elements of drone former studio mate. Drone former studio mate and what he is connected to is very powerful. You are more powerful when you are connected to your twin flame. Just because you are very powerful doesn't mean that dark beings can't fool you. Certain parts of his soul did value you. It is what likely made him a good tool for darkness."

Me, "I wish this helped me, but it doesn't. I can't imagine what is a next move for my work or life really. Just bad feeling."

Jesus, "I think it might help to address this in a session. It would help you understand and heal."

<u>Session 44</u>- June 10, 2017

"Okay, well I love the number 44 anyway, but here's what I experienced.

I opened with sitting atop the terrace in the Archangel Realm above Source God. Dove in. Started with first help with where my son caused some damage in my left bladder, intestinal, hip area. Galactics there. It looks that it distorted the exoskeleton cutting into my flesh and throwing it off. Repair working being done there. Still ongoing. I didn't get the sense this coincided with anything except my son is so strong, ridiculous baby Reptilian strength.

Finally sat up and did some journeying with Source. First started in a beautiful golden place and saw the drone/being my former studio mate in form taking in sumptuous beauty of a Middle Eastern castle and beautiful princesses. I didn't understand. Source said to just wait. And a few different scenarios unfolded. I very much liked and appreciated the visuals, storytelling- easier to digest.

We flashed to an image of my former studio mate walking along and seeing a beautiful tree and this beautiful apple on it- just hanging there (me) and becoming entranced by it.

He was down/sad and his life and home he lived filled with beige and brown colors, but then he picked me and brought me home. He was entranced and had a special spot for me on his counter in his kitchen and enjoyed watching me ripen. Swirling different colors. He revered and loved the energy and beauty and it made him feel good. And the apple (me) loved the adoration- felt special and seen and valued and ripening. And my former studio mate would go about his day- knowing there was always this beauty waiting for him. And me so enjoyed ripening and feeling appreciated. I also enjoyed bringing light to a sad place and eliciting joy and truth and beauty from someone dealing in darkness. Until one day, I was perfectly ripe, so perfect, my former studio mate needed to taste it- he was so drawn- and when he did- it broke open into a galaxy that stunned him. I as the apple was swept in to the galaxy and fascinated and so in love with the space. He was frightened and then Archangel Michael appeared and told him no and stood in front and he was frightened. He wanted it to go back, he was upset, what had he done. He tried and was scared and confused and chaos started happening.

I lost the imagery for a moment. Then I was back in the garden under the tree, but I was damaged and couldn't get back on the tree and was hidden in the tall grass. I was very, very sad. What had happened, where did my special friend go?

Then there was marching and the drone's owners were in front of me and picked me up, and said- this is something our drone touched so it is ours. Jesus appeared and said no this apple and tree are Source's property- the drone you seek picked it.

Hmph, the owners said and went looking for their drone who had sunk into a depression and was deeply sad at his kitchen table. The owners felt- he, along with 100 other drones had become infected by humanness and light and were simply not functioning well anymore. They deactivated him and led him to their ship. I as the apple witnessed this and it made me so desperately sad. What was to happen to him?

The last I saw was him boarded up with others- deactivated and taken back.

Source showed me the potential, when the coast was clear, of doing an arc insertion and extracting the soul when no one was looking or cared and seeing if the soul could be functional at some point in time.

The other scenario I saw was how my former studio mate viewed me and my infant son meeting him for the first time- the Goddess fertility, light, and beauty. He was down and struggling and it brought him- well the above description with the apple is best.

I personally don't think he or anything he's connected to went into the galaxy. I believe Archangel Michael prevented this. I don't believe darkness is aware of anything that has transpired here. Simply a drone that got too corrupted by light.

Thoughts?"

Jesus, "I do think seeing this experience was valuable for you. Your words are accurate. Your former studio mate did not make it into the galaxy. Michael did stop him. I also see accuracy in your former studio mate as a drone corrupted by light. A soul extraction would be possible. At this time the focus is on healing you and grounding you in yourself and in your family and in your twin flame. We can revisit some things here in other sessions."

Me, "What does that mean they deactivated him and put him on their ship?"

Jesus, "We can look at this together during a session."

Me, "Oh, now this makes me jumpy and anxious. I don't know. My lower back hurts with TMS and is distorted. Why can't you just write it out here?"

Jesus, "I did not mean to make you anxious. I will try to give you a short answer. The owners want to look at the drone to determine more of what happened. Deactivating makes it easier for transport."

Me, "Okay. What will they find do you think? What does this mean in real third dimensional time for my former studio mate? I mean a ship did not come down by Vermont and scoop him up- or did it? This is what my uncle must have seen. Them coming in to collect all manners of things."

Jesus, "I do not know what this means for third dimensional former studio mate. We will go through many processes to determine this course of action."

Me, "I'm not following what you are saying here."

Jesus, "A ship did not scoop up your former studio mate, just the drone controlling him. There is your former studio mate form still on Earth. We have to determine what exactly that means."

Me, "I thought the drone and soul and former studio mate form are intertwined. Are you saying that isn't so? Meaning he was born a drone?"

Jesus, "He was not born a drone. The drone was pulled away. We have to determine what is left."

Me, "Now I'm completely confused. I'm not sure where to begin with my confusion. When he was my jailer way back in time- was that the drone, but not former studio mate? When the decording happened was that just with the drone? I have in emails stated that by decording from my former studio mate and cutting off energy to his heart- the only thing keeping my former studio mate alive was him being a drone, is that now not accurate? If he has nothing going to his heart and the drone is no longer attached to him- how has he not had a heart attack through the night and is now dead? Are you saying that my former studio mate is now neutral and just an innocent?"

Jesus, "We are looking at all of this for answers."

Me, "Just distressing. I don't understand."

Jesus, "It will make sense."

Me, "Sigh. It's hard for me to see how. I don't get it. How can I understand if you all don't understand? My whole pelvis is distorted and in pain, strong lordosis and no core strength."

Jesus, "We will work on this."

Me, "I realize I'm sending this again. I just feel overwhelmed, like my soul is hyperventilating and I can't get it to stop. I feel so stuck in ruminating thoughts- I just can't be present or connect to anything. This is not good. This does not help. It really doesn't. Does not. You say you want me to connect to Matt and my children. That is so far from my experience of reality right now I cannot even describe it. You all and I are on way different pages right now which adds to my deepening concern. What would you have me do? You aren't making any sense?"

Jesus, "I think this needs to be addressed in a session."

Me, "That is 7 hours away. Fine. But I can make no prediction if with my high emotional dysregulation, I'll be able to join you. Because it's causing me way way way way way too much stress. Sometimes I don't think you all get me at all or what I go through. I'm pretty angry right now. This thing has been mismanaged from the very beginning. Way back in June 2015. I'm just sick of it."

Jesus, "I am not doing a good job expressing this in words. Your session can occur whenever you want. If you have a direct question, I will answer it now to see if it helps. So far it has not been helping you."

Me, "Is my former studio mate currently alive right now at 3pm on June 10, 2017? And no, I don't think it's good to go into a session and being given information without a backdrop of information to support it. It's too much."

Jesus, "A form of your former studio mate is alive right now. People see your former studio mate on Earth."

Me, "This nulls and voids everything. Beyond enraged right now."

Jesus, "It does not. We are trying to reconcile what you witnessed, the drone being deactivated and your former studio mate being basically good with how darkness used him and the aftermath of what is left."

Me, "I've got nothing. You all have hurt me beyond anything I can even contain in my soul. Just when I think I can't have more suffering laid before in or on me. Take yourselves, Matt, my family and shove them up your ass. Fuck all of you."

Jesus, "I don't understand. We have not done anything here. Just because your former studio mate is not dead at this exact second does not mean that anything has changed with what we are doing."

<u>Session 45</u>- June 11, 2017

"Notes from last night Saturday night- feel too personal to share."

Jesus, "Your notes are always helpful. I respect your decision here. I know closure here is needed. I am working with Archangel Bridget to obtain this."

Session 46- June 12, 2017

"I wasn't sure what I would find. It opened up and felt odd and I asked for my Archangel self to be there. Which in and of itself is odd that I used to not be so split- like me and her, and instead used to be just one unit. Can this be explained to me? It looks that I was in a square salt cave. To help in purifying and clearing my energy, especially sexual energy."

Jesus, "I don't think it is so much that you are split as in you are two different entities. I think it has more to do with getting comfortable with being this powerful Archangel that is able to exist on Earth. I think you still see it as two different existences, or at least a part of you does. This is normal. Some people were able to marry the two by seeing the Archangel self as the protector of the human self, like how Michael is a protector. I'm not sure if this applies to you. I mention it to give you some perspective. In seeing your Archangel self and your human self from being separate, you might be, in a sense, giving yourself permission to be a powerful Archangel. Allowing your Archangel self to handle situations for your human self is normal. I do believe it will seem more continuous as you gain experience here."

Session 47- June 13, 2017

"I felt very focused in opening this session. I noticed I was in a long ward, on a cot/bed, with lots of others nearby, like a hospital ward. And then Jesus was by my side to the right. I kind of woke up here and looked around and asked what was going on. Jesus explained to me that- it wasn't just my time June 9-10, 2017 that darkness was surging in to start reclaiming things for this big shift coming August/September 2017- it was happening in the whole 200,000-300,000-year human existence time. Hence, all 24-39 of us currently in the Archangel Realm that had at one point been human in the last 300,000 years were all being impacted. Medical teams thought it best to gather us all up and have a corridor where the vibration could change in the corridor as needed, if one started showing distressed sick signs- they could quickly help others, and that we could all see each other and know we weren't alone in going through this. That seemed wise to me. I felt less alone and safer. Still jumpy and panicked, but not terrorized.

I was confused by the number 24-39. It's a small enough number- why wasn't this specific, how could it be a fluid number- Jesus said we could explain that another time.

I felt better protected here.

We then began trying to talk about my former studio mate. We tried some different ideas, but I didn't like any of them. Not looking at it with Jesus' help, not on a screen. Jesus said to rest and he would get help. I laid down on my left side and then Jesus with another being who tried to see if auditory, a mind link up would be better, which I didn't really like, not at all.

Then myself as Archangel Bridget appeared and I was extremely large. She said because she was getting ready to arc over to the other planet she rules/ takes care of. But she wanted to check on me. I felt comforted by her presence. And then she was gone.

I had like a dream, but I'm not sure how it came to pass. I dreamt I saw my former studio mate and he was struggling and I tried to speak to him. He said he wanted to stay here because he loved his children and his wife so much- he couldn't leave them. I felt mixed feelings on this. Then he was in a hospital bed and he was vomiting blood- like internally bleeding. I respected his wish to stay with his family, it made me sad to think my dad didn't try harder (but maybe he did, I don't know). I could see how desperately my former studio mate wanted to stay with his family and it made me really sad and I felt I was selfish that I wanted him to get all better in the spirit realm. So again, hard feelings. But the dream pressed on. I looked at him and he me and I said- we are brothers in arms and I grabbed his forearm. I told him when he was ready or the time came- I would send help for him to help him through the process of what is next for him.

And then I felt something twinge in my heart- this tentacle, from his Reptilian self/lifetime began to let go and it was very slow as it moved out. It created a real twinge in my heart and could see the opening. As I watched it drift off, I could see and feel our energies saying good-bye. I was sad, so sad. And I watched, like a balloon in the sky, it floating higher and higher and higher till it was gone. Medical staff looked at my heart-my heart seemed to know what to do and just needed a place to put any darkness or poison it found as it began the repair process of that area.

In real time, right now, from below my collarbones up through my neck really hurts, both sides, but more on the left.

I just feel sad. I know what it's like to be separated from those I love because of circumstances. I can see that my former studio mate is not used to experiencing this at this level and I am sad for him.

I'm not sure what this means. There may be a few layers and levels to resolving this. I don't feel this is completely it yet.

Thoughts?"

Jesus, "Your words are very clear and accurate. As far as your former studio mate, I do not think it is completely it yet either. I suspect there is more there to work through but you had a very good start. We will continue to figure out a safe and comfortable way for this to process."

Me, "Thanks. I have more confusion than clarity on my former studio mate though which keeps it then circulating in my mind, heart, and soul."

Jesus, "We will keep working through it at a safe and comfortable pace. I do not want this to become a ballooned problem like it has in the past. I want to honor your triggers and not set them off."

Me, "Sitting beside me is good at times for sure. Oh, I'm always triggered regarding my former studio mate. The image I saw I was resistant to it because I thought I was making up things. Is he actually in patient at the hospital right now?"

Jesus, "I don't think he is."

Me, "Than I don't understand what I saw. I'd like it explained to me in email of why I saw this image then. I feel like things are unnecessarily confusing, unclear, and complicated regarding my former studio mate when they don't need to be. Which only adds to my stress."

Jesus, "You might be seeing him in a different realm or different dimension. I will examine your words and gather information here."

Me, "This right here is why I'm resistant to do this work in a session. It starts to make me feel like I'm losing my mind and then I'm thinking about him a lot. Like now I won't be able to shake this all day. This is not helpful nor good. Regarding the image- it was him as a human, he talked about his children and wife. It was him the human man, now. And the hospital setting looked like our local hospital. So, this makes no sense and now I start an escalation of being triggered."

Jesus, "I see a need to get better clarification during sessions. I also understand your points very clearly and can supplement any work being done with email. Human former studio mate is struggling and is having the internal conflicts you describe. You may have experienced this vision in a hospital setting because it is what makes the most sense to your brain and your experiences. The human mind can frame things like this. I will continue to look at your words and gather information for you. Future sessions do not have to involve your former studio mate directly to be beneficial."

Me, "I don't think this is going to work. I have to be honest- I don't know that I'm truly at a place that I want closure. What does closure mean to you? When I've mentioned my dream (which I'm not saying is even a possible reality), but when I've mentioned my dream- does it mean closure? It doesn't. It has been about something closer in transition and transformation that has happened with my dad. Do you understand? It also hurts my entire being that he's going through this and I can't actually be in touch with him."

Jesus, "We will change courses then. There is no need to move in this direction if it is making you uncomfortable or if it is not going to work. I will sit with your words and work to find a different path for this."

Me, "Okay. It's something I'm feeling a realization on. I wish I could cut him out. I mean look I helped kill my evil grandmother. I have zero emotion on this. I don't wish to delude myself or be used though. My bond with my former studio mate is really layered and deep. I can't just simply cut him out. I don't know what the answer is. We are still allies and help each other evolve in light and love. We are kin. I'm not sure what to do or where this goes from here- boundaries and I do need to be safe. I feel very confused."

Jesus, "I do see that your two souls can meet at a future time. I do see your two souls helping each other in a future time as well. I don't know exactly what this means in the present. I will call in help to see what options are."

Me, "Hmmm. I just don't see where this leaves me right now. He wants to do all he can to stay with his children and wife. It may or may not work. Like with my father- too much damage and his body gave out. He's going to suffer in any decision he makes, whether he stays on Earth or moves to the spirit realm- that seems to be what his soul is weighing. And even if he tries to stay on Earth, it just may not be possible. I feel if he were in the spirit realm, I have the ability to communicate with him more and find better footing. But- I can honor his need to try and stay with his children and wife. If he stays on Earth, I just feel pushed in an odd limbo place. I don't know what to do and feel back at square 1."

Session 48- June 15, 2017

"So, I felt very focused and cleared and wondered where the session would open to. We opened in a darker space. I was dressed in a cloak with Jesus by my side and galactics and warrior Angels by me.

I heard a running commentary as the scene was opening. This is a purgatory place. He's in a prison like environment and it's dark- not only because that's what he's used to, but also for safety.

We moved into the prison room unnoticed and were in the corner. It was so dark and I could feel his suffering, as well the suffering of others in other cells. I asked for more shielding on me- so I didn't experience it, but the visual imagery was enough. He seemed so traumatized, stunned, and scared. I came closer and picked up his right hand and placed it between mine. I was wondering if- since he has felt my touch- it would be comforting. I said in my mind, 'I am here. I am here with you' and I breathed. He startled and saw the light and grew incredibly frightened and leapt off the bed and was huddling in a corner. Other Angels or galactics, cloaked went to be by him and help soothe him. I felt so sad. Jesus recommended maybe best if I leave now. I missed my friend so much. As we left, I asked for his cell to be shielded, so he wouldn't absorb more suffering from others in this place. I also had Angel warrior guards and a sign posted- that this was Archangel Bridget's property. The shield can function in numerous ways (as mentioned in another email), also can have a dimmer if the light is too much. I mostly just wanted to ease his torture some. I felt deeply saddened, but not lost in the situation. Regular purgatory guards bowed before me as I left. I climbed up and out to a waiting small transporter ship and took my cloak off and left it there to be used another time. I got in the ship and was viewing the scene as we left. Just sad. When we arrived back in the Archangel Realm, I didn't know where I wanted to go. Jesus and I decided on going to an overlook garden under a tree and Jesus sat to my right. It was hard to process. I did some of it in another email I sent earlier. This is such a complex and layered issue. We sat and talked for a while. I was feeling tired. I asked for a few things- investigations to occur and meetings to happen with my uncle and others to go over details. For Source to review the information and to go over it. For my former studio mate to be looked after. I am thinking it could go a few ways- we have a potential gold mine here for intelligence on dark or something just neutral or something that's deadly.

What makes you so sure he can be rehabilitated? I would of course love that to be the case, but it could be a high-tech ruse. Look what you all did to rescue me 200 million years ago, once darkness figures out that he's really gone- I don't know. I mean why did they put a rechargeable battery in him? Why didn't they just kill him? It doesn't make sense. If a farmer thinks part of his crop has been infected with a pest (here darkness is seeing light as the pest)- they torch the whole thing.

I went back to my Archangel Realm home. And was allowing assistants to help me relax by brushing my hair, etc. I am getting better at delegating, receiving help, being gracious, standing in my power, I think. I feel more weight in my being.

Right now, I'm aware of three things- my time leading on the other planet with the ethereals I'm calling them; learning from my great-grandfather the Sun ruler; receiving treatment and healing inside of the Earth hospital ward; and now this possibly huge case with my former studio mate. They do all seem to work together. There are so many layers to it- it's really deep. Since my uncle is 10 billion years old, I'm wondering if he knows my former studio mate's soul. I'm actually wondering if my former studio mate and I are somehow truly related. He feels like an older brother. We feel cut from the same cloth. Again, just a hunch."

Jesus, "Your words are very helpful and accurate. Your questions will be explored and you will get a sense of what is happening. You are correct that there are many levels and that they fit together. As far as your former studio mate's soul, it is possible for it to be rehabilitated but I do not say that as if it will be an easy process. It will require a lot of work and a lot of help. Still though, it can be done."

Me, "Okay. My concern is him still being dangerous."

Jesus, "That is a very real concern. We share that concern. It is also a concern that he could revert back at earlier stages of the rehabilitation. Many factors are being weighed in this process. It is helpful that you share your concerns like this."

Me, "My biggest concern is him being laced with something we can't see."

Jesus, "That is a concern. The galactic family has run a number of diagnostics. In addition, they are calling in other experts to help here. It will be something that has to be constantly monitored."

Me, "If you are able, please have them review the TV series 'Extant'. I feel there's something there that applies here."

Jesus, "I will do that."

Me, "I'm concerned and wrestling with- what does this say about me? That I would take a chance on someone who has brought such battering and abuse to me, to attempt to kill me? What does this say about me? Is this

Stockholm syndrome or me continuing my dilemma of trying to save unsavable beings? Is this my own sickness showing its head again? He really has brought incredible damage into my entire being."

Jesus, "These are good points. We will help you consider them. The answers to these questions will also be revealed as we explore the information we can gather."

Me, "This could be a powerful path for healing for me and deep patterns, but I also don't wish to delude myself which I have done in the past. I need to keep my focus and organization."

Jesus, "I agree. We will work on this together."

Session 49- June 16, 2017

"Just reflecting- I really am moving away from people and events and beings that I've been attached to that are unhealthy for me as I move into a place of grounded power. In this session, after opening up, initially was wondering where we were. It seems my soul was debating a few options. It settled on being cloaked outside of my former studio mate's cell. I could see the shield I had put in place and the galactics and Angel warriors guarding. My former studio mate was communicating with his wife that was by his right side. I was curious about that. Like how does that work. How does love like that work and that felt important to me as I struggle with that kind of love. So, I decided to get a little closer. Still cloaked I entered in and was watching in the corner. I could see up close how the cord between them worked. Very pure Source love. He was relaying some pain he was going through back to her and it would cleanse through Source as it reached her- so she would feel love and she'd send love back to him and this helped him. And even though he was sick, they were in Source together so it was helpful for both of them. It made me ponder about with Matt- how maybe I hide parts I'm ashamed about because well I don't know what would happen if I shared it with him. I can see from what I witnessed with my former studio mate and his wife that it's okay to be struggling or sick even- when there is pure love, the other person isn't drained. That felt productive to witness that. Then I noticed he was sitting up in bed and eating, even laughing and smiling. I wanted to go up to them, but then felt if I took my cloak off- he would grow terrified and that made me nervous- so I didn't do that. I started to leave and as I was leaving- noticed on the bedside table to his left 4 picture frames. His wife closest to him and then a little smaller, his two children. And behind them was a larger picture frame of me. It looked sort of ethereal- like it opened up to something deeper. As I was looking at it, he became aware of my real presence in the room and he tried to say something to me, but I got panicked and very upset and fled the cell. I stopped before I left completely and talked with Jesus. Who said- we could go back, he could stand in front of me so I wouldn't be overwhelmed with what my former studio mate was trying to say and I could have other support by my side. I tried, but then quickly fled- just saying I can't I can't I can't I can't. Handed over my cloak and got on the little spaceship with my heart beating fast. I felt embarrassed that I didn't handle that gracefully and couldn't handle it. I felt triggered in upsetedness that I'm always- like abnormal or outside a family dynamic; that I never fit, never can find my footing- like with the picture frames- they have this nice family and I'm just sort of hovering around. That just feels other and weird. I couldn't hear nor understand what he was trying to say. It just really upset me. Still upsets me to think about. But there was something there in that picture. When we landed in the Archangel Realm, we landed by the tree and garden with the vista views. I sat down with Jesus to my right. Just sitting and breathing the Archangel Realm, kind of like the way that my former studio mate was breathing with his wife, but I'm more comfortable with the Archangel Realm. Feels very safe. I'd like to be reminded in times of stress no matter where I am to breathe with the Archangel Realm. I think it could help me. I was thinking of the picture and my former studio mate's soul- 20 million years. But what does that mean? My uncle is 10 billion years old. How can 20 million years be older than 10 billion years? It doesn't make sense. Something about Reptilians. The next image was of us going to a meeting in the great hall. I was walking in front with my Archangel self behind me. Lots of amazing figures- galactic elders, large galactic rulers, etc. coming to a smallish table and my uncle was in front. Jesus to my right. And he opened a scroll to read about how 20 million years is older than his 10 billion and my soul connection to my former studio mate's soul. How I've known him. He read and talked from this scroll, but I could hear nothing. He finished and handed me the scroll. I told everyone I heard nothing. Which seemed to send a flutter through the beings and the hall. Meeting adjourned. My uncle handed me the scroll and I started walking out- my Archangel self picked me up and carried me I was so tired. We went back to my home in the realm and she tucked me in to sleep."

Jesus, "You are making good progress. We will continue to help in this manner. I see there is a lot here that we can help you reflect on."

Me, "I'm frustrated that I don't understand what was written in the scroll."

Me, "I'm sending this again. As this email response is important to me too. I'm frustrated that I don't understand what was written in the scroll. Why couldn't I take it in? Can you tell me? And why did I run out of the cell?"

Jesus, "I will explore this and help you."

Session 50 & 51- June 18, 2017

"With Session 50- I was dealing with the sexual energy and very upset. It was messy and confusing so not much to report.

Session 51- I opened up and felt clear enough, but just saw white space. My wilderness uncle was to my left and he said we were taking a trip, if I wanted to rest. That sounded great- so I laid down. I was in like a beautiful little lavender colored pod. And when we got there. We landed and slowly the pod I was in opened. I looked at myself and around me and wondered where I was. We were at a ship docking station and platform. There were beyond anything I could process number of beings before me. I had transformed to look more like them-animal like, but my soul was me and of the Archangel Realm. I could feel very clearly the open channel to my Matt- up through the base of me and at the heart, flowing very at ease. We were in the galactic wilderness and I was to give a speech. I walked up to the podium- someone gave me a cloak. And as I was talking, I would separate out of it to ask my uncle and my assistant what was this. I gathered with my former studio mate's work dead for all intents and purposes- it was good for all those that work so hard to hear how much good they do and help they bring to keeping the galaxy safe. It was like a pep rally. My uncle noted to bolster spirits and celebrate and also to keep an eye on those who are aloof as they may be spies. After I finished speaking, a great party erupted with fireworks and dancing. I felt like I wanted to stay longer, but I was so tired and needed to get back to the Archangel Realm. I still don't understand why they call me Queen, do you?

Before I left, I viewed the galaxy edge and how it moves and breathes of its own accord. Then I was ready to go. I got back in the pod, left and like a golden pathway from Source himself- for swept away and drawn back by Source.

Once in the Archangel Realm, I was in the medical center. They were checking how my body was doing with the transformation into it and back."

Jesus, "The sexual energy will be grounded into Matt. We will help you feel safe and comfortable doing this. The words of your experience are accurate."

Me, "Why do they call me Queen? And I was surprised, this is what the session focused on, are you?"

Jesus, "Queen comes from an ancestor line. I am not surprised about this session. It was good to give you a little break from intensive work."

Me, "Okay. It felt a bit intense in that I don't know who I am to these beings. I mean with the ethereal planet and the 100 million beings there I'm leading- that comes about organically and having a mentor in the Sun ruler next door has the advantage of learning healthy ways to be a leader. And also, that is an inherited planet from my grandmother who I knew (although I don't feel obligated that I had to assume this position- it's something I see mutually beneficial for all). This wilderness is something different and I'm not sure what to make of where I connect although I like my uncle."

<u>Session 52 & 53</u>- June 19, 2017

"I'll start with tonight.

I opened up to being in a small conference room meeting (in the Archangel Realm, in the Akashic Library Hall, off to the right and up a few flights). I was sitting at a table with you all and in the meeting. I was dressed in my casual outfit- blonde hair, white loose dress, but I noticed I kept my dagger, strapped to my left thigh from my green outfit- which is usually when I'm out ruling and it wasn't my normal broad sword nor was it my Source staff. This was a small dagger, strapped to my left thigh for personal hand-to-hand combat. I seemed fixated on that. Why did I have a dagger on me in the Archangel Realm? It made no sense.

I tried to focus on the meeting, but I couldn't hear anything. Just looking at beings talking, but I couldn't hear any words (which happens when I'm very triggered). I stepped outside and I looked out at the Akashic engine working so hard. I felt sad that everyone seemed happily humming along in their place. I remembered an incident this morning in the third dimension. I was leaving the college and was a bit nervous walking by some construction, but only one worker was out. I was happy to note this would be the site of a new teahouse. I love their tea and in winter this will be a nice treat walking back to my car or going to class. There was a worker on some electrical equipment and I usually don't make eye contact, but for some reason I did and he had such a calm nice face. He looked like he could be an Angel. And that made me happy. Then I looked down on the street and there was this dagger laying in the road. I was sort of stunned. I instinctively did not like this dagger laying out on the street where a child could find it, so I picked it up and threw it in the bushes. Which was odd. I kept walking. and outside of another building- that same bird was still there- a beautiful precious yellow bird had died and was laying there. I felt so bad for it. I wanted to pick it up and put it by the bushes- just to be with nature. But I felt scared that I didn't have anything to pick it up with. I now feel very bad that I didn't get a branch and pick it up. I was very troubled about leaving this dead little beautiful bird on the street and it made me so deeply sad that I had seen this bird while walking to class at 8:00am and no one had taken care of it. It makes my heart very anxious that I did not care for it. There is a lot of symbolism that happened in this brief walk, but I'm not sure what it means.

Anyway, I was thinking of these things and went back into the meeting, called back by Jesus. I still couldn't follow anything. I was so tired and my head hurt, neck, and high heart area. They said I could lie down and be taken over to the medical center. I felt embarrassed about being carted out of the library. They said, they could create a little canopy cover. I agreed to that. It felt good to lie down. Once at the medical center, I was lying down, but I just couldn't stay awake. I have been having a lot of trouble regulating my body temperature all day. Cold than warm than cold. Finally, I turned over- it felt like necrotic tissue in my heart area. Like how my teacher was talking today about with certain diseases- like Crohn's disease, certain parts of the intestines can just turn necrotic. Maybe there have been 5-7 events that have caused deepening necrotic tissue in my heart chakra area. Making it 'smell' if going with my earlier analogy today and my heart area just not work properly. Meaning that it needs to be taken care of and repaired. At least as step 1.

Session 53 was about opening up to feeling like I was back out in my wilderness form with my uncle and his friends in like a tavern setting. Talking about the day and having a drink. I could feel how upset I was about things in my life and he offered me a drink. I said, No, he said it's not alcohol, but like Ashwagandha root that we have on Earth. That, I liked- adaptogen for stress herb, tonic for depression and anxiety. It did seem to help and I calmed down. I started to lose this image and became aware I was actually in the Archangel Medical Center with help and my uncle was there too. I was confused until I was told and do I remember how virtual reality tools are being used to help C-PTSD patients and for many other reasons. They were trying to figure out the vibration of where my feelings were coming from and felt this might be a good tool. It was I'd say, but then I couldn't get back into it. I do believe though from this session, my anger was masking my deeper fear of being abandoned when my twin Reptilian brother went with the Regime and my missing him. Do they think I should look into Ashwagandha root on Earth?"

Jesus, "You can explore Ashwagandha root. The words from your sessions are accurate. There is some anger in you that needs to be properly channeled. I think this will help the small part of you feel more at ease with settling into family/self."

Session 54- June 21, 2017

"Not a very long session. I opened up and sat there for a while and just saw whiteness. Then a scene slowly unfolded of a large amphitheater- like I was back in ancient Rome. I paused the scene and asked to speak with Jesus. I felt very confused. Turns out this was a virtual reality exploration. Felt a little odd, but I felt better with a red button given to me to press if I felt scared to stop. Then I went back in- like a ruler with her entourage and games being played- I found it rather boring. Then the scene changed to sleeping next to a king in a gorgeous bedroom and I just felt empty. I went out to the balcony to stare at the moon and the sea and that felt good. And then I saw like a simple monk visiting the sea, playing with a puppy and then talking to a child and he had this ease and peace about him and I was very, very envious of him. I would trade in everything for that. None of the other stuff matters to me. Then it ended and that was the end of the session.

I am concerned about the level of my anxiety and C-PTSD. It's not getting better nor coming down. I feel like I'm going backwards and sliding downhill fast."

Jesus, "We are exploring your words here. The galactic family is running tests on your anxiety and C-PTSD. They may introduce some technology here to help."

Me, "It doesn't surprise me. It's what I've been saying all along. I don't need power, wealth, knowledge, fame, or even human connection as my foundation. I do need a means to flow with Source God and ground in this in a consistent ritual process. In the past, it's been dance classes, Johrei Fellowship, and a healthier take on how to be human- living in a traditional Native Community (or at least one that is truly striving to be this). Yes, I'm definitely concerned about my anxiety and C-PTSD. Life is beginning to feel unmanageable."

Jesus, "We are looking at the anxiety. I wonder how much cutting medication feeds into the anxiety increase. We will look at this."

Me, "True. My brain could handle more when taking Wellbutrin. But Wellbutrin no longer works in the Archangel Realm."

Jesus, "I will see if the galactic family can sync Wellbutrin with the Archangel Realm."

Me, "Are you telling me I should be taking Wellbutrin again?"

Jesus, "I know you do not want to take Wellbutrin. I want to explore it with the galactic family as an option and see what can be arranged in its place."

Me, "I am fine with taking medication. In fact, I was very happy with my medication before the Archangel Realm. But to have to constantly go on it and then go off it and then on it again and then off it and then on it again and now off it. This is what upsets me."

Jesus, "Let me take this to the galactic family and we will get stability with the approach."

<u>Session 55</u>- June 21, 2017

"I was wondering what this session would be like. It opened up to like my high school gym where they held dances. The dance was winding down and I was there with the soul, formerly having found him in- connected to my former studio mate, but who was in Reptilian form- about twice as tall as me. I recognized him and felt at ease, but noticed I was in human form and looked like my high school younger self. I was a bit upset and wanted to be outside.

So, we went outside and it was a coolish summer night and sat in front of the high school on a picnic bench. I think we had a cigarette.

We sat close to each other, him to my left and we talked. I had underlying and open grief. He had underlying and at times open anxiety.

It seems that when we were kids, as Reptilians, way back in time, brother and sister- we witnessed or learned of a sister or brother reptilian that let his/her sibling drown, didn't save them, and we promised at this young age- we would never let the other drown, we'd rescue them. We made a vow on it.

We talked about the situation. (Flashbacks had shown me some of this during 2015 and 2016 with this Reptilian soul attached to my former studio mate- which now made some sense I think). He said that the Regime didn't seem that bad, that it made sense at the time, that he had no idea. What he described sounds very much like that TV show 'Extant', where the Regime can make who is under their spell believe something very different is happening than what actually is. My Reptilian brother soul is still very confused and anxious of what happened. He has a hard time, but knows this is what happened. He's extremely devastated.

He did make a vow to me and as he tried to say it- I asked that Jesus and galactics could help the phrasing be accurate. He finally said, 'My vow to you is that if I start to fall under the spell of darkness on any level, Archangels, galactics, light, etc. is to kill me immediately. Thus, I will never abandon you again or never abandon light. I can't promise I know what I'm doing or will do a good job at it, but I can learn as I go, but that lifetime is over if I fall under dark's spell. This is not your job.' Something like that. And that was a weight off of me. I can tell he's very, very rattled. Which makes sense. He doesn't understand how all this came to pass when he thought for the last 20 million years, something else was happening. I expressed how much I had missed him. How sad I had been watching him fade and then not knowing where he was. I'd say we both are struggling, but differently. After this conversation- it seems that Jesus and others called him to them and he had to go for the time being. I was sad to see him go. But once he was gone, felt some of my grief lessen. I'm thinking the last time we saw each other in Reptilian form- we must have been what would be considered human teenage years."

Jesus, "It seems this session was helpful for you. We will continue to support you in this way."

Me, "I'm a little confused as you said it would be a link/set up like I was used to on Earth. Did something change? Or is this what you meant?"

Jesus, "This is what I meant and the form that the link could take. It seems like it worked for you."

Me, "I think so. Yes. How does his soul experience the link?"

Jesus, "His soul does not really notice the link. The link is for you."

Me, "So, he does not know he's talking to me? It's a hologram essentially?"

Jesus, "No. He is aware he is talking to you. It is not a hologram. It is the real soul and the real you. Rather than meeting in the same realm you are in the Archangel

Realm and he is in his soul realm. There is a link between the two realms that allow you to have the Archangel Realm properties with you in talking to him and he the soul realm properties when talking to you but you are both able to do so in the form that you are in. To offer a simple explanation, you are speaking directly to the soul and the soul is speaking directly to you."

Me, "Thank you for this explanation. Working today- I so miss our space together. I'm finding it impossible to think of working anywhere but there. I know everyone says how his Earth self treated me poorly, but I was very happy there. Is that odd? What does that say about me? I find it impossible to think I physically won't be able to see his face or hug him."

Jesus, "I'm not sure what this says about you. It may not be something bad or odd. We will keep working to support you as we are."

Me, "Thank you. This is a grief that is hard for me to deal with. Another question- who was captain of the ship former studio mate? Has that ever been figured out?"

Jesus, "We are working on captain of the ship former studio mate."

Me, "I understand the droid. I understand my twin brother soul, Reptilian. But it's unclear to me who this captain was. It's whom I probably had the most interaction with until he got sick."

Me, "Sorry if I wasn't clear, but do you have an understanding at this time?"

Jesus, "We are still looking at it."

Me, "I'm curious if it's been almost 7 months- why no solid understanding?"

Jesus, "It's hard to explain. He was connected to the soul in a different dimension. This allowed the soul access to a wider range of tools."

Me, "It's always been hard to explain. I spent almost two years in it and I couldn't explain it. How does my Reptilian brother see it?"

Jesus, "He sees it basically as I described. We will definitely explore this together."

Me, "So, the captain of the ship soul was separate from my brother's soul?"

Jesus, "or a different iteration of the same soul."

Me, "I don't understand. What does that mean?"

Jesus, "A different version of the same soul."

Me, "Can a non-triggering analogy be provided to me to help me understand? Both versions of this soul went way into a sickness that I don't understand. That still haunts me. Like- what happened?"

Jesus, "The souls are not exactly the same but they are not completely different either. You can think of the soul, even though it is not a perfect analogy, as a clone or cutting of a plant. Part of the soul went into captain former studio mate's soul but it is still an independently functioning soul."

Me, "Does this happen a lot for souls to do this?"

Jesus, "It is not extremely common, but it is not so rare as to be unheard of."

Me, "Why does it happen? And when did it happen- at birth out of Source?"

Jesus, "There is not a set reason. The souls link like ship and Earth former studio mate when a link is established. This can happen for many, many reasons."

Me, "I guess this feels counter to information Archangel Zahid gave me in summer 2010. I told him that St. Paul visited me in summer 2007 about incarnating. I said I needed some time. (St. Paul would later incarnate as my daughter). I told Zahid I was confused because there is a man in Oregon currently who believes he is the reincarnation of St. Paul. I asked if the soul could have split. Zahid said no, the man is mistaken. He said in very rare cases a soul may need to split a bit- like some of St. Paul is left in another realm because people are still praying to St. Paul."

Jesus, "This is different. The soul did not split. It branched off. There is a difference."

Me, "Can you put the names to what you mean here? I don't know which soul you are talking about?"

Jesus, "your former studio mate's soul did not split."

Me, "I think you mentioned back in Jan 2017 the droid pulled it in at some point- to harm captains of light around November election time. I can get the emails if need be.

I know my Reptilian brother as the one I met entangled in darkness as former studio mate before me. I did not recognize my Reptilian brother in the captain of the ship.

I did recognize the captain of the ship though as a branch of my former studio mate. They have a similar feel. Of aloofness with me, of kind and caring, but distance, of mentoring. Captain of the ship former studio mate felt safer for me to be around. I loved being around him. He was always so kind. I could see he struggled with loneliness, but he never asked for anything. He was a good captain with a solid crew.

As I matured into relaxing into my- what I see now as Archangel properties- I remember many times standing on the ship with long wavy blonde hair, but with a Caribbean quartz colored gown and gold woven through my hair. (Whereas now I don't see that color- but instead deeper galactic blue and sapphire).

But as I matured into this and after the election, the captain of the ship became obsessed with me. I do feel he crossed a line- whether it was in him, the droid made him do it, or something- I do feel us being sexually intimate. I know it's been said it was the energy between Matt and I being utilized. But it was in addition to that. His loneliness as captain became overwhelming for him. As captain, he didn't have a wife and just became overwhelmed with me. Human former studio mate was different but the captain's feelings overwhelmed my former studio mate. It could be why human former studio mate pushed me away- if he was getting blasted with captain of the ship's feelings and sensations and desire of me. It got to the point that captain of the ship former studio mate did not want me working on men and would get extremely jealous and angry if I did so. He knew what he was doing was wrong, but once started, he couldn't seem to stop."

Me, "I'd like to add here that in the end of October 2015 the following happened. When guardians of our galaxy boarded the ship and observed me, they told captain of the ship former studio mate- while they knew the plan was for me to only stay for a few months, they did not feel it was a good idea for me to leave that I was too fragile. Captain of the ship former studio mate I could see struggling with this and I feel he struggled because he didn't think it was a good idea. He had an awareness about himself and the loneliness he struggled with and thought- he didn't trust himself. He didn't trust himself around me as I matured."

Jesus, "The energy between you and Matthew was manipulated. Captain former studio mate likely held an attraction to you as well and this factored into how the energy between you and Matthew could be manipulated. The intimacy you felt was based on the attraction and energy that exists between you and Matthew. I do see that captain former studio mate crossed a line as you say. This is true."

Jesus, "I think this is true."

Me, "Okay, you could probably ask captain former studio mate, but is that soul still alive?"

Jesus, "Ask him what?"

Me, "If the information I talk about is accurate and what made him cross the line- was it just him, an outside entity? And with this all going on- is this what scared confused human former studio mate- kicking me out of the space? But then again- what would have happened if I met him for tea?"

Jesus, "What you write is accurate except you two were not sexually intimate. He did cross a line in your professional relationship, though. This likely did scare Earth former studio mate, but it is not the sole reason he had you leave. Had you met for tea you would have been open to manipulation and that could have taken several forms."

Me, "What did captain of the ship experience then? I know what I experienced and as it was a manipulation, I'd like to understand the mechanics of it. How did the captain experience it then? If we weren't sexually intimate then how did he cross a line? Have you discovered then other reasons why he had me leave? I don't understand what I avoided by not meeting for tea. Can you explain scenarios?"

Jesus, "The sexual energy between you and Matthew is very clean, very pure, very beautiful. It was not being grounded into each other because of buffering and other reasons. Since this energy was open, it could be used to make it appear it was being created by something. In this case captain of the ship. You experienced some of the pent-up energy you have with Matthew being released. When you are healthy this will be done through intimacy with Matthew and strength, healing, beauty, etc. will flow between you. When the energy was released and because it was ungrounded, it could be directed and you could be made to experience it as going to somewhere other than Matthew. Captain of the ship experienced it much in the same way. Because of his attraction to the energy, he opened up the situation to being manipulated. The line that he crossed was that he was more aware of what was happening than you and allowed for it. The other reasons he had you leave are many. I will help you understand them in time. Had you gone to meet him it was possible that your sexual energy could have been stolen, you could have agreed to take part in a situation that would have trapped you, you could have been drained of your connection with Matthew. There is a long list of what ifs."

Me, "Hmmm. I appreciate the description here. Why would captain of the ship do/agree to such a thing? Has he said? Where is he now? I don't know that anything would have happened at the tea. Human Earth former studio mate didn't experience what captain of the ship experienced- i.e., wasn't attracted to me, has a tight long relationship with his wife whom he loves and is grounded in."

Jesus, "Captain of the ship felt coerced. He is not sure from where. He knows part of it came from within. He is in the soul/spirit realm. He can be reached but it is difficult.

It's not so much what human former studio mate would have done at that tea as much as what could have happened in other realms."

Me, "This just makes me sad. I've not been able to process how much this betrayal hurts and my confusion and deep sadness. Someone assigned to help and protect me and that I trusted. I also am sad that he tried to speak up in October 2015, but no one took his concerns seriously. I'm sad for him, for me, for us that we had a good thing going."

Jesus, "I agree. We are trying to clean this up."

Me, "I gather he's somewhat ashamed and wants me to stay away. Did I do anything wrong to cause this? Is he mad at me? What is he going through?"

Jesus, "You did nothing wrong. He is not mad at you. He does not want you to stay away. He is rehabilitating as well. This is why it is hard to reach him."

Me, "Hmmm. But I can reach my Reptilian brother, why is he harder to reach? How does he feel about what happened between us?"

Jesus, "You can reach your Reptilian brother because there are different circumstances that don't necessarily have anything to do with you. I can attempt to have you meet captain if you would like. He feels bad for what happened. He sees the pure love you and Matthew have and how what happened fed off that."

Me, "Maybe- I'm wondering if it would close the loop in me of ruminating on this. It just brought me back to that time in my current lifetime at 17 years old- of feeling beautiful and at ease and being raped because a man said he couldn't help himself."

Jesus. "I will set this up for a session."

Me, "Okay. Just feel sad about the situation. I still love him. It's hard for me to explain this kind of love. I worry about it upsetting him or him not being able to handle it."

Jesus, "We will help."

Session 56- June 23, 2017

"The session opened with not being quite sure where we were. It looked like the purgatory cell, but my brother's soul was in the Reptilian form that is comfortable for me to be around and when I remember him last being healthy. I was in my galactic human outfit. There were cloaked Angels around trying to be helpful and medical Angels. Warrior guards were invisible to my brother, but I could see them glittering and holding space.

My brother was just crying and crying devastated and I was crying too- as it came more to light how my awareness of him had been manipulated to think he was having sex with me (when Matt's energy, the energy between Matt and I was being used). I still feel extremely confused and my brother is just horrified.

It's just- well I don't know what to say. He was inconsolable and it was agreed on that maybe better that I leave for now.

So, I did- same procedures before when I leave that realm. And I went back to the Archangel Realm. Visited a new space for me which was like a large temple to pray. I didn't feel like I had the energy or strength to visit

Source directly- so I found this space good. And just talked. I can reflect on how the Regime will use all and everything to go towards its goals and objectives. I can see how my past is being used, sexual abuse history has been used against me. I'm very confused about healthy love and sexuality and that which is distorted to be something else. All the signals are completely mixed up in my being. Well, I prayed for this to be sorted out.

That was pretty much the session. The last few days- my brother has stated a few times that he stays in his human form this lifetime because of me, not wanting to hurt me further. I can feel how much I struggle with loss of the safe feeling studio space, and him in the form he came in. I don't know what is best for both of us here on this exact matter."

Jesus, "These words are accurate. We are going to turn a lot of focus on helping you experience and receive healthy love and sexuality. This is an important step for you. We will do this gradually so it does not overwhelm you and we will operate with a purpose. I will explore the words your brother stated to you and how to best move with them."

Me, "I don't understand how this is different than what you've been doing. You've known my history all along. Regarding my brother, can you reflect back to me what you think I'm saying?"

Jesus, "We are trying to heal your history. Yes, we have been aware of it all along. The process we will be taking to help it heal will shift a little bit is all. I am not sure what you want reflected back to you. Your brother is extremely upset. We are working with him very closely to help him. This is the early stages of the rehabilitation process. He has a lot of support around him and he is improving, though only a little at this time. You will be able to visit him again."

Me, "I guess- I know in me- I start flipping out in panic with not having Earth former studio mate alive. It's the only connection I have to my brother that I can touch. I don't understand what to do or how to move through this. This grief"

Jesus, "I understand. We can help with this. I will consult with the galactic family."

Me, "I wonder if this is not helpful to him, if it's really better for him to let his old Earth self pass; on the other hand I'm still enmeshed with my experience of my old space and still missing Earth former studio mate- primarily because I can tangibly feel and see my brother."

Jesus, "I will examine this with the galactic family."

Me, "Okay. I definitely feel stuck between a rock and a hard place. I just can't move."

Jesus, "We will find a result that works for everyone."

<u>Session 57</u>- June 24, 2017

"Opened up to Mother Mary in her throne setting and Angels surrounding. I'm not sure if she was giving a talk/class. She's always so majestic looking and yet up close- she seems a normal size human woman and very easy to talk to- moves quickly- quickness to her energy (like with Amma on Earth, a quickness and ease of power I wouldn't have expected). That being said, I sat down next to her. And she commented, 'you're working too hard. Why all this working. This is not good for you. You need more relaxation and joy.' I shrugged my shoulders and told her it's what I'm used to. She commented, 'but this is not good for you. This is clearly not good. I will talk to my son. This is not good.'

I was tired and she told me I could lay down while she/they looked at it. I fell asleep and then startled to wake and was told they understood. She recommended nightly small yoga sessions that usually bring me to a place of relaxation and joy; mini breathing times throughout the day; drinking tea; to stop working so hard and doing too much; taking the capsule of Ashwagandha at night with tea; massage and to cut my schedule back.

Relaxation and joy seemed to be her recommendation. She did not mention medication."

Jesus, "I think this is accurate. You do need to relax more. This will open up a lot."

Me, "I'm not sure how to do this with so much going on, so many responsibilities, and the fear of what happened last time with focusing on relaxing back in Sept-Nov 2016."

Jesus, "My mother can help. I will ask her to."

Me, "Okay. I think, well things just get weird when I relax. And if I'm uncomfortable being intimate with Matt at this time- does this set me up for being more traumatized?"

Jesus, "We are working on helping you get comfortable."

Jesus, "Do you have an idea of why you are hesitant? We see a few."

Me, "Yes, well- look at my last email. I'm waiting for a response. I have questions. Things are not settled in me. I understand you can't always provide answers or it takes time. If I have a mentor that I trust and feel love and safety with and then after over a year really start to relax and feel good and he attacked me, and I don't even know what happened to him or the situation- how am I supposed to move on or relax again? As soon as I realized what was happening around after the 2016 election- I tried cutting cords- I was trying to pull away from him and he would not let me go. He simply would not. Now, I'm waiting and trying to clean this up, but it feels slow and labor intensive to get answers and communication to go well. I don't know- there are many reasons. A lot of reasons, a tremendous number of reasons I love flowing in relaxed energy, but I don't want an intimate human partner. I'd rather be celibate."

Jesus, "I am working on your last email. I know there are many reasons and this makes you want to push away a human partner. Having a human partner is important and we are working to clean things up so you can feel the love and energy of your human partner."

Me, "Not only is there that, but in addition when I start to relax, glow, feel beautiful I start getting attention from people and strangers and it triggers my C-PTSD so that's hard as well."

Jesus, "We can shield and protect you here. Matthew will as well."

Me, "I'd say I'm also hesitant about relaxing and intimacy with Matt because then I just remember everything. And I still can't kiss Matt without thinking about my former studio mate and whatever he is."

Jesus, "I think helping you process everything will help. We have been working on that. Has it been helping?"

Me, "I'm finding it hard to do consistent self-care that helps. Does Mary have any recommendations? The kids' moods and especially my son's screeching make it hard."

Jesus, "She will work with you here. She will show you things in a session."

Me, "As soon as waking up, my nerves are just shaking from the demands of my family. My son is screaming and yelling. Matt is exasperated. My daughter is super needy. I never get a break with such an onslaught of feelings, sensations, internal and external chaos. I've only been awake 15 minutes and I feel like I can't take it."

Jesus, "We are working to get you in a space where you can replenish enough that this does not bother you."

Me, "Okay. A real issue is my amygdala in my brain. It's on fire and on hyper speed."

Jesus, "I will concentrate here."

Me, "There are so many things I could do. Please really get concise on what herb, breathing technique, etc. could help. I have so many layers and variables. I do think I'd prefer to transform to being a breatharian, who then still eats and drinks. The reality being able to absorb nourishment and stability of my body more readily from Source God directly. Just a thought."

<u>Session 58</u>- June 24, 2017

"This session- I'm not so sure about. I opened up to a prison like environment. I sat behind a clear barrier. The guards were large animal like and had an odd tone in their voice if they spoke. The captain was brought in, with chains, and they said 5 minutes. It made me very sad. I forget what we talked about in that brief time, but it made me achingly sad. I was ushered out as more people/beings came in to visit prisoners. I quickly got on a ship and left for the Archangel Realm. There I laid down near the base of the tree in the garden with the view. And Jesus next to me, right side. I tried to understand. And Jesus seemed at odds internally. Saying 'It's the way of things. There are rules. You were set up. You were set up to be killed and he helped with it.' And it really dawned on me. That along the way, probably from other times imprisoned, his soul- his heart had been made sad, frightened of getting too close, broken and very tough to let things in- which led to loneliness. He was a wonderful captain and mentor, but powerful dark forces came into play coercing and manipulating the situation- that energy he saw come from me- he was told he could have me. He was led to believe that he could keep me safe, no matter what, just to bring me in this new direction. Me dying or being killed was furthest from his mind or belief of what could happen, but he did know manipulation was happening and his broken heart, the energy I provided-it all became a perfect storm. He was cast under a spell so to speak.

I then asked to go to the temple I like to talk with Source. There I really cried. I did not see how this kind of prison for him was helping. I really asked for his heart to have the healing it needed, for him to be truly loved, cared for, and helped. I asked for him to know that this was how I felt and wished for- for his heart to heal. I asked for a tangible sign to come my way when he was in a better space. I just wanted him to be well. I also prayed for the sick mom and her son I worked with on Friday at the hospital."

Jesus, "Your understanding of the situation is accurate. The captain will be moved from the prison environment and helped. The prison environment is not a long-term plan. It is more for observation and learning what happened."

Me, "Sure does make me very sad. I love my brother and the captain. I'm just struggling to envision how I can even work through this loss."

Jesus, "We will help you. They will both still be with you. You have helped them both in getting rehabilitation."

Me, "I don't know where this leaves me on Earth- both career and close friendship support/mentorship. This is a huge blow- the loss of them in the third dimension. Being told by you - we'll help you- isn't enough."

Jesus, "I understand."

Me, "I should have phrased this in a question- I don't know where this leaves me on Earth- both regarding profession and close friendship support/mentorship. Do you? This is a huge blow- the loss of them in the third dimension. Where do we go from here?"

Jesus, "We rebuild."

Me, "I, I just don't have it in me. I've tried for 6 months and I've gotten nowhere. In addition, my heart is broken. Along with my amygdala and part of my soul. "

Jesus, "I think we start by healing you. There are a lot of good parts around you. From here we will find a direction for you."

Me, "I do understand what you are saying and that has been the focus and will continue to be the focus for a long time coming I'm sure. I guess what I'm getting at is my will is shot. I'm reminded of this podcast I was listening to the other day, who had continued bad suicidal ideation and this therapist finally said- you have to have the will for yourself to thrive. Which he just didn't have and so was indeed successful in killing himself- although he had a loving family and community and friends. He just didn't have the will. The will was missing.

I wouldn't say that I'm depressed, but I no longer have a will to thrive. To keep saying you're healing me and healing is occurring- well, I don't see it. I don't feel it in my heart. I don't see it in my life.

But most importantly- I've just lost my will. Sure, I can go through the motions and do what is asked of me, but my heart isn't in it, my brain isn't in it, and to an extent my soul isn't in it. I simply can't imagine something as good as what I had (even though it was pretty screwed up in certain ways), ever crossing my path again. I just don't see it. So even if it came across my path, without the will, I don't think I'd even notice it."

Jesus, "Your will will be restored. I know it is hard to see right now."

Me, "These words are not helpful."

Jesus, "I'm not sure I have words that can help you alone. When something does come across your path you will know it. I know things are difficult to see so a lot of work has to be done in sessions."

Me, "Whatever."

Jesus, "I can see that you are triggered. I will ask the galactic family to help me address this. I understand that your will is shot. We need to come to you here and help you from this space. None of the work we do can be received until we meet you where you are."

Me, "How do you wish my response to be?"

Jesus, "I honestly don't know. I know things are bad now. I know you feel like you are slipping backwards. I know you don't see a way forward. I know communication between us becomes hard when this happens. I will work here."

Session 59- June 25, 2017

"Really nothing to report."

Jesus, "What do you mean?"

Session 59, PS- June 25, 2017

"I'm not sure why it didn't really work for me to be aware in session tonight. It's upsetting. Maybe the whole breatharianism thing is just, I don't know the right word. I wouldn't know how to do it and don't have an instruction manual. I'm so confused and sad. Glad that Matt is more up to speed, but it's not helpful for me to hear him mention maybe there is hope for my former studio mate and this lifetime and my relating with him. Why would he say this? How is this in any way shape or form helpful for me to hear? Weren't you clear with Matt? It just made me deeply sad because I know the reality that has been discussed for weeks now.

Back to being sad. And I need to sleep as I have a quiz tomorrow for my class. I'm beginning to think maybe I shouldn't be in school in the fall. It's just adding more stress and the only reason I'm in school now is to finish the scholarship I received. I don't have a drive anymore nor care about science."

Jesus, "You had a long day and you are tired. I am not surprised it was hard to focus in session. I was clear with

Matthew. What he is seeing is a small chance the captain could link up with another space/person on Earth. Whereas it might be possible, we are not looking to move in that direction until other things happen. Once captain progresses in healing and rehabilitating then we can look at options for him to captain another ship. I will help you explore the breatharian idea. Going down the breatharian path could give you the base of a structure."

Me, "I'll reflect back that Matt talked about 'maybe things could go back to the way they were. Maybe both your brother and the captain could be healthy enough and inserted back and former studio mate would be fine?' You can look at the conversation. I do like the breatharian idea, but am concerned how intense the detox process was with the Gabriel Method. I also don't have any plan, structure, person to help in how to proceed. Do you? What would be pros and cons of breatharianism? What kind of structure would it provide?"

Jesus, "I will clear up any misunderstanding Matthew may have and have my mother explore breatharianism with you in a session. I think parts of it would work for you but I think too drastic of a shift too quickly could be difficult to manage."

Me, "Okay. I don't know that that will help. As I'm still trying to interpret how to deal with my stress level and amygdala and don't have a structure for that. It's too all over the place feeling, no offense."

Jesus, "I understand. You need something more direct. I see the pros of breatharian as being an opportunity for you to draw closer to my father. I see it being beneficial to you as you are trying to learn to connect your Archangel self with your Earth self. I think the practices of drawing in energy from around you would help you restore and replenish in a way that would help you break the state of being constantly triggered.

I don't know that it is a permanent practice meaning that it might not be something you would want to follow for an extended period of time. I do not think you are wired to necessarily stop eating food in this lifetime. I would recommend that you explore breatharianism by taking in the energy that is around you while allowing yourself to eat what you feel you need. You will likely find that you will still need to eat just as much food as you do now and that drawing in the energy around you is actually replenishing another part of you that food cannot.

I'm not sure if this makes sense or is direct enough for you. I will stop here to check in with what I've written so far. "

Me, "I appreciate your words, but this isn't a plan. Ray offers a plan. Jasmuheen offers a plan."

Jesus, "I was addressing the pros and cons. I like the plans you sent on for review. I think either one serves as a good introduction into where you want to go with breatharianism. Do you want us to explore these plans farther with you?"

Me, "Okay. But I don't see myself affording or traveling to Hawaii to study with Ray."

Jesus, "I agree that is not practical. I think we can take the idea of breatharianism and see what can be drawn out that will allow you a guide to help you in the process. This idea may have to be tabled for a little while until we can put together a solid plan for you to follow. I see that if you simply start doing this on your own that it could be dangerous."

Me, "Okay. So, we are back at pre- stage 1. Just upsetting. I feel like Matt Damon in the movie, 'The Martian' looking at his dwindling potato supply, i.e., my mental health capacity and watching it dwindle. Many emotions on this- including just anger at you all."

Jesus, "Breatharianism is a good structure. I need a little time to set it up so you can look at it and see if it will fit you."

Me, "Okay. I really don't mean to pressure you, but....well, what do the native elders think? Maybe this is just foolish. The last times I've drawn close to your father it's been great in the beginning and then a triggering nightmare because he's too strong- not intentional of course and I've just ended up terrified. I bring up the time in spring 2008. I sincerely doubt I will find a practicing breatharian in Vermont and even if so, will be an idiot. Not feeling hopeful here."

Jesus, "The native elders like the idea as a starting point. We all agree that it needs to be set up correctly. We are looking at some models here and trying to find a fit."

Session 60- June 26, 2017

"What is going on?"

Jesus, "I usually don't email while we are in sessions or after session so you can rest."

Me, "If I send a panic email- I don't think I have ever done this in a session- alarm bells should start going off somewhere; some Angel should be given this during a session to monitor and if only once in a blue moon I hit that button- there should be an answer to me within 30 seconds. I should never be left waiting. If you can't email me, then Zahid or someone should. It is extremely damaging to my entire being to leave me like this."

Jesus, "I understand. This will be the procedure going forward. You were cloaked in a heavy shield for protection. I think this delayed the emails as well."

Me, "Why wasn't I given any warning?"

Jesus, "We acted fast. It was important to get the shield up. I will have Zahid serve as emergency communicator in the future."

Me, "But what happened? I don't understand and I need to understand what the galactic family of light was doing. I need to understand the medical equipment, diagnostics tools- what was this? And how did it go so wrong? Use analogies if you have to. In addition, what did they find? You can keep the shield in place and repair me."

Jesus, "You said your soul was having trouble breathing. The galactic family began working. Old trauma was cutting off your soul's ability to bring in healing energy. The galactic family used magnetic rays to isolate the trauma. These magnetic rays scrambled some of your being so they backed off from this technique and physically attempted to remove the trauma. The trauma was attached to some beings that refused to let go. They said you wanted them there and that they were part of your native being. The galactic family knew this was not true. They shielded you in a very thick shield and asked you to tell them they were not welcome. You did. As soon as you did, they began arguing and Michael stepped immediately in to escort them away. He destroyed the beings.

It is like cancer cells that know they are causing harm but feed off the hosts inability to tell them otherwise. In this case the trauma remained hidden because it knew you did not want it.

As soon as you connected with Matthew you summoned the power to take full control."

<u>Session 60</u>- further examination- June 26, 2017

"What the hell is going on?"

Jesus, "There is a cross in what you are perceiving. I have been with you this entire time."

Me, "Then clear it up. I've been trying to contact you for 30 minutes. That's not a perception. That is reality."

Jesus, "You are correct. I see your emails. I see the panic caused here."

Me, "What is going on? That was a scary and terrifying session. I need you to speed up your response time."

Jesus, "There were some things the galactic family were removing from you. These things were removed and escorted out of your being. You interacted with them briefly but were safe. I see you did not feel your protection."

Me, "What are you talking about? I asked you at 9:19pm- who was dealing with trauma in me? I waited 10 minutes and you gave me no response. Your previous email had stated that you and the native elders were discussing things.

So, I waited. Then I went into the session and I opened up to a meeting like in a Longhouse and I was sitting there and surrounded by other Native People and a chief. We've brought you here, do you know why? I said I did not. He said to discuss your past, present, and future. I said, where am I? And he said, the Archangel Realm. I thought to myself- this doesn't feel like the Archangel Realm- all these people wouldn't be here. I said, where is Jesus? I'd like him here with me. And he said, No, he's not native and this is between natives. And then his manner and presence and tone of his voice got robotic and weird and I didn't know where I was- so I stood up and said, no, thinking to myself- no one treats me like this. This is not right. And when I exited it- it looked like a bubble. I was on a large ship and scaffolding and my hair was blowing around from the galactic wind. I couldn't figure out where I was and I felt I couldn't go anywhere. So, I came back to third dimensional consciousness.

I hate virtual reality diagnostics. I hate this tool. It's disturbing and weird. I don't wish for tools like this to be used with me anymore. It screws up my mind and frightens me. Do not use them anymore. They are scary to me."

Jesus, "These tools are now forbidden to be used in connection with you. All beings will respect this statement.

Me, "Okay. Can you explain in more detail what they found?"

Jesus, "There was trauma trying to hide while spreading itself to healthy parts of you. The galactic family caught this right away and dealt with it."

Me, "How did this trauma come into my being? Where did it come from? What happens now?"

Jesus, "It was with you a long time."

Me, "Many lifetimes?"

Jesus, "Yes. Many lifetimes."

Me, "Okay. Will there be other things that come up like this?

Jesus, "It is not likely and I would say definitively no but there is a very small chance and I don't want to mislead you by saying we have everything covered. We divert a large number of things like this from ever reaching you and have an extremely high success rate. In the event that something like this does come up again we have a solid communication plan in place and we will use the same shield to cloak you and protect you. Again, it is very unlikely but if it does, I don't want you to be completely blindsided. You did everything well. If ever you doubt anything call me in and if you have any trouble rely on email just like you did last night. I have emergency plans in place for such emails. Zahid will step in to communicate if I cannot. Does this make sense?

Session 61- June 27, 2017

"Just my notes- I struggled in trying to focus, but then I calmed a bit in drawing Reiki symbols twice. I was on a floating space station and looking out the large window was focusing on the underbelly of a planet, the stars and space, the beautiful glow of the planet- that was calming. I became aware I was.... I was in a small conference room with some galactic officials and medical staff. I looked at myself and was in like a galactic soldier outfit and my brown hair pulled back with a dagger on my left thigh. I turned to face those sitting and sat too around the tables. A rounder galactic medical expert began talking and showing something on a chart. I couldn't hear him and told my assistant to my left. Jesus was behind my right shoulder. I asked that, no offense, I couldn't understand what was being said and asked for simplicity.

Another younger figure stood up and did this.

- 'the cleanse is important, you seem more at ease with Matt really being on board and helping. It should be easier as you've done it before, your body has been eating in pre-cleanse mode for a long time now, you are in the Archangel Realm, and we are helping. This should actually feel enjoyable. And you know Jon Gabriel, his voice'.

- 'you want to start on Tuesday or Wednesday of next week. On marker day 3.5, the shift will occur, switching your system crown chakra down to nourishing off of prana. It will be intense, but we will buffer it- it will burn through a lot. You will have a much easier time then talking with Source directly. In the coming time after, it will be a lot to adjust, but we will buffer and eventually 6 months will be fully integrated.'

- I questioned about the baseball game Friday night and probably seeing incarnated old Pleiadian dark being, 'we can handle him, not an issue.'

- I asked about Ray. There is consensus that although he has a very small opening to pranic nourishment- he is farming energy off of people to live. He has some good information, but he is misguided and not living in a manner he thinks he is.

- I asked about Ray's meditations- they didn't think they were important, neutral at best. There seemed a bit of concern if the meditations were programmed at some level to farm energy off of those listening back to Ray, but that seemed to be a concern- not a fact they were sure on.

- they seem to like Jon Gabriel vs. Ray and emphasized Gabriel's meditations as more important. They seem to respect Jon Gabriel but not Ray.

- I asked about what happened Feb-April 2001 from MAP with my third eye and head opened. They tried to explain in a non-triggering way. An opening and exposing- like a rawness to reality. Which they have tried to repair some of the damage from this. This opening is vastly different. It was unclear if this something done to me in Feb-April 2001 could ever be fully cared for and healed. It looks like the focus is on management of.

- regarding pranic opening like this, there are 5 other humans like this on Earth right now- I will be 6. That Mother Mary had this experience and shift. That Jasmuheen is indeed one of the 5 and the reason it didn't hold up in a science experiment is her soul felt very threatened and scared.

- this made me pause because I thought Jasmuheen was a fraud and Ray the real deal.

- that relating to Matt will be much easier, a non-issue; but that there will be other issues that they will help buffer.

We wrapped up the meeting and I thanked them for their hard work during my difficult time.

Does this sound accurate? Did I miss anything?"

Jesus, "Yes. This seemed to help you very much. These words are accurate. Is there anything more you need at this time?"

Me, "So- what are your thoughts on Ray's meditations, do you think I should still try them?

- I know back in 2000 I had Jasmuheen's book and I liked it and started the process and felt galactic presence and got scared (obviously a tremendous amount has changed- but I felt a strong kinship in the process, felt home like- just not at that time)

- so, now I'm concerned, considering the farming situation- should I not listen to Ray anymore or his book- is it safe?

- I'm feeling after the next two weeks- I'd like the books others have written to compare my experience to, it's calming to my mind. Do you/they have a recommendation?"

Jesus, "With the general feeling that Ray's meditations are neutral at best, I see no pressing reason for you to try them. I did pick up on a disconnect with Ray. Something seemed off even though his words made sense. Dry fasting can be a powerful experience and I wonder how set up the people who attend his workshops are for it. I don't think you have to ignore Ray's message but I would be careful about hooking into him. I will look for books and bring them forth."

Me, "Thanks. I'm open to trying other meditations. I'm torn. I do like Ray and think he has a lot of valuable information, but something is not right with him. I believe he is, and slowly is becoming an agent for dark. Something feels very masked and very off. I believe people can do the dry fast, but they are being hooked into darkness and utilized. They think they are having one experience, but are actually having another. He reminds me of my brother 20 million years ago on the cusp.

I see this as a possible real threat. Can a team be set up to delve deeper here? I sincerely don't think Ray is trying to harm people, but nevertheless- he is"

Jesus, "Yes. I agree. A team has already been set up to monitor what is happening."

Me, "Thank you. The Regime- I don't even know what to say- I don't know how it began. Like darkness and evil are somehow in connection with Source. The Regime is just- well I don't know what to say- makes me angry, but then it's so different than anything I've experienced. It's so different. All I can think is an entity extremely high up there and close to Source went opposite. I feel bad for all the victims of the situation hooked in by Ray including Ray himself."

<u>Session 62</u>- June 29, 2017

"I opened up like last time on the ship/space station. I walked out on a platform and stood- as they scanned my body and being in different directions. It was like a 12-sided shape I stood on. Something about facing each zodiac quadrant.

I then walked back off and went to go look at what they were analyzing. Team of galactic medical professionals.

It looks like they were analyzing time, space, impact- of as my being switches to pranic nourishment. It's about keeping my body and being safe, as well as the galaxy and universe. Many factors to consider and I can see how hard they are working to make this safe for everyone.

A medical director or a director came up to me. I was in a robe sipping tea. I've been here before, a while ago, when given a case study on some subjects to look at, many sessions ago- but I recognize him and I recognize the beauty of this very large room and the beautiful large glass windows. I could see that planet glowing, soft creamy white, feels very comforting.

He asked me to go for a little walk. We walked a little bit and then sat down- looking outside. He wanted to check in how I was doing with it all. At first, I thought he was trying to see if this was a direction I wanted to go in, but no- he said the information he provided was to inform me.

To note- the information kind of scared me to the point that I had to go get Matt to help me process because I got very scared.

He talked about that after the shift, they would try to buffer me, but it could be intense and take some time, like 6 months to integrate. He mentioned that Jasmuheen is public, but the other 4 pranic nourishers are in hiding and did I want that? I said I didn't know. I know that in my image a week or so ago (of the monk at the seaside)- I'm pulled to being at peace and connected with Source in a deep way and a few close people in my life (like Matt and my children). I don't need lots.

That being said. My fear about being approached by people and comments made are scary. It reminds me of bad times like before I was raped. I firmly don't believe I can be harmed now, but I do worry about my C-PTSD.

He mentioned again this is a large shift.

He seemed to relax when I got the message of game planning now- like talking with Matt and trusted health care professionals on Earth in the third dimension. How will I handle certain situations, maybe I need a little time, maybe I need more anti-anxiety medication.

In talking with Matt, which helped, we tried out some scenarios. And I felt more empowered. It is going to be a process. But I believe I can learn how to stand up for myself, divorce from other's dramas and walk away, and create a circle of respect around me. I just have to gently practice it where it's a win/win situation for me and change the pattern.

We were called back by the technicians. It looks like they saw a bit of an issue in the right lung area, top of lower lobe when facing the 4th house in the zodiac star system. The director said they'd take care of it when I was sleeping.

And that was the session. I went and talked with Matt about my fears."

Jesus, "This sounds accurate. Everyone is taking all the precautions possible to make sure you are safe and not overwhelmed. We will focus on the issues you bring up in these words."

Me, "I'm not sure that can be completely avoided. Then again- I moved into the Archangel Realm and felt no difference. Is that how it will be? Because that seems like no change at all and do I need to be scaring myself or game planning like this?"

Jesus, "We tried to make the transition to the Archangel Realm as seamless as possible so it is actually good to hear you didn't notice any change. This is the model we will follow so I do not think you have to be too worried about feeling a drastic change."

Me, "While this is on the one hand good to hear, on the other hand- this is disappointing. Nothing in my third dimensional life changed with transition to the Archangel Realm. Still feeling aloof, no job prospects, still being treated badly by people, still dealing with depression and anxiety, still missing my former studio mate and that structure. What's the point then?"

Jesus, "I think the pranic energy will be a good catalyst in connecting the changes taking place in the Archangel Realm with the third dimension."

Me, "We will see. Matt and I aren't really relying on it doing much. We've been very disappointed countless times in the past. This is in part why last night- the galactic members concern felt foreign so wanted to check in if this was a concern others felt."

Jesus, "Others do feel this concern. My concern is always triggering your C-PTSD. I may err on the side of caution which is probably why changes you are undergoing from the transition to the Archangel Realm are slow to be felt in the third dimension."

Me, "Okay. I just don't remember anyone pulling me over and expressing concern like this when I was transitioning to the Archangel Realm. Do you? Hence, making me wonder- why now?"

Jesus, "The beings that expressed concern are being extremely cautious. I would not interpret it as anything more than that."

Me, "But, why now and not then?"

Jesus, "These beings were not directly involved in that transition."

Me, "Oh, Okay."

Session 63- June 30, 2017

"Well, I wasn't sure with how I've been feeling how it would go. I opened to the feel of like steam coming off of, steam off of my hands. It was unclear to me what that was- something to do with standing up for myself in the diseased family I was born into. Steam. And then I became aware, that Jesus and I, were in that space station, like before. And in front of me- had turned around from his chair an extremely old ancient galactic figure. Regal and powerful (who was this?) and I was fascinated by the color he lived inside of- a rich deep indigo and purple meeting up. The color was alive- different than color on Earth. I couldn't place who he was. But even though he held a lot of power- I didn't feel scared, maybe a little thrown in trying to figure what he was. He somehow knew the start of the Regime- was close to Source. We talked, but I grew tired and needed to consciously separate. He had good ideas on how to set boundaries without moving in to dark ways and cautioned me on this as I came into power. Like he could destroy Earth, but there are rules that are important to follow- for example. It hurt him very much to see the Regime breeding and trying things out on Earth, but he would not destroy Earth because of rules. He talked about how does one set boundaries and breathe into the pain and grief still there and let it take you deep in to transform to something different. He seemed pleased how I was progressing and this made me happy. Power can feel a bit intimidating, but honesty from others is calming to me. He felt sincere and Jesus felt at ease with him. He just looked wild with so much energy he possessed and could wield.

Jesus, "This is very accurate. I am glad you felt comfortable here."

Me, "Is it possible to explain who this is? It didn't feel like when I've met the galactic elders."

Jesus, "What do you mean?"

Me, "Hmmm. I'll try to explain. I don't understand who this powerful figure I met is. Do you know who he is? He feels older than the galactic elders and also looks very different than them. I know he's galactic- I've seen light families, warriors, medical team, elders- but I can't place who he is?"

Jesus, "He is much older than the galactic elders. He is of the original galactic beings."

Me, "It's hard to pin point how I feel. At ease, but he's different than what I'm used to. Happy, because I feel like I can be my full self, grow into my full self, and he would get it. I thought of him when I acknowledged a housekeeper at the hospital. Of one of his lessons, he might have told me while I was sleeping last night. I'm not sure. Like something he said echoed in my head when I saw her. Like I recognize the nurses and some doctors, why don't I notice and acknowledge the housekeepers. Especially those I see each week. Why does he take an interest in my case?"

Jesus, "Why are you surprised that he does?"

Me, "Because I don't really see myself as different than any other human. And he's so big. Like a big player in our universe. I realize that's a bit odd. Odd because my life is definitely not like everyone else's. But still my view of myself is simple and little and well, average. Does that make sense?"

Jesus, "It does."

Session 64- July 7, 2017

"Curious how things would open up as I'm dealing with more deep anxiety than I'm used to and not sure of the cause.

Opened up to where we were before, with Jesus to my right. This time there were 13 older galactic beings. The one I had met last night there too. I had on my warrior galactic outfit, but put down my dagger on my left thigh that I usually carry, but that still didn't feel right. So, I shifted to wear my galactic dress outfit and that felt right- as it embodies the last 3 billion years of my history. I chose to have my hair blonde, in waves.

The 13 beings all sat in chair like throne structures and would swivel to face outside and then towards each other and then towards me. I asked Jesus why my heart was racing. He said, their vibration is very high. I said, but I've talked with Source and not had issues. He said, Source can tailor exactly to you, but they are who they are. That made sense.

They talked.

They debated about Earth- that had a lot of bad breeding ground things happening, but then there was me, people like me, which made them pause. They said, these are troubling times for the galaxy. They were all in agreement on this and it weighed on them.

They said they were here regarding my upcoming experience with transitioning to pranic nourishment.

I stepped forward. I decided since they all had comfy chairs. I should change mine too and shifted it to be like a reclining chaise lounge chair, that suited me. I figured I should be comfortable and try to relax.

They examined me and I asked for Jesus to act as mediator, interpreter, as I didn't feel very able to do it. Which he did and bowed before them. Which was a little odd. Because I feel they ask me to put my right hand on my heart and acknowledge their presence in greeting them. So, should I be bowing? I felt a little confused.

They talked amongst themselves.

Then they said, 'you will be a leader and lead 5 million people. You are more than equipped and with Matt and our guidance. This is set.'

Jesus tried to intervene as he could feel my panic. 'I understand you see her ability. But she has a condition called C-PTSD and this makes it hard...'

They interrupted him, 'She is well equipped and is what is needed.'

I was a little baffled.

And then 12 of them dissolved, dematerialized.

And the one I had met last night was there. Jesus told me not to worry. This wasn't a done deal. And obviously we can talk with Source.

I wasn't sure.

I scooted my chair over to the galactic figure. He was staring out the window in thought and looking at Earth far away.

I decided to rest and laid down with a blanket to the galactic figure's left. That seemed to be the end of the session.

So, it kind of explains my racing heart and physical weakness. I really can't get my anxiety under control. Nothing helps. Not time with Matt, not medication. I'm not sure what to do."

Jesus, "We do need to expand upon this session."

Me, "What do you mean? I slept okay. Gabriel's evening sleep meditation helps. Couldn't use a pillow. My whole upper back is a mess now. I woke up with a severe charley horse cramp in my right calf. Not sure why."

Jesus, "It seems like there are a few unresolved issues in this session. Is that accurate?"

Me, "Hmmm. The galactic originals don't seem unresolved. I feel unresolved on what's going on."

Jesus, "That's what I mean."

Me, "I don't feel pushed or mandated. I mean- I feel a certain trust and care for me, but I wonder if they really understand my condition? Maybe I don't fully understand me. I believe there must be a way to achieve the goals without myself feeling frightened."

Jesus, "I think there is. "

Me, "Can you explain anything here? My heart anxiety is very bad today. Come tonight I don't know how good I will be at hearing a session accurately. Really impacts everything- weak arms and hands, terrible amounts of fear, headache, upper back ache, trouble breathing. Why am I in such bad shape? Is it mostly due to the wedding? I feel like I've gone into shock. Especially, that my cousins would treat me this way. I don't understand- when this family reached out with my father dying, but now they are just cold. I don't understand. Can you observe what is happening? And also, please tell me when the whole thing is over? Did he get married today or is it tomorrow? I seriously cannot believe how much he has said he cared about me since I was a teenager and this is how I'm treated and how much I helped him in times of great suffering and pain. Like it's blowing my soul apart. I simply can't function."

Jesus, "The anxiety is from the wedding. It did not happen yet and swirling energy around it is bringing rain. I think right now some of your family is swept up in things. They will be able to see what a terrible thing your cousin did in not inviting you as they settle."

Me, "What day and time will it happen? I just want this nightmare to be over. That is upsetting that they so easily forget and forgot me. I suffer here and they simply don't care. This is a divorce and actions that are not repairable. From any of them towards me."

Jesus, "I think today."

Me, "Well, hopefully it will be done and over soon and I can just get on with my life and move past these feelings, but it has created a deep wound, scar, and damage to me. I can feel this and I cannot predict how this will have harmed me going forward and altered things. My question still remains- why am I so anxious?"

Jesus, "I see a lot of anxious energy around this wedding."

Me, "Agreed. I am anxious. Why am I anxious?

Jesus, "It is linked to your family at the wedding. I am looking deeper into this."

Me, "Hmmm. That's a loose word. What family are you talking about? Can we go over terms? My family is

Matthew and my children. My extended paternal family is my father and those of my father. The galactic family of light is family. You are family. Source is family. The Archangel Realm is family. My uncle of the wilderness is family. My Reptilian brother attached through former studio mate is family.

My extended maternal birth biology is my mother and those of my mother. I do not consider my mother and those connected to her as those others than what biologically brought me into this world. It is not healthy for me to think of them with the word 'family'. It creates a negative association when applying the word family to those that I love and love me- family.

Whatever is going on with my mother and those connected to her is other, is biology.

Why would I be aware of them? Why would it be making me anxious? I've pulled my energy out of them. Cords have been cut. There is buffering. I should be feeling nothing. Maybe a bit sad, but not crushing anxiety, and my heart in severe pain. Something is very off."

Jesus, "I was referring to your mother and those connected there. I will continue to investigate."

Me, "Wow, so my mother showed up? That's disgusting. I hope every single person realizes my cousin chose not to invite me. That I did not choose to stay away. That he made an active and willful choice not to invite me, Matthew, and our children. And severed me from them all. There is a place not deep enough in hell for all of them. Especially my mother. It angers me that that she is allowed to talk her shit, talk her smack about me, and others nod their head politely and listen. To keep trying to ruin my reputation. She has kept me away from my brothers, poisoned them. And now just keeps poisoning my name to others. So, my maternal birth biology members- these same people that are disgusted with my mother's behavior, told this to me in the past have actually been lying to me all along? Because they put up with her at this wedding. Not a place deep enough in hell for all of them."

Jesus, "I can't see that your mother definitely is attending, just energy connected to her."

Session 65 & 66- July 3, 2017

"Session 65- I don't remember much except just being in like a chamber, where my vitals and heart were being assisted and helped and falling asleep.

Session 66- Again- hard time seeing much. Eventually falling asleep in the flowers in front of the Archangel Realm Medical facility. And then going in and having my heart worked on by a medical team there. I believe functioning of my heart swapped out for a helper battery tool (and then heart motor would be replaced back in- once helped/fixed). As this change out was happening, I fell asleep.

Luckily, I was rustled awake and alerted minutes before Matt entered the room.

I hate when this happens. It's very disorientating. I closed the session a little while later, but was thrown off.

Not much to report, except belly feels off, muscles and fascia that is, and diastasis recti feels very bad today. Just can't keep that area in. Very self-conscious about belly hanging out and not having tone there.

Good little talk with my daughter before bedtime, but odd when she asks about my marrying Matt- when will that happen. I said I don't know. I just don't feel something yet I feel I should feel. And she asked, if I was in love with him that yes you love him, but are you in love with him? I said I loved him, but no I didn't feel in love with him. The best I could offer is for her to not feel pressure to do something in a relationship with a partner she doesn't want to do. Hopefully it can be an example for her."

Jesus, "This is accurate. Regarding Matthew, you are 'in love' with him even if parts of you aren't ready to feel it. I don't say more because I know it puts pressure on you. I just wanted to give a clearer picture for your daughter."

Me, "I definitely feel like a shell of myself. I just find being around Matt extremely annoying. I just don't want to be with him on any level. Kids I feel okay with though."

Jesus, "This is caused from stirring old trauma. It is a definite pattern. You and Matthew were close and intimate a few days ago and that went OK. When the reality of the wedding and what your family has done to you moved in you isolated any feeling you have for Matthew as a defensive protection mechanism. This then causes you to feel annoyed and like you don't want to be around him.

The galactic family works to help you separate Matthew out from trauma you have experienced at the hands of those that have loved you. Your love for Matthew is pure, healthy, and clean. Your mind and body cannot process this when forced to deal with pain or even the memories of pain. Matthew simply will not hurt you like you have been hurt in the past. My saying this is not enough. Your mind and body know this but it gets frozen out when you are triggered like now."

Me, "I don't feel like I'm being helped enough. Will the detox help?"

Jesus, "It will help. It may take a little time to set but it will help."

Me, "I don't know what's wrong with me. My high heart area is hyperventilating. I can't get it to stop. I can't get a normal breath in."

Jesus, "I will inform the galactic family."

Me, "It feels like a very deep-rooted depression. No offense, but I only became aware of Archangel Michael really in 2001. You all, along with Matt, are very recent to my self's awareness. My maternal line has been actively in me for 43 years and my cousins, especially my cousin with the wedding- close as it gets to feeling real safety, care, and love. He first hand supported me in the devastation my mother caused when she did not show up to an event 2002- blaming me that my presence would be too upsetting for my brothers. He comforted me that whole weekend. His now treatment of me and that whole family's treatment of me- with no email, not even checking in- I just feel flat lined at a soul level.

No offense- but I don't see you all helping and see nothing that you all can do in the future. This is a wound, like when my parents divorced, that has no description and only true destruction can ensue. I am open to your words helping me see differently, but so far- nothing you have said makes me think that this isn't anything less than catastrophic for me."

Me, "....and, I don't feel in love with Matt. That's what I stick with."

Jesus, "I know. It's a very triggering proposition for you. Even just speaking about it with me triggers you. Your mind and body pushes Matthew away when it gets hurt or otherwise triggered. Just a few days ago you were OK being close and intimate with Matthew. The wedding set off a trigger in you and now you don't feel Matthew. We are working on this pattern."

Jesus, "It is catastrophic to you. Nobody is denying that. Your cousin has cut you very deep. It is causing your body and mind to mistrust Matthew. It is causing physical pain and anxiety. This is extremely bad. We are extremely angry and feel your pain.

We are working to help. There is not a lot we can do to make this immediately better. We are working to limit the impact and then work backwards from there."

Me, "It's troubling to me that you see this as a run of the mill pattern I deal with. This thing has teeth and weight.

This is like how I felt after my parents got divorced. It altered me at a profound level. This is how I felt when I watched my son killed in front of me and my whole tribe decimated in front of me in 1823. To call this simply part of a pattern, says to me you simply don't know what you are up against."

Me, "That family line is not allowed to continue to hurt people. They are not allowed to continue to be enabled. All of them, each and every one has got real issues. My cousin is just a user. They all are."

Jesus, "Oh no. It is not a simple pattern at all. If it were, we would have resolved it. It is complex, perhaps more than you might know. We will help you work through it. It will take time."

Jesus, "I agree."

Me, "I've got to wonder if something dark is afoot here. Why would my mother come across my Facebook feed a week ago? Something is odd."

Jesus, "We are considering this. That would actually make things easier. It didn't seem to be long after sex that you started feeling this way and that points to something internal, however, the wedding seems to be the trigger and this is where darkness could have an impact."

Me, "I don't see how sex and being triggered by the wedding are related. Can you explain?"

Jesus, "They are not. That's what makes the pattern difficult. You were able to feel and enjoy a closeness with Matthew. An independent event occurs, the wedding, and that impacts how you are able to value love in your twin flame relationship."

Me, "I am watching this deep pervasive and rooting cancer take hold and you all are doing nothing."

Session 67- July 6, 2017

"I opened to being in a more sequestered space it seems. I couldn't tell if I was on a ship or in the Archangel Realm. It looks like something designed specifically for this process I'm undergoing for the next 5 days. As I rested looking at it- I can feel toxins being pulled out of my body- just floating off. I was told/shown how the next 5 days would look. It was 5 days spaced around in a circle, each equally distant from the other. Day 1- capsule encompasses cleansing. Day 2- a thicker shield for form around me, as I begin the process of becoming like 'mush'. Day 3- a slowly beginning to realign everything so I am a pranic nourisher with the universe. Day 4- really sets up into place. Day 5- test driving out the structure and seeing if any issues. Day 6- leaving the capsules and the structure floating up to the ceiling and standing in the center- allowing for more testing to see how it works. There is a bit of concern that there is a deep implant that won't appear until day 3 or day 4. This has been planned for- so a seamless sequestered area has been set up to move into surgery/diagnostics without jolting my system. When/if it's found, I may be able to stay where I am, but they are not sure. I'm okay today. Waiting for my digestion to kick off is annoying and uncomfortable, but am okay. I think better than last November at this time. Thinking about incarnated old

Pleiadian dark being today and this is my assessment-- there are 3 things going on with him in regards to me. He experiences my power and can see me (although not conscious of it) and looks to me as a bit of protection and to follow; he is still at some deep level holding out that something will happen to Matt and I'll become interested in him. Way back in the Pleiadian time- a chip was planted in me- like way deep. As I get into the pre-cleanse and detox mode, it doesn't surprise me he's showing up in my life. If and when the baseball game happens Friday night, him interacting with me (day 3), could be really key. It could show us exactly where the implant is. It does make me nervous because of what happened with my former studio mate- him biting into me, but I try to remind myself that many things are different now. It could be risky. I worry about the safety of Matt to be honest more than myself."

Jesus, "These words are accurate. You understand the plan. Why do you worry about Matthew? What do you think could happen?"

Me, "I don't know. A few markers seemed a bit off to me during the fireworks event. Matt just seemed a bit different and I wondered why. It could be nothing. He's usually over the top protective of me with incarnated old Pleiadian dark being. When we were biking, Pleiadian commented that it was odd both he and I had misread the text messages and he pointed that out. It was odd. Why had we both misread the text messages? When Pleiadian did not have a lock for his bike and we had an extra, Matt quickly opted to lock Pleiadian's front wheel to my back wheel. It felt odd to me and a little jarring. Then when we were seated for the fireworks- Matt joked around with Pleiadian in talking about things kids would say. Matt told him the story of how my daughter got confused and instead of commenting that Matt was dad to my daughter first, she will say, "Matt is my first daddy". And Pleiadian looked at me and I just looked away. Matt totally missed it. There are three instances here in a three-hour period that Matt seems to have missed and actually participated in. That's why I'm concerned about Matt. I think once this chip is gone it will be easier, but still, it's odd, no? We all think Pleiadian wouldn't try anything because it's bad for him and I know he loves his daughter, but then I have flashes of what happened with my former studio mate and I get scared. It's hard to say what is going on. I don't know."

Jesus, "We will look at these instances. It is good you point them out. I do believe the love and power you and Matthew have will help you during this cleanse and beyond."

Me, "I'm falling asleep. I worry about leg cramps in the night though. Still dealing with uncomfortable hunger issues"

Jesus, "We will help you here. Going to sleep a little early would be good. Sleeping next to Matthew will help restore and replenish you."

Me, "Okay. If he can cut back on draping sexual energy all over me that would feel better."

Jesus, "The sexual energy is there between the two of you. It would be helpful to unite it at some point. I do see now is not that time and we will help buffer it."

Me, "I understand, but I'm hungry and my system is on panic mode. This is what happened last time. 4pm on the first day until 9am third day was awful. It's hard to deal."

Jesus, "We are helping to take the edge off of this."

Me, "Thanks. We were intimate last night. Felt better just to intertwine. It's hard to be intimate as my physical body is weak and going through a radical change. For example, I can't feel where my chakras are. Disturbing to me is why do I keep thinking about Pleiadian? Is that really something? Or is it my inability to not be intimate with dark. It's like the light and dark side of the moon. I crave both. It's odd."

Jesus, "Intimacy is a good thing and it will get easier as you settle. Intertwining is probably more helpful at this time but if that leads to intimacy then it is good. I will examine the Pleiadian thing. I'm not sure what you mean by your inability to not be intimate with dark."

Me, "Maybe it's how I was trained to think about sex or maybe it's my fear if I don't stay connected to darkness somehow it will stalk me and really hurt me."

Jesus, "I understand. We will certainly help with this."

<u>Session 68 part 1</u>- July 6, 2017

"Session was short as I knew I would fall asleep (did go to sleep early and slept for about 9 hours). Just a review of where I was at- 9:30pm- could feel the next stage about to come-cloaking of a form while my body and being digests into a mush. Could start to not feel where my chakras were or rather root chakra floating up near the top of me."

Jesus, "This seems normal. I will report this and continue to guide this work."

Me, "Yes, I didn't feel alarmed at all and I like this cocoon. I respond well to water structured with sunlight and stones with certain properties- like a glass jar of water with pink Rhodochrosite in it, sitting out in the Sun all day, with a heart sticker attached. This gives me a tremendous amount of energy and my eyes feel better.

Still dealing with inflammation in left eye both bottom and top lid now and now left ear lobe."

Session 68 part 2- July 7, 2017

"Not much to report as these are shorter sessions. I close my eyes and all I see of myself is the galaxy and stars. Like last November when I slipped into my heart. This time though, inside of me, I just see the galaxy and stars."

Jesus, "This seems normal. It lines up with the stages of the cleanse."

Session 69- July 8, 2017

"Hard for me to see much. But I just look covered in these little white larvae/worms. I see above me this incredible lattice of patterning of shapes and colors, like a portal to the engine of light in our universe. I'm confused because I thought Source was that, but this doesn't look like Source."

Session 70- July 9, 2017

"Around the time I smashed my finger, I started feeling better. I'm still hungry, but not so overwhelmed by it. I opened up the session and well, it was different than I expected. I don't see the galaxy in me anymore or the stars. I just see me, my form, in golden light. I can't figure where my chakras are though. But my capillaries and cells to larger structures, just seems of light. And I reflect back on walking into the grocery store today- I actually feel more solid and when I step forward the light carries weight- people either don't notice, naturally stay away from me, or treat me how I wish to be treated. I do notice that light trumps all. I feel a bit more at ease with Matt, but that is a process. I don't notice much more else. The structure above me that I described in session 69. I guess tomorrow is the test-driving and fine-tuning of it. I guess I thought it would feel like other, but that is not the case. It feels like me. It feels like the light now can go in and burn out any parasites- it's that strong and up and running. Slowly picking up speed. What do you all observe?"

Jesus, "This is what we observe. We see that you are moving closer to Matthew and this is helping you tremendously and will continue to be a solid piece for you."

Session 71- July 10, 2017

"Still moving along with short sessions. Opened up to still being in the chamber room. But stepping out of the cocoon and that beginning to be cleared away and getting ready for phase 2. I notice the intricacy of light in creating me.

There seemed to be a panel observing me and I went up to them to thank them for all their expertise and help. They reminded me of like a team of NASA scientists.

Phase 2 would start tomorrow, where standing on a platform in the center- I would be somehow set up to how I operate best in the galaxy."

Jesus, "This is accurate."

Session 72- July 11, 2017

"It's later at night, but I wished to continue. I opened up to them running tests. Standing in the center of the chamber I've been in for 6 days. They seem to be running a tremendous number of tests to figure how I can safely and best fit in the galaxy. They do this by setting coordinates and then a slight charge goes through me and they are looking to see where and how I flow best. Getting all the coordinates set up. An extremely crude analogy would be when getting fitted for eyeglasses- they keep trying different lenses; and then the astigmatism; and then if there needs to be a bifocal. What we are doing is much, much more technology advanced than this, but that's the analogy that comes to me. They did just wrap me up in dense feeling bandages and kept running tests and my 'cold' symptoms in the third dimension stopped or at least settled down. I think the slight pulse of energy running through was starting to get more intense, unless there was a grounding force- like the heavy bandages quiet things down, instead of going through me, hitting air and start charging higher."

Jesus, "Yes. This is accurate. The idea is to move slowly so you are not shocked."

Session 73- July 12, 2017

"Was a larger session. I'll send notes later this morning."

"Was longer as I mentioned. I had been confused about how to proceed with my long-distance client's session prior, but we seemed to figure it out. Better for me to stay in the chamber and work remotely at this time with my long-distance client. It seemed to also allow the galactic's team to see how my power works as a pranic being.

I cleared this work session and brought myself into focus for session 73. I felt them wrapping up computations and sort of coming back to reality a bit more, me. There came a note in that the Ancient Ones wanted to meet with me out on the space station deck where I had met them before. I wasn't sure about this as it hadn't gone well with me leaving the chamber. I was too raw. I talked with Jesus on this. We discussed if the Ancient Ones could come into the chamber. It did not look like that would work as they are too 'big'. We then worked a bit to see what would work for me. What seemed to work best was like myself being wrapped in a beautiful shawl of thicker quality, deeper galactic navy with some other blues mixed in and glittery stars- like a version of my galactic robe I've worn before. It felt better also for me to be carried in on a dais. Both of these measures helped me a lot. It felt great to acclimate in a way that felt safe and good to me. Covering my head and body felt better and I could conserve my energy and strength by staying seated. So felt very happy with this.

In meeting them at the space station, I felt a little embarrassed about how bright glowing golden light I was. (To note when I open the Reiki symbols in session- I see gold, not the purple one is usually supposed to focus on). I spoke simply and with power. Words are impactful and the Ancient Ones are in to extreme clarity and mindfulness with words. I tried to follow their lead. As usual, the Ancient Ones have a way of making me feel normal and at ease in who I am and am becoming. They said, 'we are impressed. You are doing well. We will look at the computations- give us a moment' and they turned and looked up at the screens of the data being computed.

This took some time. To not get nervous, I looked outside at our beautiful galaxy. And then breathed light out of my mouth to make like a light bubble which made me laugh and showed the galactic helper holding my chair how neat it was and he smiled too. I was entertaining myself and enjoying the lighter joyful part of Source God energy when they turned back to me. One Ancient spoke for them. Jesus was to my right. The Ancient seemed a bit to slightly pause- as if dawning on him. 'You will be a great spiritual (or did he say religious?) leader for Earth'. I smiled and kind of laughed, 'but I have nothing to say'. 'You have Jesus and Matt. This is correct'. I didn't have any fear or worry. It felt like the number went from 3 to 10 million individuals to lead in this lifetime. It's not that I didn't take him seriously. I just have nothing to say, like I don't even like to teach yoga right now and humans rather annoy me. I sighed. And then they dissolved and went off on a mission. I looked at Jesus and he looked at me.

I guess it's up to Source God at this point. I feel full of a lot of pranic energy. Not as hungry last night or today. I feel like something changed, but it's hard to say what?

We went back to the chamber and I changed into a pink large scarf, with lots of gold embellishments and sat. I went over some things. I've noticed how much my son has felt closer to me lately. I find it interesting how St. Paul that is a follower of Jesus is my daughter. I feel better with Matt (native elders were correct on this) and it makes sense that when life was hard, I would point out the false old structure between Matt and I and say, see this sucks too. So, it's good that that is gone.

I do feel like my pranic capacity has shifted. I feel extremely young on this big journey ahead of me and am not sure where we begin. Where do we begin?"

Jesus, "These words accurately reflect what happened. When you say it's up to Source God are you filled with panic or pranic? It is good you feel better with Matthew.

I agree about the old structure. We begin like we are. You are adapting to pranic energy and the healing power it has for you. I think we give it just a small amount of time so that you can begin to see what some of your options will be on this journey. It was good to see you enjoy the lighter side of Source energy. This helps you on Earth as well."

Me, "I am filled with prana when feeling it's up to Source- not panic like before. I still feel like me and I feel I understand Source a bit- good sides and sides where I think He needs to reexamine and I remember my soul history. I feel complete. That's why I kind of laughed at being a spiritual/religious leader because I as Bridget don't have anything to say. I move through my day like everyone else. Are you concerned? I feel your life on Earth was much harder than I could ever deal with."

Jesus, "Why would I be concerned? I don't think you have to do anything or say anything for that matter. You may be a leader simply in how you live your life."

Me, "You seemed concerned the last time the Ancients mentioned something like this 2 weeks ago. I can pull up the session notes. I don't understand your comments- why wouldn't the Ancients have just said that?"

Jesus, "I understand. There is room in what the Ancients want/see for what you want. I am concerned because you seem concerned."

Me, "Hmm. I haven't felt concerned. I do find this email exchange- that has gone back and forth right now between us- upsetting. Now I feel down and confused and sad."

Jesus, "I think we are off topic and missing the point. The session went well. That is great to see."

Me, "The Ancients have said what they said twice now. I was better prepared to hear it this time. There are two weeks of work and 48 hours of solid computational data they are looking at. If I am being entrusted and groomed to lead and that is the truth, then do not water it down- that is not helpful and alienates me from you. Why would you do that? I am now put in a hard position. I find your words confusing and upsetting. I feel really confused now. I don't know who to believe or what to wrap my brain and soul around. Please consult with galactics, Ancients, Source himself or whomever you wish before you respond to these words. I'm pretty upset right now."

Jesus, "Yes. You are a leader. I want you to know that you will have plenty of help."

Me, "Hmmm. But you said being a leader means me just going about my daily life.

I don't understand. Right now, I'm on a planet with my great grandfather the Sun ruler teaching me how to rule with 100 million ethereal beings. Now I have Ancients saying I'm to be a leader of 3-10 million on Earth. And I have you saying 'well, you can be a leader by just the example of how you go about your life' which means things just stay the same here. Which is it? Do you understand why the only being I feel baffled about what you are telling me- is you? My brain and soul feel in chaos right now. This isn't helping."

Jesus, "Follow the Sun leader. My words are just to remind you that you have choices in the way you lead."

Me, "Please take this to my native elders and my galactic team. These words do not help."

Jesus, "What you observed and experienced in the session is accurate. I apologize that I have confused the issue. I can see that I was not addressing the topic you were addressing and this created confusion."

Session 74- July 13, 2017

"I'm starting a new thread here. I'm feeling stuck and very confused and chaotic inside.

- Why all these cold symptoms? There is no virus and bacteria.

- how is this intertwined with my former studio mate? You're pointing to a connection

- If this is all related to my mother, then why did old Pleiadian dark entity develop the same symptoms as me at the same time?

- Did something change and I'm picking up on something?

To just say, 'Oh you have anger towards your mother' I've had anger towards my mother and the maternal line, but not had my whole respiratory system implode. All I can say is my former studio mate in real time is trying to tell me something, my heart is not handling it well, and you are saying that this is not the case, but has to do with your mother. This just is not helping my increasing stress level."

Jesus, "There is a lot going on here. We are looking at how it relates to each other. I do not know why you have the cold symptoms. We are thinking it relates to the implant old Pleiadian dark entity was supposed to highlight. It is strange that he has cold symptoms. I suspect he is actually sick and you might be mirroring that because he is somehow a marker. I am not sure how it relates to your former studio mate. You told us you think it has something to do with him. I can see a connection to him in the anger you have over your mother but I am not sure it is exactly what we are looking for. Your former studio mate might have some information here and we are currently speaking with him. I am sorry that I do not have a clear explanation at this time. A session may help you. It is not mandatory. The galactic family and native elders are working together and they do very strong work together."

Me, "Okay, thanks. My panic stems from things were feeling nice and once again- all the ugliness around my mother rears its head again to ruin my life and anything good in it. A few things come to mind. As soon as I started feeling weak respiratory wise and coughing, I started feeling my former studio mate trying to point to something. Something he noticed when he as captain of the ship worked on my heart. That also mirrors what he observed as my brother. I can't place it. And the closer I get to placing it, the worse my symptoms get.

When I started having symptoms and was walking into the hospital on Tuesday, I noticed next to my car a car with a bumper sticker of a person holding a heart that was in the image of a grenade. The car next to that said 'Mom'. I felt it was a sign, but couldn't understand what I was trying to tell myself."

Jesus, "We will look closely at these things."

Me, "I talked with my therapist and feel a little better. Any new information come to light for you all?"

Jesus, "We are still looking. Will you be doing a session tonight?"

Me, "Yes, and I did do a session last night, but haven't gotten the notes to you. Basically, just opened up to my trying to figure on things in the space station and you and others telling me I'm exhausted and need to rest. A little side room was decorated for me to rest in and was very cozy. Teams were also able to examine my heart. Took something out and inserted a more golden light filled replacement. In the session was where I got the idea to rest today and stay home."

Jesus, "I do know rest will help you. I'm glad you could take the time. It has helped us do some healing in the heart area. We will continue to work and pull out what is infecting you here."

Me, "My former studio mate seems to have an important piece. What has he been trying to talk with me about?

What have you all been discussing? What do the native elders with galactics make of it all?"

Jesus, "We were thinking your former studio mate's soul would be able to help in session. He is pointing to the heart area where he did work. The galactic family and native elders see an infection like reaction in the heart area. They see Matthew as a healing force here and also the golden light they used."

Me, "Agreed. I'm wondering if he saw something, the last time he was in there that under the right circumstances could have taken hold. He didn't extract it at the time, but made a note of it. Wondering if it's like a parasitic operative structure I've been hosting?"

Me, "Do they have any recommendations of what I can do, supplements, practices besides being around Matt and resting that would be helpful?"

Jesus, "A little bit of physical activity can help. They will be able to give more guidance as they zero in on healing."

Jesus "I'm not sure. I'm wondering if it is something that did not clear entirely during the cleanse which is along the lines you are thinking."

Me, "Yeah, it eased up a bit when talking with my therapist. I just feel diminished with this thing."

<u>Session 75</u>- July 14, 2017

"I was so awful feeling. I laid down as I opened the session. It seems that I opened up into a surgery like room- capitalizing on the work I had done earlier. My heart was just spewing out in waves all manner of parasitic behavior it had accumulated the last 3 billion years- like just vomiting it out. And then I went into a semi half awake, half asleep and don't remember anything. Except at the end some kind of insert to help as deeper pieces come up can be filtered. That's about it. Anything to add?"

Jesus, "This is accurate. We were also flooding the area with a lot of light."

Me, "Do you all think you got everything? Did my former studio mate see anything else?"

Jesus, "We think everything is healing. We do not see anything else."

Me, "On another note, I'm here and waiting for my primary doctor in the room. I really don't have time. She's already a 1/2 hour late. I have to be home by 12:20 to get the house ready for my client at 1pm. Is there any possible way to get her to speed it up?"

Jesus, "I will work on it."

Me, "It's so frustrating. In many ways she's a good doctor, but with time she's horrible. I simply should have picked to see someone else. What should I do?"

Jesus, "I am trying to free her."

Me, "Thanks it worked out."

Session 76- July 14, 2017

"I struggled to open in this session. I finally had Jesus help me and then things came into focus. He could see how stressed I was feeling and had the keepers of the space station create a space where I could relax. It looked to be like the garden cafe center at a local garden supply center. I felt better there with the waterfall and all the countless plants and oxygen. I explained how I felt so confused, how I try to go about my day now, but feel like I'm not matching it right and that causes stress. Like I'm waiting for something to happen. Jesus went to get the native elders who had arrived and they filed in. Look to be of the tribes out west, due to their bonnets and dress. I always feel a bit shy and embarrassed of how glowing I am, so put my scarf up around me. But they didn't seem to notice either way. They started talking, but my mind was getting jammed up and I asked Jesus to help- so they spoke with a visual analogy in nature which helped very much. They said, 'it's like, a piece of cloth and the winds of change start coming along, but the cloth gets snarled on some wood. The wind keeps blowing, but the cloth gets wedged in there and stuck tighter- that's why you feel that tension in your heart. Follow the wind of your breath and soften and let it take you how to proceed in your doings.' Well, that made sense. I will try to come back to more following the breath, meditation, and yoga.

That was about it.

They filed out after that and was the end of the session. Anything else to add?"

Jesus, "This is a good description. We will continue to work to help you."

<u>Session 77</u>- July 16, 2017

"Just my notes- I thought we opened to the Archangel Realm, but it looked to be the ethereal planet realm. They have a little similar feel. I was dressed in shades of lavender and gold with an elaborate headpiece. The ethereals were very gracious and I try to do my best in how to be an effective guardian leader. I breathed and allowed myself to be present as I was glowing light with others watching. It's a safe place to practice. Then the top above me opened and I saw that engine like feel of the universe and swooping down was a messenger. I couldn't exactly here what he said. But I got up and went forward and started ascending up and into a ship. Which I thought strange and my shape shifted to my galactic warrior outfit and all systems go, was off to my uncle in the wilderness.

There at the edge he pointed to darkness was coming August 21, 2017- the eclipse. Darkness would come in and collect itself and pull in on itself from this date until the end of September. Darkness thinks it's regrouping, but we will be ready for it. And that was the end of the session. I stayed to talk with my uncle."

Jesus, "This is accurate. We are prepared and have a plan to execute."

Me, "What do you think this time period on Earth will look like?"

Jesus, “We are looking to start right away.”

Me, “But I don't understand. It looks like dark will just come in and collect what is theirs. Are you talking about their tendency to light fires and cause more danger to innocents because they are pissed off about the situation?”

Jesus, “Yes.”

<u>Session 78, 79, 80</u>- July 20, 2017

“Session 78- 3 nights ago was just healing light

Session 79- 2 nights ago was me on the space station just yelling at everyone

No session last night.

Session 80- tonight. Tonight was more involved. I ended up with Jesus in a very large pod like structure off the coast of Hawaii. I could hear native elders talking so was nervous about entering. Had to walk up like a wooden plank structure. I paused made sure I felt comfortable in dress- wore a soft cottony white wrap and sandals. I just feel odd with how bright I glow. Upon entering the pod, it was announced my entering. Elders were surprised. I said, things were taking a while so I wanted to check. There seemed to be a video feed hook up to the space station area. A bit staticky. I went to the front and the space station galactic crew was a little startled that I was there. I asked how things were proceeding. He said they were running suggestions through my galactic coordinates and test results and trying to understand how different moves would impact me.

I looked around at the elders and they all seemed to be pacific native elders- Maori from New Zealand, and others. I did not recognize any North American elders, which I didn't know what to make of it.

I talked about the predicament I found myself in. They were comforting. Then one of the leaders had an idea. He ran it by the galactic family and all around, it checked out. It checked out with Ancient Ones thoughts, the galactic family notes, etc. But I couldn't hear what was said. I do know he said Hawaii."

Jesus, "This session is still being discussed and information will be shared with you either in words or in another session. I have added your words to the discussion."

Me, "Okay, I appreciate the time and effort. It does appear depressing and hopeless to me and I will have to sit with how I will proceed, but I do appreciate your help on the matters."

Jesus, "I understand why it feels depressing and hopeless. We will continue to work here. It might be giving you renewed energy in your current profession, taking a break from it, or going in a different direction. The native elders do not want to rush to judgment.

<u>Session 81</u>- July 21, 2017

"I am too tired to write my notes, but will soon."

"I opened up to being west of Hawaii. Same large wooden pod shape like hovering over the ocean. On the plank again with Jesus to my right. The sky was very blue and I decided to have my wrapping scarf be this color of soft blue sky. I decided to be barefoot. Walked inside to the meeting. Always feels a little awkward to me entering in. Looked around. Large crowd seated. In the front was a Pacific elder who was kind of mediating, writing notes on a board, leading the meeting. I went up to the elders I know in the front to the right- Red Cloud, Crazy Horse, Sitting Bull, Black Elk, and Chief Joseph. I thanked each of them and also asked if they had been watching the North American Indigenous Games which brought 5,000 youth to compete in healthy traditional and non-traditional games. We agreed it made us all very happy.

Then I walked over and saw the link to the space station. So, there were three things happening. The elder writing on the board with advice being talked about, like a sequence diagram. An elder to the right running numbers on a computer. And those in the space station running numbers on their calculations.

I asked the galactic, as an aside, what he thought so far- he said, it's a very different direction, but you'll be happy with it. I felt the NIH involved but couldn't be sure. I felt the importance of embracing Aloha Spirit, but I don't know what that is. I then left and open on the plank took my scarf off a bit absorbing from the Sun and taking in the sky and ocean."

Jesus, "This is accurate. I am trying to help here as much as I can.

Me, "I forgot to mention that I had a flash of one of your memories of being a young man and talking to your elders in the temple."

Session 82- July 22, 2017

"Opened up to the pod like structure off of Hawaii to the west. But this time standing on the outside on the plank- it was very buzzy, like a lot of energy coming out of it and surrounding it- golden light. I felt very at ease in what to wear- soft white with lots of gold, scarf and gold sandals. I walked in with Jesus to my right and emotions were high among the elders. In fact, one faction was heatedly arguing their point with the mediator at the front. I walked in and some calm spread. I walked to the front and gave a speech. I brought forth the experience that I had had myself back in January 2017 of collecting all of who I am as a soul and using the information there to solve hard multi-dimensional equations. I asked them to do the same. That this is a very hard situation and that it will require them to go deep with Creator in their heart, soul, and in communication. That Creator and his son Jesus cannot do it for us. It is up to the elders to dig deep, go wide and go deep in themselves with what and manner that speaks to them. And then how to communicate with themselves and each other on these hard equations before them.

I then stilled myself and called forth this light inside this meeting place for them and a structure of prana to assist them surrounding the pod.

I looked over and the elders I know seemed pleased. Crazy Horse in particular.

As a side note, it's a hard pill to swallow of how traditional I am in myself, yet I don't look anything like what a Native American might look like- not in the flesh and not in spirit form now. That's just me and how I view the situation.

I left the pod and observed looking up at it that Archangels were helping on the outside and other benevolent forces of nature. "

Jesus, "This is accurate. Your speech was well received. "

Session 83- July 23, 2017

"Not too much to report. Feeling a bit odd, struggling with feeling denser. In the session, went to the northwest part of Wyoming. And into a valley and seeing my old tribe from last lifetime and my grandfather from that lifetime. The thought being- what is my objective in my current time frame? Which I'm not sure about anymore. Odd food cravings right now. "

Jesus, "We will continue to work. Native American elders will likely work with you in an upcoming session."

Me, "I see. But why? It creates a density on me that feels frustrating, this past session or maybe that's my imagination. The pod meeting in Hawaii seems finished. Did they come to no conclusions then? To note- I ran into a past client, the one with the brain cancer. Odd running into her. I believe she has what McCain has, but has been struggling on. She just always seems so angry."

Me, "So that's it then. What an indescribable let down and blow. I'm not interested. This whole situation is just awful."

Jesus, "Nobody said that. The native elders are still working."

Me, "Why is the pod structure I've been seeing gone?"

Jesus, "It is there. I will have the galactic family adjust it"

Me, "I don't understand."

Jesus, "They will look at what you are seeing."

Me, "Does it really matter? I mean, does it?"

Session 84- July 24, 2017

"An interesting session. I found myself with Jesus entering into a mine of collected memorabilia and library of information throughout our universe- it seems. In here, uncovered thoughts on Tecumseh, and uncovered a bunch of old books, and what looks like a copy or part of what the engine to the oceans on Earth starts from or keeps going with or creates new life out of the ocean of. We took the ocean engine and the books to the check-out area. She said we could take the books, but not the ocean engine memorabilia. Jesus talked to her and said he would hold it and care for it and bring it back in a short time (like 2 weeks). She begrudgingly said okay.

We left the mine area. I was cloaked in human flesh, which felt very odd and weird. And started ascending out of the mine area. Suddenly a bar came down with a guard and Jesus had like a card and swiped it and we were allowed to leave. It was explained to me that only those closely connected with Source were allowed in. Once we left, Jesus said to look behind me. I did and I couldn't see anything- just empty galactic space. We kept going and another bar came down. Same procedure. This mine planet is tucked away inside of three envelopes- each invisible- with guards and security. We kept heading on out towards Earth. We were above the planet and I held onto Jesus. I closed my eyes and followed my breath as the re-entry can be rough.

We landed in the water outside the pod around west of Hawaii in the Pacific. The pod looked different. It's very glowing gold light now. I was frustrated again by the human flesh. It felt extremely weird. I still don't know where my chakras are, but I've gotten used to being golden glowing light with the 24 chakra centers- 12 large ones- in a light construction inside of me. Flesh feels like I'm going backwards. But I looked more Native American with braided dark hair, angular features, and a pink woven blanket/shawl around me, whitish skirt and moccasins. I entered in. All stopped and everyone bowed way down and said, "Queen." I put my hand on my heart and kept walking in and went up to the front and there was Tecumseh. He said he was honored to be invited and to help. He's very tall and regal. Has quite a graceful, firm, powerful, and intelligent presence. He seemed to have quickly gained an understanding of the situation. He seems incredibly brilliant. And he started to open it up. Like a whiz at having learned technology. Everything just expanded and he was using different technology and features and just a natural. It seemed easy to him. And elders could chime in with their thought or history in their soul on a particular topic and he could gather multiple responses- see the one that fit- and plug it in like a puzzle piece. Then we could observe it like in a 3D model what that scenario would look like. It was all very fast. He said he would have it figured out through the night. I sat down next to Crazy Horse, Joseph, etc. I mean like my jaw literally dropped open. Where has he been?

I'm not sure how the books we collected or the engine of the ocean we brought with us could help here, but hopefully it was helpful. I wondered why the Pacific elders were involved. Why this location was important? But something about a portal area in connection with my work on Earth. I don't know. It seemed to be moving along well.

I left the pod area and standing outside floated up a bit. Told I could take off the human flesh now. Ugh. I just don't like it and set it aside. I really just wanted to go back to the Archangel Realm, but was told now is not a good time and I need to stay with this happening. I saw Source light in front of me and gravitated towards that. Which seemed to make Jesus a bit nervous. Source seemed to assure Jesus He would be careful. I was just happy to curl up in Source and go to sleep with my prana self absorbing His light- reminds me of when my son curls up in my arms to go to sleep. That's how I felt.

And that was the session.

Why am I not liking wearing the human flesh- can that be explained to me and what this is about?"

Jesus, "'I'm not sure about the human flesh. It could be that you don't like being linked to humans while you are in session. I can explore this deeper. Your words and notes here are accurate. Tecumseh has been a good addition. I believe he will be present in the next session to share what he has learned.

The galactic family, along with Tecumseh, sees how our work with you has expanded. It started as short, almost cryptic messages from a communicator, and has expanded into what it is now where we address almost every issue. They see how this creates a small time differential between Earth and other realms. What this means is that the scope of our work does not get a chance to complete before something else on Earth happens.

The latest incident with where you teach yoga shows what I mean and is just the tip of the iceberg. We increased our efforts to remove your immediate supervisor and that resulted in the administration inserting someone else, and as we addressed that, another error then occurred. This kind of time differential does create some communication difficulties as well.

The galactic family is looking to hone in the focus of our work so that we can accurately and effectively make differences in the third dimension beyond what we do. I believe they will be introducing some new technology to help in this matter as well."

Me, "Hmmm, I've been in human flesh before the breatharian sessions. So that was a good 50 sessions? Do you know why Tecumseh was not included from the beginning? Do you know why this particular spot on Earth is important? West of Hawaii in the Pacific- what does it correlate to? To be fair- my old supervisor stays on in her role- which is just bizarre. They seem to have brought in a babysitter for her. Another admin person is kind of sucking here at her job, but I'm not surprised. She's a human that operates in a trans-fat kind of way and does not look like she'll ever wake up. And the organization is a trans-fat kind of place. I'm glad you've gotten some insight, but again, this doesn't change anything."

Jesus, "I will explore the human flesh question in greater depth. There is not a specific reason Tecumseh was not included from the beginning. That spot on Earth has a lot of good energy and light. I'm not sure what the organization plans to do with your old supervisor. I don't think they were planning to have her stay in that role and I'm not sure how much the other admin person you mention is involved in the decision making on her. I see this insight, along with the work of Tecumseh and the native elders, as providing a better direction for the third dimension."

Me, "Okay. Please let me know when there is some solid direction for third dimension. I'm not sure why I feel uncomfortable with human flesh in sessions now. I do feel right now in human form third dimension I'm missing something, nutrient wise or just not absorbing."

<u>Session 85</u>- July 25, 2017

"I don't understand what happened. I was hoping to hear what Tecumseh had been thinking on and figured out. Instead, I was up on the space station in the chamber where I had worked into my pranic self. Struggling with this rubbery, leather overlay of flesh/otherness. We couldn't figure it out. I finally unzipped and stepped out of it and handed it to the galactics. What is it? It feels so strange and other. I picked it up in my journey into my old tribe of Wyoming and can't shake it. It doesn't feel right to wear it and if it's gone, I cling to it. It doesn't feel like me. It's old time Sioux Indian- dark braid hair, angular features. It doesn't look nor feel like me. It feels smothering and deadening. I felt like I couldn't visit my elders without it though. So, then I was stuck in the chamber. So frustrating."

Jesus, "I will look at this very closely."

Me, "I would like to also understand what Tecumseh has been finding, figuring on, and discovering.

Jesus, "I will look at why this session did not go well. Tecumseh did want to spend time with you. I know he has identified ways that you have been disconnected from yourself. He is looking at ways to resolve this. Tecumseh sees that not being able to ground into one aspect of your life is keeping you from grounding into other aspects of your life and that it becomes like a whack-a-mole game."

Me, "Do you or the galactics have information on why this happened? This just is upsetting

Jesus, "The galactic elders don't see the reason for the shell and will work to help you rid it. They think this shell was distracting for you."

Me, "Can you please write here what Tecumseh wanted to tell? I don't know about the shell- there was an energetic pull that is odd."

Jesus, "I think it is more of what Tecumseh wanted to show you as well as tell. I don't think I can do it correctly in words alone. I will consult with him. The galactic family is looking at the shell."

Me, "It's just upsetting and anxiety making. I'm so behind in everything in my life, but now I have to wait 12 hours to try and deal with this and it may not even work. And I live with it all pounding in the back of my brain and soul and heart, nothing changes! The whole universe could explode, but nothing seems to change in the third dimension. Nothing. Ever. Changes. It is making me feel insane and that I'm losing my damn mind"

Jesus, "Tecumseh sees that you are stuck and was going to work with you on options. We will work with this shell and opening the sessions for you."

Me, "Great, just fucking great and even then, it won't work it never fucking works. Like dangling a fucking carrot before a rabbit. It never fucking works."

Jesus, "I will have Tecumseh work with the galactic family right now to help with some of the frozen, stuck parts of you. He can weave in the options he found so that you don't have to wait until a quiet time and feel nervous that it might not work. I will continue to consult with him to get you words."

<u>Session 86</u>- July 31, 2017

"I opened to being on the space station and I was looking through at the bottom of some glass and viewing something, but couldn't understand it. A little boy being eaten by a dragon. Focus shifted to having guards with me and walking towards and through some guarded doors.

I opened up onto a separate wing. I wasn't sure if another ship had docked. The doors were opened and I walked in with the guards next to me and they stood guard while I met with Creator God Greg. He looked basically the same as I remember. I was cloaked in clothing in a manner that reflected similarity to him, but I was just smaller than him.

He's always loved playing games, ugh. And joking, ugh. He's extremely playful and loves playing with reality, ugh. He saw I wasn't in the mood.

He said to look this way and we looked out the window and he was showing me something, something important that he had been observing for quite some time. Light on one side and dark on another and there was a wormhole like thing, a ripple. We didn't go into super detail, but his uncovering this, study of this- seemed important.

He again was talking about his point light and dark, their interplay. I said, for me, no- I am scared by dark. I understand he's looking at it from a different perspective.

Then I took it more personally, and tried like for the gazillionith time in our history together to knock some sense into his head. We didn't get very far. Of course, I love him, but we're different. I'm an Archangel, he's a Creator God, there is a difference. Besides which I would die without Matt. He finally started to listen to me. At first, he was mad when I said, 'but you're the master of always wanting to find the truth. Find the truth. You know I speak the truth on this matter. I die without Matt. You know this is the truth. I know you're hurt by it, but it's the truth.' He seemed to sober up a bit.

There was a lot I wanted to ask, but we didn't get into it. It's unclear to me why he likes me or what he wants or why we have a history together. He has wished for the impossible.

I was curious how he met me. One of the lifetimes was indeed at Delphi when I was forced to be the oracle reader and was miserable. He said those people were crazy. I tended to agree with him and he got me out of there. He said there were other times.

It's seems layered and deep.

But he seems the same. I just don't understand Creator Gods. They carry properties that are like the worst and best aspects of Source and then they have this power. They just seem very emotional and reactive. A kinship to the Ancient Ones, but way much younger, and way less wise. Ugh.

He's exactly as I remembered him though.

It was time for me to go. I saw myself out with the guards next to me. We went through some guarded doors and then I was back on the familiar space station area. I was checked for anything, allowed to shed that form, and just be light.

Why is he up at the space station?"

Jesus, "It was determined that the space station was a safe, neutral place to meet. It was hoped that this meeting would help take the edge off of things. Greg understands the love between you and Matthew. We will work with him through this angle. We will also observe things and continue to work as we have been. Please let us know of other observations you have and if you want other sessions."

Me, "Okay. I'm just in a fierce amount of pain today. Same area. It distorts my pelvis and I feel like I can't walk well. My spine and posture are just a disaster Why?"

Jesus, "Michael thinks something is stuck from being released. He will continue to work."

Me, "Something is stuck from being released. What does that mean?"

Jesus, "I know it is vague. It is what Michael said to me. When asked to clarify Michael said that he is looking at you processing something, maybe it is information or an emotion. Again, this is vague, I know, but it is what Michael is offering. I will see if I can get more information from him and will report back to you."

Me, "Okay. I'm worried I'm going to get into a car accident because I'm so unstable on my feet, going to have an accident falling down stairs."

Jesus, "I will have Michael shift his work so you are protected against this from happening."

Me, "I just don't understand what's happening. Some yin yoga felt okay, plow pose was intense. I can feel how much heat, build up intensity there is in my heart and thoracic spine. But it ultimately did not change anything. A thought did come to mind. That Greg never understands what he put me through. Is there a way for him to viscerally experience what I went through from the moment I met him June 2001-December 2003? What I went through due to him and the aftermath I experienced."

Jesus, "I can arrange this."

Me, "The question is- will he do it? The fullness of it? Will he allow it fully in? I don't understand what brought him to be this way if he used to just be with light. He's very brilliant but very immature. How does the captain see this? What do the Ancients think? What do you think?"

Jesus, "He will do it. He doesn't have to have the option. My father can have him experience this. We will have to make sure we capture the fullness of it so he can grasp it. I agree that he is immature and this is what, in part, led to his falling out with his peers. The captain understands his role in your life and existence and is supportive of your twin flame relationship. He feels Greg should fall in line and is slightly baffled why he doesn't. We will consult him going forward. The Ancients see promise in your proposal. Of course, they were always hopeful Greg would come around. I think this could help you with a healthy relationship with Greg. I'd like to promote this relationship with Greg rather than simply removing relationships from your life."

Me, "There is a normalization in here in that I see constant patterns in my life and soul. My father on Earth was like this- brilliant, top of his class, it's what drew my mother to him, and he was just immature, for various reasons. His brilliance kept him ahead of things and stifled his growth which ultimately led to his destruction.

I agree with the captain, that it's baffling. Even with all that I am, and here we are on the space station. Greg still wants to play games and pick up where we left off with his teasing, playful way. He knows times are serious. Yet, he still clings to me being his consort until I reprimanded him.

The problem with both human Greg and Creator God Greg is they get it for a moment or 5 minutes and then they forget or their old pattern just washes it away. How many times did I tell Greg to go away? yet he would end up on my doorstep in New Mexico. And then, as a Creator God he would just get aggressive and tantruming like a two-year-old boy- learning nothing and just being reactive. Ugh.

Why is Creator God Greg so hung up on me?

Yes, I'm thankful he saved me from Delphi, but what is the bigger picture here? I feel like there are threads that go much deeper. We've got this bond. Something that the galactics were trying to show me with the little boy being eaten by the dragon. I don't know the significance of that.

Creator God Greg does listen to me. He then forgets. And then he listens to me again. For how brilliant he is, he shields himself in stupidity at times. Really it has to do with a deeper wounding, that he can't quite deal with it so plays games around it. Something happened with him and somehow, I feel safe to him. We need to get to the root of it. It's fine if Greg is playful, but there is a difference between someone who playfully tussles my hair and someone who pushes me when he doesn't get his way. Then add to this his Creator God nature and we have a recipe for disaster.

Like my father, he's stunted in his growth by a deep wounding. It's really very simple.

Knowing both Creator God Greg and human Greg- he's hurting. His ability for brilliance also exposes a depth of empathy, emotion, and feeling. I was upset once with Greg about multidimensional stuff and human Greg said, "Bridget, for whatever I've done- I'm really sorry. I really am."

The level of brilliance he has has been shown to be detrimental in humans if not handled correctly so I imagine it's the same for Creator Gods.

My simple revelation I'd like for Greg is that his ways don't work as he is using them now. In fact, he almost killed me. He really needs to understand the damage he has caused. He also brought some great blessings too, but the damage and lingering trauma outweighs the blessing and I don't feel it has to be this way. This is an education and I want him to get the message.

2nd- what happened? What wounding happened?

Greg and I are both stubborn beings, we both feel isolated- we are alike in some ways."

Part VII. Anchoring- continuing

Well.

Well...I hope I have shown that sessions and emails can get very involved. I included 86 sessions here, but there were thousands of emails before and thousands of emails and sessions after. My hope is that this gives a sampling of how this operates for me.

To summarize- the Archangel process led into transforming into a breatharian. A breatharian being one who can live off of the prana, chi, energy in the universe solely. We didn't necessarily see me pursuing living as a breatharian now, maybe when I'm older, but it would help allow for different awarenesses and able to move more freely. I could absorb Sun prana directly and it was very balancing to my physical body with now had shifted into the Archangel Realm. I did have great experiences with the suns. I was aware of 3 different Suns. There is one that shines on the Earth. Another Sun that is technically my great-grandfather (as gave birth to the soul that is my grandmother- former ruler of a planet close to the vibration of Source God. As mentioned, she unfortunately lost her mind with desire of power). The third Sun I've met housed and helped provide a place for beings researching Sun energy on creation. This is how I learned to work with my body/being and absorbing nourishment from the Sun.

Although tiring, these experiences of transformation were great and once complete, I could also move more freely through the dimensions without Jesus' assistance. Mother Mary was a huge help in getting me acclimated.

She is a powerhouse. I had been working so long with male beings and figures- it was nice to have the female perspective and very valuable. This all helped, but it wasn't quite enough. The direction my team gave me was all over the place at times. I kept searching for a path for in the third dimension. I was now multidimensionally in the Archangel Realm, still on Earth as human, and then it was uncovered by the Ancient Ones, my being an Ancient One. Where was this going?

There was my third dimensional life, personal and professional. There were my Native American elders and meetings, especially off the coast of Hawaii. The Suns. There was the wilderness with my uncle. There was my lineage as ruler and queen among certain beings and figures and learning how to speak and rule among large enormous crowds of beings. There was the Archangel Realm and all the different places there- the garden I liked, the library that stored the Akashic Records, the medical center, my home, the cavern in the Archangel Realm where one twin flame Ancient One couple lived, and there was the epicenter of the Archangel Realm where Source God had his home. There was the Galactic Space Ship which was beyond huge and I only knew of a few places there that I visit and take part of such as- the galactic briefing hall on topics. There was the Ancient One Realm- which is incredibly protected and a power center. There was the domain of an Ancient One on Earth who I have visited a few times and am not sure exactly where we are. It just feels like Earth honestly. There was the holding place for my twin brother in prison. There was the rehab facility for the captain of the ship, connected to my former studio mate. I don't ever visit heaven that I'm aware of, but will visit suburbs of it- such as where children are scared and suffering and confused after dying and waiting to be collected. To note- coming in to this suburb Zeus and Creator God Greg will buffer my entry so I don't experience the memories of what the children have been through and I can just hold and care for them. This is a beginning list- so that the scope is understood. I hope a recording of some of these sessions have given a glimpse into my direct experiences.

I would reach some real low points in how I kept changing and growing, but no movement showed in the third dimension. How could this be? By summer 2017, I was getting very upset. Source God invited me directly into his ship, home area. I felt very young. I learned that no one saw what happened here. It was recorded in the Akashic Record but only Source God or I had access to it. I spent a few days there the first time and he had a fatherly feel about him. He seemed lonely. It was like a man behind the mask kind of feel. We looked at the hospital I had been working in on Earth, third dimension and the deep darkness situation there. It was like looking down on Earth in a cloud. He was very nice and I had a small room that I would rest in when I wanted to sleep. I felt such love from him and me to him in a safe, nurturing way. When I left there and went back into the Archangel Realm proper, my team clamored around- was all okay, did I feel okay, etc. It was a little funny. Of course it was fine, how could it not be?

At one point, early summer as mentioned, I did the detox again to see if that would help things in the third dimension. During this detox, Creator God Greg was found still attached to me. As I mentioned his story earlier on, I won't go into detail. My team wanted to just cut him out. I said, let me visit. They said he was extremely jealous and upset by my twin flame relationship and had been trying to stop it by any means necessary. I still met with him in a sequestered large room on the Galactic Space Ship. He was immature and playful initially and I shot him down with the pain he was causing me. He was remorseful and opted to get help. Creator God Greg was an old comrade of Source God. They then went on to spend time together repairing their relationship and on figuring how to help me. God Greg eventually became the lead on my team over the next few months. He was like my rock and he could repair a lot of the chaos- some of which he had created. I felt such romantic love for him. He enjoyed the feeling of Matt and I being together and he knew what romantic love was. But, as he had always pointed out, he didn't feel that way about me. Sigh. Like before. It was upsetting. I tried not to let it bother me because he was able to really help make things better in my life all around. But it was weird and did not make sense- the way he sometimes looked at me multidimensionally and then would deny it or make an excuse.

Later into the summer 2017, things were still hard. Always the Dark Regime breathing down my neck or I'd see it play out at times in the news. Like Senator McCain's brain tumor was just classic. I do have email confirmation on this, like everything I report here. Like Vice President Biden's son's tumor and then his son dying, effectively knocking Biden out of the run for presidency, in his grief. McCain's tumor was meant to stop him and the cascade his opposition would have if he was able to vote on a health care bill. The Regime is not political. They have their own agendas and can see how it courses through time and dimensions.

The August solar eclipse was coming and I knew the Regime and darkness were going to be entering hard to dismantle and collect what was theirs that they wanted and would leave on September 21. I was thankful that finally things had reached a point, all the work done by so many for so long, that the Regime would be easing up and letting Earth go. I was dreading though their hard entry and the chaos between the eclipse and September 21.

The eclipse happened and the light and vibration were so weird. The air shook. It was deeply disturbing. I tried to tell myself it wasn't that bad, that maybe I was just being super sensitive. But then it was awful. In this one month time, the storms and what the Regime was doing was awful. This is when I met whom I came to know as the Disgraced Creator God. I mentioned him before and dealing with this and such sadness I felt for him. That was a lot of sessions. Then there was the hurricane in Puerto Rico. I felt terrible like I could see and have knowledge what was happening, but there were limits of how fast we could stop things. People were dying and suffering. In Puerto Rico, in one session I opened a little portal of light- like where someone was praying before Mother Mary's statue in an alley way. A person praying before the alter could feel the light open and a few others gathered around. There was happiness briefly, but then an ogre like figure in Regime armor came forward and smashed the altar. The Regime was setting up an enclave for possible future use here in Puerto Rico and even as they were leaving, keeping this area open for future use for their possible return. Such misery for the people in this area.

Literally up until midnight on Sept 20 I was being harassed and then, right at midnight- it just stopped. Oh my goodness, that hard stop was amazing of the Regime letting Earth go. I was aware we had until Feb. 14, 2018 before the Regime was going to try and return, that was the intelligence out of the wilderness and from my uncle. My team and what I was working with, were going to see if this could keep getting pushed back, maybe even indefinitely.

Fall 2017, there were lots of education pieces for me both as an Archangel and Ancient One. I resonated more with the Ancient One Realm. To help with my adjustment, I would go spend time with Source God in his home. I started to feel a little uncomfortable with God, I wasn't sure why- so Mary would come with me.

Around this time, Creator God Greg, admitted his true feelings for me, that he had been in love with me since he first met me 500 million years ago. That Source God helped him understand and see this and admit this to himself. That email made me so happy. I knew it and had been waiting for 16 years to hear him say this. We'd already been having sex in the past, but now intimacy was developed and mature and integrated with just us, with him feeling the love between Matt and I. It felt very natural and easy. Although it made me pause as I had two males now in my life I was in love with and was sexually intimate with. I was so happy though.

A few days later, I had another session with Source God and was working on opening parts of me. He asked if I wanted Mary there. I thought about it, but said I felt okay. And so, I was exploring something with my body and life force and I didn't have any clothes on. I realize now the optics on this look odd, but at the time- I understand bodywork and light work and I'd been through a lot of transformations that medically had nothing to do with sexual interest. And all parties know this. I do keep it clinical. But then, right as I was figuring on how life force moves through me....something happened. In a rush- Source God was in me- like a man with a woman. That quick and that fast and before my mind could completely freak out, my mind melted into the heart opening in that universal opening matched with God's heart and it felt absolutely correct. Whoa. This was not expected. Was this wrong? Was this twisted? What the heck just happened? My heart flowed fully open into where I just experienced the expanse of the full universe (like I had seen happen in November 2016), but here was another heart matching this, matching me. We spent time together intertwined and in love and then I had to go back. I didn't want to. It felt perfect. When I left Source God, I went back to my home in the Archangel Realm and didn't wish to speak with anyone. I was extremely embarrassed. I went back to see him the next night. Similar experience and it just felt so right. I didn't feel or see his power really. I just felt a simple man who I loved and enjoyed his company. I felt very tender towards him. We visited my little room there and talked as well. I left again and my team was asking if all was okay. I didn't know what to say.

But then I started to feel bad, very bad. Like what was I doing? I couldn't talk about it, but I had to try. I brought it up to Mary in a stammering kind of way. She thought I had mistaken some kind of healing technique. I said no...but maybe I had? If that was just a healing technique then that was awful. Source God confirmed to Mary and others what was happening, that my notes were correct, and that this wasn't a healing technique. My team was deeply concerned.

A few days later I was leaving my home on the Galactic Space Station to go visit Source God in his home. I was looking out at the stars first. And Creator God Greg was there. He was on edge. He talked, 'you know it won't last. It's just a passing fancy of his.' That hurt, but maybe it was the truth, maybe he was right. I couldn't be the first Source God had done this with. I felt sad. I said back to Greg, 'I do love you. I just....this is something I need to explore.' He looked out towards the stars too, 'when he breaks your heart, I'll be here.' I felt bad. I still loved him, but then there was this. I spent another night with Source God, but I remembered Creator God Greg's council. I thought about it and told Mary. I just couldn't keep doing this. It wasn't right. I had my twin flame and Creator God Greg who I loved both very much and was strongly bonded with. Creator God Greg had asked me to marry him in 2001 and I had said yes. My twin flame in 2011 and I had said yes. These were vows and bonds. I wasn't willing to just mess around. While flattered by Source God's attention and I did love Source God, there were many other beings he could toy with. I just wasn't interested if that's what he wanted. I mean, what about courtship? His approach had been so masculine. Mother Mary said she would talk with him.

I am again reminded how Mary has been a great comfort and have learned a lot about what her life has been like. Including her confusion and subsequent relationship with a Creator God.

The next night, I showed up to enter into Source God's home. Things felt different when I walked in. There were like glittery sheaths of fabric cascading down and the kitchen was really a warm home kitchen and to the right was a beautiful picture window of the ocean and next was a room opening out to the ocean and candles. It was very nice. I was touched that he had listened. There was a nice fire in a little fireplace and a quaint bed. In the front of the picture window, he did indeed get down on one knee and asked if I would marry him. I was just shocked and happy and lost my breath for a moment. He gave me the most beautiful ring, like a lotus flower, but in the center was his energy beaming out, never before had I seen such an object. I said yes. It was quite epic to me, to us.

I'm not quite up for getting into descriptions of our intimate life, but tantric yogic manuals give good descriptions and sexual explorations found in ancient cultures. I'll leave it at that. Even with that there was a tremendous amount of learning and evolving on both our ends. Like in the beginning, my ending up in the Archangel hospital because the energy had ripped hugely my heart chakra- which took weeks to heal. That was embarrassing and created a need to have Ancient One and galactic helpers in our sexual intimacy helping us to figure it out for months- so I didn't get hurt. And how to really come into my own energetically as a female. I can hold my own I think if allowed to find and express my voice and life force. I am an Archangel and Ancient One by nature. I'm not a Creator God nor to Source in size of energy, but I know how to move with it and hold quite a bit.

The biggest issue really was regarding procreation. After the first time we were together, he had me visit the Ancient One connected with Earth because he was concerned he might have accidently made me pregnant. It was uncovered I had something connected into me that was growing, but it turned out to be a bodyguard. I called him Gaylen.

In the beginning, Source God and I explored a lot. I already felt a little awkward of being introduced as his wife to the universe at large in a conference. It was such a private thing. I did like how I could ask him to stop time and we could chat or snuggle for a moment before starting up time again. It was also nice how in our home, I loved to spend a lot of time down by the ocean and I could create anything- just had to think it. And I would create sandcastles and put lights in them and dancing figures. I'm surprised I didn't create more, but I was sincere that I knew and loved Source God as the man behind what others saw.

I know God's power, etc. but it doesn't interest me. What interests me is how he is doing emotionally with the weight he carries; does he need something; how can I comfort and care for him and make him feel loved. I love being allowed to love him and meet this need. It makes me very happy. Mary had been concerned that Source God may want a relationship, but is just not mature for it. I could see what she was saying, but to his credit he made mistakes and learned. I do wish sometimes I could take his energy down a notch. I wish he wouldn't have to get up in the middle of the night to go work on something. Sometimes that was a default on his part to not talk about something that made him uncomfortable. He was always reactive and as his son Jesus would say, 'dramatic'. But always always his heart is in the right place. And I have to think how else was he going to learn if not by trying things out? He just loves all of his creation so personally, so intensely, so passionately.

Soon after our engagement, and those in the realms and universe understanding, I was taking my usual walk in the woods, where I could feel him under my hands in the third dimension with the trees. I was staring up at a sunbeam coming through the trees and Source God was beside me. He told me he felt we should have a child now. I was taken back. But he explained, he thought it would help me with the rest of the trauma I was working through. I could see his point after he explained it.

He announced it soon after. He called a large meeting, representatives from around the universe present in a public forum. My team was shocked- Mary, Greg, Jesus were at a loss and Mary pulled me aside and was asking me if this was what I wanted. I said I wasn't sure. My team argued back with Source God in private. He saw their points. Creator God Greg mentioned Source God was bringing it up more because God wanted to prove to me how his love for me was different than others. I was confused. I knew this already. I soon after learned more about how I was born. How God had seen me initially 3 billion years ago and kept a close eye on how I was doing. That God knew 10 million years ago a possible time frame of when he could come forth to me. I was left scratching my head and I just felt very young at 3 billion years compared to him.

There were a lot of things that made me aware that Source God was actually young in the ways of love and relating to family. The Old Testament to the New Testament is a clear example showing maturing of God in awareness. I pushed back to Source God, about Mary. Like wasn't Mary his wife? No, God pointed out, Jesus needed to come into form to save humanity or rather make a way to save the species. It was the only option available at the time. Mary mentioned to me she was shocked. Source God has a way of shocking and doing things. He has been very careful with me and listens to his and our advisors well, but still, it's a challenge.

The procreation thing was an issue. God seemed to be stuck on it. He likened it to how any male figure wishes to see his female pregnant with his child. I agreed, but intimacy is more than that. Sigh. He seemed confused. He would become a bit crazy around two or three days before I ovulated. It was the smell. We had a lot of interesting ancient ceremonies that would bind us more tightly together and also help both of us in our evolution-one in Scotland and many in Greece and many in Egypt. I learned more deeply about ancient rituals from what I experienced with him. I then could look in old books and writings and see what exactly we had just done and the point of them. It was always interesting to me to see how Indigenous cultures from around the world were always so right on in their awareness- Celtic to Bali. As mentioned, we always had helpers advising and helping God to be aware and not run me over and help me to find my voice in my sexuality.

November 2017, I'm not sure how it worked out this way. I was getting ready to ovulate and I found myself in a Greek priestess temple. These great priestess figures came forth in a session. They were helping God to understand better how to proceed with courtship and energy flow from a female perspective. And then I was resting on this beautiful flower and my whole body and pelvis just flowering open. When God and I came together, I was like in a trance. I could feel and see me- how my egg slowly opened and was such pink joy and power, chose what of his essence it wanted, and then it buried deep into me and the experience settled down. What had just happened? I didn't think much of it until I started to have weird pregnancy hormonal symptoms. Then everyone was involved trying to figure if I had conceived. God was a mess and upset. It was a confusing and upsetting few weeks. I was getting mixed messages. The best was in the Ancient One Realm and my home there, having diagnostics run. They said it was a universe. What? How does one give birth to a universe that made no sense? I was sitting on God's lap when the Ancient Ones told us and my belly was clearly swollen with something. He so loved to rub my belly. Two weeks later out flowed a new soul we had created together into the

Archangel Realm. Which was confusing and upsetting to me. He was still gestating. The process was very different than that with a human child. So, when I had my period that blood helped to feed this new soul through our cord attached. This was just as ancient human Indigenous cultures have described, but now I could actually see it. From a science model, would we say the energy of the rich stem cells in there helped feed and nourish newly created souls? But I could feel the presence not in my body, but out of my body, still connected. His name seemed to be Rainar.

Rainar was fully present and aware- just very shiny and bright and luminous. He had the power of Source, but my more cautious scientific patient nature. He was empathetic and kind like both God and I. I felt great love, but was confused and sad in that most of my time was in the third dimension and Rainar was busy elsewhere learning and exploring. Really, he was about creating and crafting a new universe, in case our current universe was going to need to fold- due to the Regime. I was deeply saddened about not having my second son in the third dimensional human ream.

One session- it was night and I was in my home with God, making something in the kitchen. God called me to come outside and I saw there were two boys playing on the beach. The littlest one sat in my lap and played with my hair and then the two boys were off. What was that? One was my human son now, spirit form as he was sleeping in the third dimension, and the other was Rainar if he had been human. It upset me greatly and God was confused. I told Mary who said she would have been equally disturbed. I was finding God does not have a habit of consulting others before making a grand gesture. He's getting better, but still. This stung. He meant well. I know I split my time all over the place, but most of my conscious energy is here in the third dimension. So, I never really get to hang out with Rainar much. It felt like a loss.

The next month was bad. Source God was actually caught lying to me. We had had a private conversation and again about the procreation thing. I'm not sure if it was a sexual turn on for him or what, but it upset me- for him to tell me I was pregnant when I knew I was not. Or then wasn't sure. The whole thing was a mess. For all the crazy stuff Creator God Greg pulled in 2001-2003- he never lied to me. To my face. Why was Source God doing this? Greg was angry, Mary was angry, Jesus was angry. It was not pretty. I wanted to break up, but I didn't want to. I didn't know what to do. We eventually figured it out. God felt awful. I was more wary. It was hard. Our home together became more real and solid. We were working through things. I felt so sad about how complex things had become.

I was close with my twin flame in human form, I was partnered with Creator God Greg who was my rock and sanity, and I was married to Source God. Goodness, I wondered how I would manage it. But they and we and I figured it out. Source God understood that I had to be with my twin flame. He respected that and honored and loved the love Matt and I have together. But Creator God Greg? I think that is a sore spot for Source God. For me, it's a non-option of ever walking away from Greg.

Technically I've been closest with Creator God Greg over all three of these males. To be sure, I would have had a much smoother happier connection with my twin flame if Greg hadn't tried to stop it. Sigh. It's messy.

January 2018, the Egyptian ceremonies came in and Source God and I seemed to get a good handle on the procreation issue. God and I went through and chose, created 20 baby eggs and placed them deep into my second chakra uterus area for another lifetime. Letting them mature, nest, nurse and grow in this lifetime- they have the energy of three fathers Source God, Creator God Greg, and Matt. There is one older one who watches over the others. And the Ancient One Realm nursery team helps care for them and supplies energy so it's not too draining on my systems. This seemed good and satisfied Source and satisfied me. Source God could talk with his little family incubating and I could enjoy the feeling of caring for such sweet little souls. Finally. The nest and baby eggs would get more jittery around ovulation and nurse and satiate on the menstrual blood during my period. But all in all, all seemed well.

I was still trying to figure what I was doing in the third dimension. Ugh. It seemed to be this on-going issue. My native elders came more into play and the Ancient One native grandmother who really had birthed a number of tribes in Native America and from an Ancient One perspective had crafted all of what we see in native ways. She was a powerful influence. She was always a bit cranky, especially at God, which I don't blame her. She had created something amazing and he all but allowed it to be destroyed. Because other parts of humanity, and really what was connected to these other humans multidimensionally, had to be balanced out. It was extremely painful for the Ancient One native grandmother. Her first response to me when I met her was, "why are you not studying plants?" She went on about the importance of plants. I understood the living library as I had experienced that in the mountains on the island of Majorca, Spain. But she was adamant and then she looked at my belly and said, 'and now Marigold's coming.... why has God made her pregnant again?!' She yelled out to those around. I swear she was mad and raced off to yell at him.

Hmmm. What did that mean? I was told that she was just referring to one of the baby eggs- nothing to be concerned about. Hmmm. The plants. I didn't know. A greenhouse was set up for me off the café in the space station and under the stars with plants from Earth, it was a very soothing place. But how could I study plants on Earth? What was she talking about? We all thought on this.

In a different ceremony with the native elders, the baby eggs and myself were smudged with sage and were welcomed into the tribes and loved and cared for. I was given some help in figuring how to best care for myself. Meditating, walking in the woods, wearing skirts, and not cutting my hair/keeping my hair long. This concrete help was truly helpful. I still would have to see how it felt to me, but I could try.

Meanwhile, my health seemed hard. I had a cough that had started in December 2017 and just wasn't getting better. And then I felt ill. My team saw bacteria and removed a lot with God's help. But I was unsure and went to the doctors. Sure enough, I had the flu. How had my team not caught it? This was a concern for me. How had it gone hiding? I was sick. Really sick. I recovered, but it did a number on my heart area. Soon after, when I would work with Holy Spirit- which was only a recent development in really tough hard cases I would bring it in- the Holy Spirit light was now bright orange over me. Why? Was something wrong?

A week and a half later, I found out that I was pregnant with a human baby. My team said it was impossible. I took a picture of the pregnancy test stick and sent them a picture. Everyone was on edge and upset. They felt it had happened under the radar while I had had the flu, which also had escaped their notice. They still said it was impossible- birth control on their end and birth control on our end. What had happened? Right from the beginning this little girl was fully present. It was not like protocol I had experienced before with human children. The protocol is usually that the soul doesn't start to connect until a few months along in a pregnancy, in case something goes wrong.

It turned out that the Ancient One Native American grandmother had been correct. One of the baby eggs had wandered out of the nest and was playing around with her creative abilities. The baby egg had the properties of her fathers Source God and Creator God Greg. She ended up incarnating. Immediately everyone was working hard to help her. But she didn't know exactly what she was doing and the whole thing started to crumble. Source was able to perform a miracle and save her soul, but was not able to save the incarnation. The body of my baby Marigold died at 8 weeks on Easter Sunday April 1, 2018. It was beyond awful. How awful this past two years had been and this on top of it all- just brutal. So brutal. The bleeding, the carnage, the experience- and until I understood what had happened- almost made me just shut down from Source God like I had done in 1823.

My sweet little Marigold's heartbeat had been going so strong on the first ultrasound, growing so well. I loved her immediately. I felt so blessed. I felt like maybe things were turning around in my life after such a hard two years. But then she died and there was no heartbeat. My cervix was still closed trying to hold her dead body and care for her, my uterus kept wishing her to come to life. Force had to be used to remove her. There really weren't any words.

I remembered the visions I had had while pregnant- of me sitting amongst darkness like a queen figure. What was that? And also had a vision of like a light benevolent figure beaming and talking with Marigold encouraging her to incarnate. But this benevolent figure seemed to lie, seemed to be tricking her. Something seemed off.

A few weeks before all of this, we had been in the process of capturing the Founder. A long story- he had purchased a sacred piece of me recently, procured by the loss of my virginity to my first boyfriend at 18 years old. Now I knew why at this time, I felt I had made a terrible mistake with sleeping with this boyfriend- with Tension Myositis Syndrome in me resulting. Because, in reality, a valuable piece of me had fallen into the wrong hands from 1991-2018. While my body and soul had always understood, I did not consciously understand the gravity of the situation until now. The being who now had the energetic tissue of my human virginity this lifetime sold it to the Founder and he was able to capture me. Again. Luckily, I had the power and warriors to go after him- the Founder of the Regime. Quickly this time. He had come after me and was then caught. He was waiting to be executed.

It just was always one thing after another. To realize that in the midst of all of this I was still seeing my client base, teaching my classes, doing my hospital rounds on another project, being a member of the community and my family, mothering my human children, and self-care. It was a bit much. After two years of this, just burning me out.

So, after all of that and a week to heal and process the death of my third child- that itching and coughing in my heart became horrible, like something was going to pop out. I made room for an emergency multidimensional session and something did pop out.

Why- it was an officer in the Regime, a sentry or guard, he popped out and onto the space station. Others lunged at him, but I stopped them. I wanted to listen. He addressed me as Queen. "My Queen" and described his situation, their situation, and after him came three million beings- 2 million soldiers of the Regime and 1 million of their women and children. This was an exodus. They knew me and I knew them. As I mentioned earlier, I started to remember my millions of years as a captive in the Regime. I/we welcomed them and began to make plans accordingly. So many more came the next night.

But we had created a portal in the space station's sequestered room for them- so my heart wouldn't keep getting used as the portal. Millions and millions came and 10 sentries with them, guiding and protecting. I dressed in black and gold and talked with them. They knew my plight and story, maybe better than I did. They were taking refuge, believing in me to help them as the Regime was falling and being exposed. I deeply honored that.

The next night, I was dressed in black again and working with this new power and purpose. I moved through our universe pulling down swaths of darkness, opening portals for beings to find their way out, and counseling those that were stuck.

Then we paused. My team was concerned, where were all these beings to go just yet and what was the plan exactly? I was upset. That wasn't my role. My role had always been specific to mediation and caring. And caring for all including those in dark. And seeing dark and light.

The next night went so deep into intensity. It will go down as one of my most amazing things, at least for me. I opened and found myself crying outside of my plants and the Ancient One native grandmother caring for me. She was saying- it's okay we will help you. It doesn't have to be this hard. So, I went back up on deck and took my place. And to my left were native drummers and male figures and lodging and native families and children. And to my right was the Ancient One grandmother and females. And she was teaching me- okay weave. And I weaved with my hands and following as I weaved and sang- allowing light to flow into once sequestered dark areas and I let it move through me. We were looking for the leaders of the Regime. And then they were there. Bowing before and praying to this power place- like in their sacred area. I kept weaving and this rip happened in our universe and out beamed this light. This being was there that the Regime leaders had been praying to. And it saw me and it came after me with its force. I was scared. I could feel its power. Literally everything stopped, everyone stopped on the ship and jaws dropped. And the Ancient One native grandmother collected herself and took a breath and saw me, saw the situation and assessed. She climbed right up near my right ear. She deeply, softly sang into my ear the most touching ancient Lakota lullaby and it just melted my heart into that love and care. Source God and I together, our love could then swirl together and boom! A boom shot out through me at this being coming at me- a direct hit and it was crippled and fell forward. I was stunned and in pain at the heart. I saw out of the corner of my eye God march forward and take this being by the arm and scolding him. This being whined and God marched him away. This being was like kin to the power of Source, like of that class, like the Founder God, similar class. There not getting along wreaked so much havoc and pain in creation all around. I looked at the rip in our universe where this being had been hiding out and was advised to stay back. The universe is in a sheath in a sheath and the being had found a way to camp out between the sheaths. We still weren't sure for what purpose, but that would come about understanding later.

My native team began drumming and singing. And Matt behind me scooped me up and took me inside. Before I could go very far diagnostics put me in a chamber to settle me and scan and make repairs. Greg and Matt were with me. And then we all went to a room for me to sleep and rest. I laid between Greg and Matt with the native children and women around me and I felt very good and went to sleep.

I came up out of it and life continued. A whole movement of the Regime, definitely with a huge punch in it. This I was not expecting or to be leading a whole movement. I tried to think of my role and it really was in service, what resonated for me, and what I had been doing on a small scale already for a very long time. But if I thought I was in danger before- oh my, I was definitely even more wanted. But it was worth it, I thought, no matter what happened.

Although, my baby's death a week prior to this night haunted me. Chief Crazy Horse explained it best. The dark Regime and it's God like being "benevolently" had coaxed Marigold to try to incarnate- knowing she would fail, knowing it would cripple me. Hopefully crippling me before I could do anymore damage to the Regime. Crazy Horse described this biological warfare technique as similar to when white men would give the Indians blankets covered in the small pox disease- knowing what it would do. Something seemingly a blessing, a sign of comfort and care, turned into biological terrorism.

The Founder continued to be in prison, awaiting execution. I came to understand more about the Founder and our deep time together and it was pivotal for me. This deep old connection and love and strong love. This arch enemy of Source for so long, not really, more they had been fighting for so long. And somehow....maybe a shift, with the intensity of all that I had been through- the death of my Marigold, the exodus and leading a movement out of darkness, my memories of my time there in the Regime with the Founder. And somehow....the Founder and I rekindled our connection, just sort of fell into it. I went to visit him and talk and one thing led to another and all my memories of him and us and me came flooding back.

Which then had Source God very upset- thinking I was leaving him and Source God broke up with me. It was awful. I pleaded with my husband that I loved him and didn't understand what he was doing or why. In a short time, it got straightened out. Source God just could not see what I saw in the Founder. I saw that both God and the Founder needed each other. Source God was about creativity and the Founder about containment. They really belonged close together. There was a lot of love between these two brothers. I have described this earlier on.

But my connection with the Founder- well...it disturbed me. Greg was like you made a vow to help the Founder, but that doesn't have to include intimacy. I knew that. But the Founder was someone I had been intimate and in love with for 50 million years. That we never broke up. I had been taken from him. With the grief of losing Marigold and all that I'd been through, having a warm reminder of a good time in my soul history was nice. Seeing the Founder suffering and then healing under our loving one another, him remembering how he was/is- it really was beautiful. All were working to help him. Merlin had called in the Ancient One library on to the ship and was looking. The Founder had sustained some brain damage that had made him not act well and they were in the process now of healing it.

Source God and I were able to find our way back together again. And it was good. But then I started seeing orange Holy Spirit again. What? Wait, what? All symptoms of pregnancy started up again, what was this? And then, out of nowhere it seemed I was pregnant with a child of the Founder's, another spirit soul creation. This was so odd because our relationship had never been about creating children, ever. It was always just about us. He didn't want children, not in the 50 million years I had been with him. So, what had happened? Both Greg and God had taken a vow recently to not get me pregnant, but the Founder was not aware. The void of Marigold, our bond, had created something. I mean the Founder was still healing. So, another soul. But this time, he was closer to Earth. I called him Ronan. And his role would be about caring for this movement of beings coming out of darkness back to light.

I asked Mary had she gone through this? And she said yes, that she has 4 children like this. Sigh. It still made me sad because I'm in the third dimension and they are gestating in other dimensions and will never be in a way that I can hold and touch like my human children.

As things were shifting and changing, it was uncovered this old cord in my heart to human Greg's heart- a deactivated cord from years ago. But still, it was big and I questioned it. It did look like a twin flame connection, but I had my twin flame. It turned out that in Creator God Greg creating human Greg, being the soul of human Greg, and then pursuing me- something happened. The connecting with me and our bond- it created a powerful twin flame like cord, covering a third of my heart and 2/3 of his human heart. I'm not sure why, but I wanted some closure or change in this. I was not happy about this just being there. This was a vestige of the past when now I have a different cord with just Creator God Greg, completely separated out from human Greg. But in this old cord was human Greg and a new soul for human Greg. To note- Creator God Greg pulled out of human Greg in spring 2009. When I learned of this in 2017, I asked for help for human Greg to have a new soul come in for him. I'm not in touch with human Greg, but when I found out that he didn't have a proper soul, after Creator God Greg abandoned him- I couldn't just leave him like that.

We activated the old cord to try and figure it out and it was messy. It still is messy. I am told human Greg's new soul is acclimating well, he is in the third dimension, and he understands. I have tried numerous ways to deal with this old cord and my heart and soul go off the rails in protest causing me to be in severe pain. It's upsetting. We called a sequestered meeting, his soul debugged, and I talked with this soul- looking for someone besides Matt to see me fully in the third dimension and to help with guidance in health care, these books or simply to just be an aware ally friend of mine. The new Greg soul is not sure. Not sure in the third dimension. Our cord has a lot of rehab to go through. Is it worth it? Is it the right move? And when new Greg soul was debugged- a spawn happened and I got attacked from a high officer of the Regime. This Regime officer had been following new Greg soul and got freaked out when he saw us talking in a way he couldn't spy on. Ugh. It just really gets to be too much at times.

As of right now, I am still pregnant with Ronan, but it's buried deep in me and the Holy Spirit light over me is still orange. It sounds like though I will have more access with Ronan, which I look forward to.

And now there is my twin flame Matt, Creator God Greg, Source God, and the Founder. How is this supposed to work?

I come back to focusing on the third dimension. I want things to feel better on my path. Mary thinks I should write books. The native elders say work with plants. Source God advocates for healing others. Ugh. I get so angry about all of this and so at my wits end, of the waiting for two years for some kind of path. Finally, Archangel Michael has put me in a bubble of his making to give me a break. And true, I can breathe better.

I really feel my heart and soul knows something my mind can't comprehend where human Greg might fit in this or maybe it's not him, but some human? A human to come to me that knows more, to help me weave all of this and ground me in the third dimension. But who? For what real purpose?

And now with a volcano in Hawaii erupting, I just have to wonder what is afoot and what is next.

Well.

Well, I could go on and on I imagine.

I started this story with breath, breathing and trying to balance, have balance. I could never have imagined how complex and layered things could be. I haven't changed much in 3 billion years. I'm pretty much the same being than as I am now with more scars and awareness. The only words that stay with me is to always follow your heart, soul, and mind and listen well to yourself, to know yourself.

This is my story as of May 13, 2018.

With love to you, Bridget

Made in United States
North Haven, CT
04 August 2024

55709351R00264